THE CHURCH
AND THE
FOUR-YEAR
COLLEGE

THE CHURCH
AND THE
FOUR-YEAR
COLLEGE

AN APPRAISAL OF
THEIR RELATION

BY

GUY E. SNAVELY

Executive Director Emeritus,
Association of American Colleges

HARPER & BROTHERS

NEW YORK

r 378.73
S669

TO

LOUISE

WHOSE AID AND CONSTRUCTIVE CRITICISM

HAVE BEEN INVALUABLE

CONTENTS

PREFACE   vii

I   The Church College Today   1

II   The Church and the Colonial Colleges   10

III Baptist Colleges   66

IV Congregational Church Colleges   74

V   Disciples of Christ Colleges   79

VI Lutheran Colleges   83

VII Methodist Colleges   87

VIII Presbyterian Colleges   102

IX Roman Catholic Colleges   115

X   Other Church Colleges   126

XI Church Colleges That Became State Colleges 137

XII Church Boards of Education   176

XIII The Church College Tomorrow   184

BIBLIOGRAPHY   199

INDEX   205

PREFACE

This book results from a request of the Commission on Christian Higher Education of the Association of American Colleges. It was the desire of this Commission that the book would serve as a reference work as well as record the evolution of the American church college and its supporting agencies.

Chapters II, VIII, and XI were the bases for three lectures delivered by the author under the auspices of the John Findley Green Foundation on November 9-10, 1954, at Westminster College, Fulton, Missouri.

"The John Findley Green Foundation was established in 1937 by Mrs. Eleanor I. Green as a memorial of her husband, a prominent St. Louis lawyer who was graduated from Westminster College in 1884, and afterward served on the college's Board of Trustees twenty-seven years. The deed of gift provides for lectures designed to promote understanding of economic, political and social problems of international concern, and because of Mr. Green's lifelong belief that the most practical application of the Christian religion is the improvement of human relations, the Foundation is considered an especially fitting memorial of his life and work."[*]

The Green Lectures became internationally famous when, in the spring of 1946, the phrase "behind the iron curtain" was used for the first time by Winston Churchill, Prime Minister of Great Britain, in his celebrated speech under the auspices of Green Memorial Foundation, Fulton, Missouri. Other Green Foundation Lecturers have included Harry S. Truman, former President of the United States; Charles H. Malik, Ambassador to the United States from Lebanon; Count Carlo Sforza, then Italian Minister of Foreign

[*] An excerpt from a Westminster College printed announcement.

Affairs; Roscoe Pound, Dean-Emeritus of the Harvard Law School.

The author is deeply grateful to the members of the Commission on Christian Higher Education of the Association of American Colleges for their encouragement in the initiation of this study of the church-related college in the United States. Thanks and gratitude are due also to the Board of Directors and to the whole Association for approval of the plan and for an appropriation for secretarial and travel expenses.

G. E. S.

CHAPTER I

The Church College Today

THE church and the four-year college have been the chief agencies responsible for the rapid rise of the United States to its prominence as a world power.

As the pioneers moved westward and sizable communities were settled, there soon arose a movement for the establishment of a college. This movement can be readily traced from the founding in 1636 of the frontier college at New Towne, Massachusetts, now Harvard University, to the establishment in 1853 by the Presbyterians of the College of California, now the University of California. These colleges were different from their British prototypes in that they were open to rich and poor alike. There was no distinction of rank, although a few attempts had been made in this direction in the early days of Harvard.

The rapid multiplication of colleges along the developing frontier was rudely stopped for a while by the financial panic of 1837. Many of these "mushroom" colleges were kept alive at times by contributions from men of strong religious faith in the East. To stabilize the situation somewhat a number of educational societies were organized. The most influential of this group was the Society for the Promotion of Collegiate and Theological Education at the West, organized in New York City, June 30, 1843. The Annual Reports of this society contain excellent source material on the development of the church college for the twenty-five years between 1844 and 1869.

The Fourth Report of the Society, issued in 1847, contains these significant observations of its author, Absalom Peters:

1

And this is the very thing designed to be effected by this Society. It is to unite the appropriate and the best energies of the older and the new States in harmonious cooperation, to concentrate them upon the most important points of the West, and thus to plant and cherish Colleges and Theological Schools when and where they may be most needed, and to aid them in succession, until they shall have in themselves the elements of strength, of expansion, of improvement, and of continuance.

For such a purpose as this our society was called into being, as by the voice of God. It was felt to be needed. A hundred beginnings had been already made, moved, in some instances, by religious principles and a high sense of duty; in others, by the hope of worldly emolument, and the multifarious impulses of a discordant and enterprising people. But they were without concert. Their conflicting applications came to us from every portion of the West. Benevolent men were interested in their appeals. They wished to aid the general cause. But what they gave was, in many instances, scattered and lost in ill-directed and impracticable efforts, and good men were becoming weary of the work, in the exhaustless multiplicity of its demands.

In such a state of things, it became necessary to arrest the progress of causes, which threatened not only to weaken, but even to destroy the benevolent sympathy of the East in the great cause of Western education. Western men desired it, and we saw the necessity of an organization to harmonize the diverging and scattered action which was wasting itself in this impracticable way.

Our object was to protect the churches of the East against the ill-judged and discordant appeals of the West (with which we are thronged), and, at the same time, by a Society, representing the Eastern Churches, to welcome all worthy applications from the West, and combine them into one, and thus commend them to our churches, on the effective and economical plan of a single and concentrated agency, which should have its place among the other agencies of our great Benevolent Societies.

In his pamphlet, *A Plea For Colleges*, issued in 1836, the Reverend Lyman Beecher gives this excellent analysis of the value of the church college:

Colleges and schools are truly the intellectual manufactories and workshops of the nation, and in their design and results are preeminently republican institutions. They break up and diffuse among the people that monopoly of knowledge and mental power which despotic governments accumulate for purposes of arbitrary rule, and bring to the children of the humblest families of the nation a full and fair opportunity of holding competition for learning, and honor, and wealth, with the children of the oldest and most affluent families . . . giving thus to the nation the select talents and powers of her entire population.

Another excellent characterization of the early church college was made in a pamphlet on the place of the college among American institutions, issued in 1857 by the Reverend William S. Tyler, professor of classics for nearly sixty years at Amherst College:

American colleges bear a general resemblance to the English colleges, from which they sprung; not, however, without important modifications, which bring them into nearer conformity to the genius of our institutions, into closer connection with the wants and wishes of the people . . . the people have built them with their own hands, and cherished them in their own hearts. They are the people's colleges. . . . Scarcely anything in America is more distinctively American than the relation between the colleges and the common people. The people have made the colleges what they are, and the colleges have, in no small measure, made the people what they are. All classes have contributed to the establishment and the support of colleges, and all classes have reaped the benefit.

Yale College developed conspicuous leadership in the organization of church colleges across the nation. Yale was the center of the educational and missionary interests of the Congregational Church in the early days of the nineteenth century. The so-called "Yale Band" was responsible for organizing such well-known colleges as Western Reserve, Beloit, Illinois, Grinnell, Pacific University, to a total of some sixteen colleges.

The other "Mother of Colleges" was the one located at Princeton, from which radiated the influence of the Presbyterians on higher education in the early days. One of its historians claims that twenty-five colleges were organized through the influence of Princeton alumni.

The other large church groups like the Baptists, Disciples, Methodists, and Roman Catholics had a much later start in the establishment of colleges. When the Methodists and Baptists came to realize that higher education was a necessary handmaiden to zeal and enthusiasm, they established rapidly a great number of colleges. These two groups with the Presbyterians and Catholics now have by far the largest number of affiliated institutions.

The rapid proliferation of colleges throughout the nation caused the lowering of standards. In the early days there was no clear-cut distinction between the academy (high school) and college courses. Often many institutions were publicly proclaimed as universities, when they were hardly little more than junior colleges, really often not more than high schools.

To the credit of the consecrated leaders of the church colleges, they were in the forefront in establishing standards and in enforcing accreditment through the organization of accrediting associations. Notable is the record of Vanderbilt University, then controlled by the Methodists, and the University of the South, to this day under the control of the Episcopalians, in taking the lead in organizing the Southern College Association in 1895. Administrators of church colleges continue to work harmoniously with their colleagues of the state universities in the maintenance of proper standards for colleges and universities.

The accredited colleges listed in later chapters are members of one of the six accrediting associations in the United States. These groups are named according to their respective geographical areas:

1. Middle States Asociation of Colleges and Secondary Schools
2. New England Association of Colleges and Secondary Schools
3. North Central Association of Colleges and Secondary Schools
4. Northwest Association of Secondary and Higher Schools
5. Southern Association of Colleges and Secondary Schools
6. Western College Association

In recent years the accrediting movement seems to have become as expansive as the rapid growth of the colleges in the early days. Not only has the college or university been required to meet standards for professional schools but also has been put under pressure to affiliate with associations desirous of accrediting single departments of the curriculum.

It is understandable that professional associations like the medical, legal, engineering, and theological groups would be expected to set up standards peculiar to their type of vocation. In the fields of law and medicine, accreditment is in order so that the institutions concerned will be able to educate their students to meet the licensure requirements of the various states which must be passed by the prospective lawyer or physician.

The tendency to accredit an individual college according to the status of its various departments like chemistry, psychology, journalism, and philosophy would seem to put the whole undergraduate program into a strait jacket. It would prevent experimental variation of program and freedom of action on the part of alert faculties.

To check the proliferation of accrediting agencies there was organized a few years ago a National Association of Accrediting. This group was originally comprised of representatives from the Association of American Universities, Association of American Colleges, National Association of State Universities, Association of Land-Grant Colleges and Universities, and Association of Urban Universities. This National Accrediting Association cooperates fully with the regional associations. Most of the latter, in their annual surveys on inspections of member institutions, work with a large team of some forty members which include all interests, both vocational and nonvocational.

As indicated in detail elsewhere, the curriculum of the early colleges was designed primarily for the education of prospective ministers of the Gospel. Most of the early church colleges also slanted their curriculum toward the education of those interested in becoming leaders in affairs of state. Later the curriculum was altered to serve the interests of those desiring to enter other professions like medicine, teaching, engineering, and journalism.

The theological character of the early curriculum illustrated the great influence that clergymen had not only in religious affairs but also in political, social, and intellectual areas. Thus the curriculum was attractive to any ambitious young man.

Obviously the products of such a curriculum would be predominantly clergymen. According to the records it has been discovered that by 1855 the American colleges had graduated 40,000 students, 10,000 of whom had entered the ministry. This is truly an impressive record.

In his book, *The Founding of American Colleges and Universities*

Before the Civil War, Donald G. Tewksbury gives many supporting data which are convincing as to the results of the curricular offerings of the colleges. Significant are the following statements concerning the situation as it prevailed about the middle of the last century:

More than half of the graduates of Harvard, for the first sixty years of its existence, became ministers of the Gospel. Nearly three-fourths of the graduates of Yale for the first twelve years, entered the ministry, and a trifle less than one-half during the first thirty years.

About seven out of ten of the graduates of Marietta have become professional teachers or preachers of the Gospel.

Of the eight hundred graduates of Middlebury, nearly one-half have devoted themselves to the ministry.

Of the first 65 gradutes of Wabash, 45, or more than two-thirds have devoted themselves to the Christian ministry.

Of the first 94 graduates of Illinois, 45 have devoted themselves to the work of the ministry.

Of Knox in 1850 it was stated that "of 25 alumni, 11 have devoted themselves to the work of the ministry."

Dartmouth gave from her first ten classes of 99 graduates, 46 to the ministry.

Amherst gave "from its first six classes of 106 graduates, 68, or 15 more than one-half of the entire number to the ministry."

Of Western Reserve in 1849 it was stated that "of its 153 graduates about one-half of those living are either in the ministry or in actual preparation for it."

In a statement issued in 1847, it was said that "Since its charter, ninety-two students have graduated from Hanover; of these forty-seven are now preachers of the gospel."*

The curriculum of the early college was uniform and rigid. In all cases the required curriculum included Latin, Greek, and mathematics. Some colleges did include courses in English and natural philosophy. From the latter evolved our strong departments of physics, chemistry, biology, astronomy, and geology. History gradually edged its way into the curriculum as did the study of Romance languages. The latter interloper got into the sacred hierarchy first at Harvard about the middle of the nineteenth century.

* Donald Tewksbury, *The Founding of American Colleges and Universities Before the Civil War.* New York: Teachers College, Columbia University, 1932.

Two distinguished professors in this field at Harvard later became known as famous American poets, Henry Wadsworth Longfellow and James Russell Lowell.

The gradual evolution in the expansion of curricular offerings by the colleges reached a climax near the latter part of the nineteenth century when Harvard, under the leadership of Charles W. Eliot, its president for forty years, announced the Elective System. Although the Harvard Plan named English as the sole required course for all graduates, it did specify various combinations of courses for certain goals and aims. However, many smaller institutions jumped at the announcement and adopted a sort of cafeteria style of curricular program.

The stronger and better known colleges met the Harvard challenge with some modification in the stipulated program requirements, but did continue the requirement of "majoring" in one subject or area. For example, when the Johns Hopkins University opened primarily as a graduate school in 1876, it organized also a College Department wherein the requirements for the Bachelor's degree included fundamental courses in English, history, science, and foreign languages. Students planning to become teachers or ministers were expected to "major" in the languages, those desirous of becoming physicians would major in the sciences, others wishing to be lawyers would major in social sciences, prospective engineers would major in mathematics.

The church college of the present, like all other strong colleges, follows much the program just outlined. To their credit they also offer courses in the Bible. Many of them indicate that a person with a well-rounded education should also have some knowledge and appreciation in the fields of music and the other fine arts.

Obviously the presidents of the early colleges were clergymen. This type of administrator predominated for more than 250 years. At the turn of the century the typical college or university president nearly always wore a Prince Albert suit and most of them were distinguished with whiskers. Likewise most of the faculty of the early days were careful as to their dress, wearing Prince Albert or cutaway suits, as well as scholarly looking beards or mustaches.

Within the past two generations the clergymen have given way to professors, business men, lawyers, and in a few cases to physicians or journalists, as the various types who now serve as college and university presidents. In most cases the president is chosen from among college teachers who have shown previous administrative capacity, frequently through service as deans.

The evolution and the ups-and-downs of the church-related college in the United States have depended mostly, if not completely, on prevailing economic, political, and social conditions.

The demise of many hastily organized colleges and the amalgamation of many others bear testimony to the unrelenting pressure of economic conditions. By 1860 the records indicate that there had been organized 500 colleges. Scarcely 180 of these now survive. There were 260 existing at the beginning of the War Between the States. These colleges enrolled some 25,000 students taught by some 1500 professors. Over half of them were in the Deep South where the number of colleges had doubled between 1850 and 1860.

Vivid is the evidence of the influence of social forces in the story of the founding of the University of the South at Sewanee, Tennessee. Under the able leadership of Bishop Leonidas Polk of Louisiana, the Episcopalian dioceses in the Deep South organized the college in the fall of 1857. Although a charter was obtained from the state of Tennessee on January 6, 1858, and some buildings were soon constructed, the institution was not formally opened until 1868 because of the intervention of the War Between the States. Bishop Polk was unable to see the fruition of his dreams. He had yielded to pressure from his West Point contemporary, Jefferson Davis, to accept a commission as Major General in the Confederate States Army. After gallant service in the Mississippi, Tennessee, and Georgia campaigns, he was mortally wounded in 1864 at Pine Mountain, Georgia.

Remarkable and appropriate was the transfer by church groups of their colleges to the states when it seemed evident that the best interests of all concerned would be better served. The passage of the Morrill Act by the United States Congress in 1862 which provided for the establishment of land-grant colleges in each state was largely responsible for this movement of transferral of church colleges to state control. A later chapter gives some detailed information on this movement.

Most of the colonial colleges received from the Old World aid of various kinds—books, cash, and personnel. During the latter half of the nineteenth century the majority of the better college professors had studied abroad, many obtaining their doctorates from German universities. Since World War II the process has been reversed. Our colleges have been aiding many students of foreign lands to complete their higher education in the United States. The church-related colleges are notably active in this area. An example is the Methodist Board of Education which has a sizable scholarship fund allocated to the sole purpose of bringing to the United States capable young students from Europe, Asia, and Africa. It is inevitable that this international interplay in the college realm will result in better understanding on all sides, and, it is hoped, much improved international good will.

As the title of the book indicates, the record for each college or group of colleges will be definitely circumscribed. When a college loses its church connection and its presidents cease to be clergymen, its destiny will be no longer recorded here.

CHAPTER II

The Church and the Colonial Colleges

THE aim in this chapter is to indicate church support, church control, church contributions, and controlling church influence in the early colleges. When it becomes clear that all connections with the church have been severed, the story of the individual college ceases in this volume.

HARVARD COLLEGE

The Massachusetts Bay Colony might justly be considered to have had a theocratic type of government. Only church members were considered free men and allowed to vote and hold office in the colony. Thus Harvard can be considered as the first church college in the United States when the "Great and General Court of Massachusetts" passed on October 28, 1636 the Act establishing a "Colledge or Schoale" to be opened a year later in New Towne, promptly renamed Cambridge.

Another evidence of church interest is the reason given for the establishment of the college:

After God had carried us safe to New England & wee had builded our houses provided necessaries for our liveli-hood reard convenient places for Gods worship and setled the Civill Government: One of the next things wee longed for and looked after was to advance Learning and perpetuate it to Posterity dreading to leave an illiterate Ministery to the Churches when our present ministers shall lie in the Dust.

The early colonists settling on the shores of Massachusetts Bay included some thirty graduates of Oxford and seventy of Cambridge by 1640. From the above quotation it is clear that their orthography resembles greatly that of many modern college freshmen and is reminiscent of Shakespeare and Chaucer.

Among the early settlers was the Reverend John Harvard, a Master of Arts graduate of Emmanuel College, a Puritan foundation of Cambridge University established to provide a preaching ministry for the Church. In Emmanuel the chapel services were of an evangelistic type; no surplices were worn; there was no prayer-book ritual. In John Harvard's day it was second in size to Trinity of the Cambridge group. Other Emmanuel fellows helpful in founding Harvard were John Cotton, Thomas Hooker, and John Preston. The climate of the New World was not salubrious for young Harvard for he died of tuberculosis in Charlestown on September 14, 1638, at the age of thirty-one, a year after his arrival in New Towne. By an oral will the college received all his books, totalling 320, and one half of his estate, amounting to about 380 pounds, which he indicated were to be used for endowment of the college. In recognition of this interest the General Court ordered on March 13, 1639 "that the Colledge agreed upon formerly to bee built at Cambridge shalbee called Harvard Colledge."

Nathaniel Eaton, who probably came over in the same ship with Harvard, was the first "Master" of the new college. Eaton was a graduate of Trinity College and had done advanced study at the University of Franeker in the Netherlands under a celebrated English Puritan living there in exile.

Master Eaton comprised the faculty while his wife operated the boarding department. He wielded the cudgel so briskly and his wife served such poor food and drink to her boarders that the trustees were obliged to accept their resignations before the end of the second year. Mrs. Eaton admitted that she had never given the students beef, one of the standbys of a thoroughbred Englishman, but she denied that she had ever served "ungutted mackerel."

After the college had been closed for a year the trustees, consisting of four Puritan magistrates and four clergymen, re-opened the institution in the fall of 1640 with a new president and sole faculty member in the person of the Reverend Henry Dunster, a thirty-year-old graduate of Magdalene College, Cambridge. To

Dunster is due the credit of organizing the administration of Harvard through which it still operates by the charter obtained from the General Court in 1650. The Corporation comprises the president, the treasurer, and five other fellows. The 1650 charter continued the Board of Overseers which had been organized in 1642. Roughly speaking, this larger group corresponds to the usual college board of trustees with the Corporation serving as an executive committee practically responsible for full operation of the institution.

Rules drawn up by President Dunster required that the students read the Scriptures twice a day, attend church regularly, eschew profanity, have good manners, and *mirabile dictu* accept positions in commons, in classroom, and in chapel according to their social rank. In these same regulations was one prohibiting the use of tobacco "unless permitted by the parent with the consent of parents or guardians, and on good reason first given by a physician, and then in a sober and private manner." The Master's degree was to be conferred automatically on those who had been A.B. graduates for at least three years and were willing to write and "defend" an essay or thesis at commencement time. Most of the graduates who aspired to the Master of Arts degree entered the Congregational ministry.

Although the founders were strict Puritans they claimed to permit freedom in matters of theology and made no religious requirement of college officers. President Dunster had increased the equipment, enrollment, and financial conditions but soon found that theological freedom was not really in vogue. He had come to believe that infant baptism is "unscriptural" and refused to allow his youngest child to be baptized. This action created much excitement which the overseers were willing to overlook if thereafter he would keep quiet about religious matters, but being a man of convictions he resigned in 1654 to become a Baptist minister in Scituate of the Plymouth Colony.

President Dunster was succeeded in 1654 by sixty-two-year-old Charles Chauncy. He too was born in England and was a graduate of Cambridge University, having ranked at the head of his class in Trinity College. After graduation he left the Church of England to become a Puritan and to emigrate to the Plymouth Colony. Like his predecessor he opposed the total immersion of infants as he considered it "not so conveniente in this cauld countrie." Unlike Dunster he was willing to heed the advice of the Harvard overseers about keeping silence on his baptismal ideas, particularly since college presidents had no need to administer such rites. He served as president for eighteen years until his death in 1672.

He was followed by three undistinguished clergymen who served short terms. In 1685 the Corporation succeeded in persuading the Reverend Increase Mather to become president. He accepted on condition that he could continue to serve as pastor of the Second Church in Boston. This distinguished and somewhat belligerent conservative clergyman, father of the more distinguished Cotton Mather, had great influence on the progress of the college and doubtless would have been more influential if he had not treated the position as a part-time job. From 1688–92 he was in England on a political mission and on his return gave more time to his church than to the college. His continual aim was to keep the college under control of the Congregational Church and free from the politics which had crept into the Board of Overseers, which included a number of ministers of Anglican faith and possibly some of other sects. When pressed by the General Court to choose between giving full time to the church or the college, Mather finally resigned from the presidency to be succeeded for six years by an acting head, Vice-President Samuel Willard, brother-in-law of fellow Harvard alumnus Joseph Dudley, who had just been made the royal governor of the State of Massachusetts.

The loss of Congregational control was indicated in the election of John Leverett in 1708 to the presidency. Leverett was not only a layman but was decidedly a liberal in the eyes of the Mathers and their supporters. Maintaining the old custom of having the students "translate the Scriptures from one ancient tongue to another at morning and evening prayers," he did make it clear that Harvard was no longer to be considered a seminary for ministers of the orthodox Congregational faith. Like most college presidents of all times, he had critics of various types. A young journalist writing under the name of Silence Dogood in the New England *Courant* on May 14, 1722, noted that the Temple of Learning was veiled by Idleness and Ignorance, and reflected on the extreme folly of those Parents, who, blind to their Children's Dulness, and insensible of the Solidarity of their Skulls, because they think their Purses can afford it, will needs send them to the Temple of Learning, where, for want for a suitable Genius, they learn little more than how to carry themselves handsomely, and enter a Room genteely (which might as well be acquired at a Dancing-School), and from whence they return, after abundance of trouble and Charges, as great Blockheads as ever, only more proud and self-conceited.

The writer of this screed was none other than the sixteen-year-old Benjamin Franklin. From the other end of the social scale came bitter criticism from the Mathers. They were particularly concerned by the practice of using liberal ministers of the Church of England to teach divinity courses. It is generally conceded that Cotton Mather was particularly antipathetic because his father had been dropped from the presidency in 1701 and he himself had been overlooked when Leverett was elected in 1708.

A man of much more liberality of spirit was Thomas Hollis, a Baptist and a wealthy merchant of London. In 1721 he gave sufficient funds to endow Harvard's first chair, the Hollis Professorship of Divinity, "for the education of poor, pious, and able young men for the ministry." In 1720 he had sent the University about 700 pounds to endow scholarships for divinity students. The first man elected to the Hollis professorship was Edward Wigglesworth, who was not able to obtain a parish because of his deafness. To him was given the credit of training "the ministers who led the way out of the lush but fearsome jungles of Calvinism, into the thin, clear light of Unitarianism." Surely such religious evolution was never expected by the loyal Baptist Thomas Hollis.

On the death of Leverett in 1724 the sixty-one-year-old Cotton Mather felt sure that he would not be passed over a second time by the Harvard Corporation. This they did in spite of his 350 imprints, of the fellowship awarded him by the Royal Society of London, and of the Doctor of Divinity degree given him by the University of Glasgow. Since it seemed necessary at this time to have a conservative president, the Corporation elected the Reverend Joseph Sewell of the class of 1707, minister of the old South Church in Boston. When his church declined to give him a release, the Corporation went to the opposite extreme in electing the Reverend Benjamin Coleman, a foremost liberal Congregationalist who also declined when he found that the conservatives were unanimously opposed to him. Benjamin Wadsworth, who for thirty years had been pastor of the First Church of Boston, was then chosen as a compromise candidate in 1725. Two years later another large gift came from Thomas Hollis to be used in establishing the Hollis professorship of mathematics and natural philosophy.

On Wadsworth's death in 1737, the Corporation and Board of Overseers spent the entire forenoon of May 4 in the college library in prayer to God "for his gracious direction in the Important affair of Chusing a President." When neither group received a divine inspiration, it was agreed to postpone action for three weeks. The choice was finally made at the dinner table of Governor Belcher, chairman of the Board of Overseers. When one of the conservative guests indicated that the Reverend Edward Holyoke of Marblehead under consideration by the Corporation "was not sound in his religious principles" but another guest insisted that "he was as orthodox a Calvinist as any man, yet too much of a gentleman, and of too catholic a temper, to cram his principles down another man's throat." Thereupon the governor explained "then he must be the man!" Thus President Holyoke was elected unanimously to the Harvard presidency which lasted thirty-two years.

The new president was nicknamed "guts" by his students because he showed great courage in dealing not only with them but with the royal governors and members of the provincial legislature as well as with renowned faculty and meddlesome overseers who were quizzing new tutors on their religious beliefs. Despite the efforts of the latter group, Harvard college and a large part of the local Congregational Church groups evolved from Calvinism to Unitarianism. The evolution was interrupted in September 1740, by a visit of the Reverend George Whitefield who was reputed to have addressed on one occasion fifteen thousand people on Boston Common. Remarkable is the influence wielded by this "whirlwind revivalist" as indicated in the mention of him in the discussion of the progress of at least five other colonial colleges. In spite of being entertained by President Holyoke and being listened to eagerly by the students, he was blunt enough to surmise that "piety and true Godliness" were not much better at Harvard than was true at Cambridge and Oxford. It is understandable that White-field was not invited back the next year.

When Holyoke died on June 1, 1769, shortly before his eightieth birthday, the community was in the turmoil that resulted in the Revolutionary War. Nearby Boston was occupied by the British troops, with the result that the Massachusetts House of Representatives met in the Harvard Chapel. After the aging Professor Winthrop and one or two others had declined the offer of the presidency, the Reverend Samuel Locke of the class of 1755 was selected. He not only had grave financial problems, with one lottery proving a dismal failure, but subsequently resigned when the maid servant in his bachelor president's home gave birth to a child, a fact that did not come to light for nearly one hundred and fifty years.*

In 1774 Locke was succeeded by the Reverend Samuel Langdon of the class of 1740 who was then preaching in Portsmouth, New Hampshire. A good friend of Samuel Adams and John Hancock, his accession to the presidency "gave great delight to the Sons of Liberty," but the Sons of Harvard got rid of him as soon as they could, which was not until 1780.

With reduced attendance due to the war, with currency deflation, and with the incompetent service of the college treasurer, the great patriot John Hancock, Harvard College fell again into a desperate financial plight. After much delay the Corporation voted to choose a treasurer that "shall constantly reside in the State," thus releasing from his arduous and delinquent duties as treasurer the great signer of the Declaration of Independence with the impressively bold chirographic flourish.

When Massachusetts evolved from a province to a state during the Convention which assembled at the First Church in Cambridge on September 1, 1779, John Adams, who drafted the constitution, carefully prepared the Harvard charter so that the Board of Over-

---

* Many other human interest stories will enthrall the reader who peruses Samuel Eliot Morrison's exciting chronicle, *Three Centuries of Harvard*. Cambridge, Massachusetts; Harvard University Press, 1936.

seers would include the governor, lieutenant governor, council, the commonwealth senate, and the ministers of the Congregational churches in Cambridge, Watertown, Charleston, Boston, Roxbury, and Dorchester. This composition of the Board of Overseers lasted until legal authority was given to have the overseers elected by the alumni.

Although President Langdon had worked hand in glove with the patriots, he seemed to become unpopular by "abolishing Sunday evening singing to give more time to his harangue," which sometimes lasted nearly two hours. With pressure increasing against him he resigned in 1780 to take another pulpit in New Hampshire.

For a while the Federalists and Unitarians dominated the situation with presidents who were more or less distinguished. When the new "Medical Institution of Harvard University" was opened on October 7, 1783, the Corporation still required that each professor be a Protestant Christian.

After the subsidence of belligerent political and religious contests, the Unitarians and Federalists elected the Reverend John Thornton Kirkland as president in 1810. The Calvinists then founded Andover Theological Seminary under the leadership of Eliphalet Pearson who had been acting president of Harvard from 1804 to 1806.

President Kirkland maintained his popularity throughout the eighteen years of his presidency. He extended the reputation of the college so as to attract students from great distances, particularly from the South. Two kinsmen of Archbishop John Carroll of Baltimore were given permission to attend the Catholic Church rather than the services in the college chapel.

During Kirkland's day there were notable additions and changes in the college. Particularly noteworthy was the addition of the Modern Language Department, the first professor of which was George Tichnor, an alumnus who had spent several years of preparation in Europe. On his resignation he was succeeded by Henry Wadsworth Longfellow, who in turn was succeeded by another famous poet, James Russell Lowell.

The Harvard Law School and the Harvard Divinity School were also established under Kirkland. In this connection it should be noted that over 50 per cent of the Harvard graduates up to 1721 had become "settled ministers," while during the next eighty years the average was 27 per cent. Quite evident was the predominance of Unitarians not only in the Divinity School but on the faculty. Charles W. Eliot, who became president in 1869, deemed the proper way to keep Harvard "nonsectarian" was to appoint only Unitarians to fellowships and key positions.

Between Kirkland and Eliot seven presidents, mostly laymen, were appointed, with none attaining particular distinction save Josiah Quincy. During this forty-year period the contest between church factions was interspersed with hot political battles between the Whigs and the Democrats.

The potency of continuing church influence from 1636 to 1692 is Quincy's positive assertion that during that period the college had been "conducted as a theological institution." Of the alumni of that era more than half had become ministers.

It is a curious fact that Harvard students did not become enthusiastic about participating in the War Between the States as they so magnificently did in the last two World Wars.

With the passage of the legislative act on May 22, 1851, that removed all requirements for election of clergymen to the Board of Overseers, the Harvard story no longer falls within the purview of the purpose of these annals. It should be added that the college has become world famous under the leadership of layman Charles W. Eliot who served as president for forty years and his distinguished lay successors A. Lawrence Lowell, James B. Conant, and Nathan M. Pusey.

COLLEGE OF WILLIAM AND MARY

The College of William and Mary was the second of the colonial colleges to be founded under the aegis of the church. It has survived terrific political upheavals and catastrophic economic changes that developed in its environment. Its charter was granted by the British Crown on February 19, 1693.

As early as 1619 some fifteen hundred pounds had been collected by Bishops of the Church of England to endow a college in Virginia for the Indians. Additional gifts of land and money were made in 1621. George Thorpe, "A gentleman of his Majesty's privy Chamber,"

was sent over to be the "Superintendent of the University." The
Indians were not in a mood at that time to profit by higher education, so on March 22, 1623, they murdered not only George Thorpe
but some three hundred and forty other colonists.

Troubles in the Mother Country and Bacon's Rebellion in Virginia,
engendered by the arbitrary and tyrannical actions of the royal
governor, Sir William Berkeley, prevented further activity in the
founding of a college for two full generations. Shortly after the
revolution in England which established William and Mary on its
throne in 1688, the Virginia Colonial Assembly approved the plan
for a college. The Reverend James Blair, D.D., was empowered to
seek a charter from the Crown. He received a cordial welcome
from Queen Mary, to whom he made his first enthusiastic appeal.
King William promptly concurred in her plans of support and
ordered a grant of two thousand pounds "out of the quit-rents."

When Doctor Blair conveyed the royal commands to Seymour,
the attorney general, he was sternly rebuffed. The latter saw no
need for such liberality in a time of war, nor did he see the "slightest
occasion for a College in Virginia." When the persistent clergyman
insisted that Virginians also had souls to be saved and that an
educated ministry was necessary, Seymour bellowed: "Souls! Damn
your souls, make tobacco!"

In spite of Seymour's antagonism, the Sovereigns granted the
requested charter which is in itself a most interesting lengthy
document. It fixed the location of the college on the south side of
the York River near Yorktown but gave authority to the Virginia
General Assembly to change its location if it were deemed advisable.
It stated that the Charter was granted "to the end that the Church
of Virginia may be furnished with a seminary of ministers of the
Gospel, and that the youth may be piously educated in good letters
and manners, and that the Christian faith may be propagated
amongst the Western Indians to the glory of Almighty God."

The royal charter of the College of William and Mary required
after the establishment of the college and the appointment of
competent "Masters or Professors," the transfer to the "President,
Masters or Professors, or their successors, the lands, inheritances,
chattels" belonging to the college. It was further required that

the trustees elect every seven years a "discreet person" to be known as chancellor of the college. In the charter "The Reverend Father in God, Henry (Compton), by Divine permission, Bishop of London," was appointed the first chancellor.

This position, more or less honorary, was held by the Bishops of London until 1776, with the exception of the year 1764, when it was held by the Earl of Hardwicke. George Washington was the chancellor from 1788 to 1799. John Tyler, ex-President of the United States, held the title from 1859 to 1862.

The indefatigable James Blair, the first president, held his office for fifty years, until his death in 1743. He was followed by a succession of distinguished Episcopal clergymen, who served as presidents until the election in 1836 of a layman, Thomas R. Dew. Only two of these presidents held the office for any length of time, the Reverend James Harrocks who served from 1764 until his demise in 1771 and the Right Reverend James Madison, Bishop of Virginia, who was president of the college from 1777 until his death in 1812. Like many present-day presidents, this James Madison (born two years before United States President James Madison) was a versatile and industrious person. After graduating from William and Mary in 1772, at the age of twenty-two, he studied law and was admitted to the bar. However, he soon abandoned the law for the ministry. He became professor of mathematics at his alma mater in 1773, but after two years of teaching he went to London in 1775 to be ordained by the Bishop of London. On his return he became professor of natural and moral philosophy, international law, etc. This post he continued to fill after election to the presidency in 1777. In 1790 he was consecrated Bishop of Virginia by the Archbishop of Canterbury in Lambeth Chapel, London.

During Madison's presidency the college buildings were occupied at various times by American, British, and French troops. For a brief while in 1781 the main theater of the War of the Revolution was so near at hand that the college was forced to close. By that time it had lost most of its endowment through the ravages of the war.

The original college building, now restored through the Rockefeller munificence, was planned by Sir Christopher Wren, England's foremost architect of the time.

For nearly ninety years William and Mary continued as the "nursery of pious ministers" for the Church in Virginia. In 1779 under the influence of alumnus Thomas Jefferson, then Governor of Virginia, the college discontinued its divinity school but became a university by adding schools of law, medicine, and modern languages. Jefferson's continuing antagonism to clerical domination in higher education finally led to his establishment of the University of Virginia in Charlottesville in 1821.

That the classical curriculum was strictly in vogue in the early days of William and Mary is indicated by this excerpt from the Virginia *Gazette* under date of November 12, 1736:

On this day sen'night being the fifth of November, the President, masters and scholars of William and Mary College went, according to their annual custom, in a body to the Governor's to present his honor with two copies of Latin verses, in obedience to their charter, as a grateful acknowledgement for two valuable tracts of land given the said College by their late King William and Queen Mary. Mr. President delivered the verses to his honor, and two of the young gentlemen spoke them. It is further observed that there were upward of sixty scholars present.

The records indicate that this is about the average number of students enrolled in the earlier years.

An unusual department of the college was a school maintained expressly for the education of Indian youth. This school resulted from a bequest by the famous British scientist, Robert Boyle. He left his estate "to such charitable and pious uses" as his executor should deem fitting. After considerable litigation it was decided by court decree to allow the executor, the Earl of Burlington, and the college's first chancellor, Henry, Lord Bishop of London, to give ninety pounds to Harvard University and the rest of the annual rents to maintain a school at William and Mary for educating Indians. This division of the college was maintained until the Revolution. The venture did not seem to produce the expected results. Colonial governors and others felt that the Indians were lazy and frittered away their time in idleness and mischief; that when they returned to their homes, "they relapsed into idolatry and barbarism." Other observers of that time were of the opinion that the Indians would have done well if more personal attention were paid them and some continuing interest manifested in them on completion of their studies. "They have admirable qualities when their humors and tempers are perfectly understood," is a penetrating observation voiced in an official report published in London in 1724. Only about ten Indians each year received board, room, and tuition from the Boyle bequest. This would make a total of less than eight hundred: some came from as far as four hundred miles away.

Before the War of Independence and up to the period when the church was no longer in control, William and Mary College could count among its alumni many who became illustrious. Mention can be made of Thomas Jefferson and James Monroe, Presidents of the United States; Carter Braxton, Benjamin Harrison, Thomas Nelson and George Wythe, signers of the Declaration of Independence; Peyton Randolph, President of the First Continental Congress; Edmund Randolph, Attorney General and Secretary of State; John Marshall, Chief Justice of the United States Supreme Court. Three professors and thirty students left the college to join the American Army when the Revolutionary War began.

Faculty and student problems have varied greatly over the years. In a report of the college Visitors (trustees) for September 1, 1769, there is a vigorous complaint about the professor of divinity, who had gotten married and taken up residence in Williamsburg, thus failing in his responsibility to be on hand in the dormitory to pay heed "to the conduct and behaviour of the students and scholars."

One of the "Old Laws" forbids the keeper of the college table to admit as a boarder any but students or faculty. Nor is he allowed to sell to the students "wine or any other spirituous liquors, to be drunk at any other time or place, than at their ordinary meals." This would seem to cause no severe hardship on thirsty students for another sentence in the same law states: "No liquors shall be furnished or used at table except beer, cider, toddy, or spirits and water."

Before leaving the story of William and Mary while it functioned under the domination of the Church of England, we should recall its significant contribution to improvement in higher scholarship in the organization of America's first college fraternity, Phi Beta Kappa. The date of its first meeting was December 5, 1776. The meeting was held in the Apollo Hall of the old Raleigh Tavern, located in Williamsburg about a mile from the campus. The charter members numbered forty-three and included scions of families famous in Virginia, like Washington, Lee, Madison, Cocke, Page, Cabell, Mason, and Stuart. John Heath was the first signer of the charter while late in the list came John Marshall and Bushrod Washington, both later to become members of the United States Supreme Court. Unlike current social fraternities, Phi Beta Kappa long ago gave up esoteric features of its initiatory ceremonies to become a society whose members are limited to a small number of outstanding scholars in colleges and universities that have been recognized with chapters of the society.

YALE COLLEGE

Yale College had the most obscure and humble origin of any American college. For in the beginning its campus was uncertain, shifting from one small town to another, and on occasion operating in three towns at once. On October 16, 1701, the General Court (Assembly) of the Colony of Connecticut voted a charter for a "Collegiate School" together with an annual subsidy of 120 pounds "in country pay." The trustees elected the Reverend Abraham Pearson as rector. The original site of the school was fixed at Saybrook but it met in the Pearson parsonage at Killingworth until his death in 1707. At that time the trustees elected the Reverend Samuel Andrew, one of their number, as rector. Since he was the pastor at Milford, he had the seniors come to live with him to finish their course while the two younger classes stayed at Saybrook under the guidance of two tutors.

The college was organized by ten Connecticut clergymen who met in the home of the Reverend Samuel Russell at Branford. They started the enterprise because of the distance and expense involved in sending their prospective preachers to Harvard, doubtless also because of their feeling that the Harvard clergymen were drifting away from Congregationalism to Unitarianism.

The preamble to the charter which appointed the ten clergymen "trusty partners-undertakers for the School" expressed well their aims and beliefs:

Several well disposed and Publick spirited Persons of their sincere Regard to & zeal for upholding & Propagating of the Christian Protestant Religion by a succession of Learned and Orthodox men, have expressed by Petition their earnest desires that full Liberty and Priveledge be granted unto certain Undertakers for the founding, suitably endowing & ordering a Collegiate School within his Majesties Colony of Connecticut, wherein Youth may be instructed in the Arts & Sciences, who through the blessing of Almighty God may be fitted for Public employment both in Church and Civil State.

The first two rectors were Harvard graduates, the second one having taught there from 1679 to 1684. The next ten presidents were also ordained ministers of the Congregational Church. The first layman, Arthur T. Hadley, was elected in 1899. His distinguished successors were also laymen: James R. Angell, Charles Seymour, A. Whitney Griswold.

Like most of the other colonial colleges, financial aid was obtained from England; the college also acquired about seven hundred choice books, some of which were given by distinguished persons like Sir Richard Steele and Sir Isaac Newton, who gave their own works. The curriculum was of the classical type then prevalent at Harvard and in England. It included a study of the Greek Testament, the reading of the Psalms in Hebrew as well as the study of such Latin authors as Cicero and Virgil. About 1710 the course of study was extended from three to four years. One of the graduates of this era was Samuel Johnson, who became a tutor in the college on his graduation in 1714. After a pastorate at Westhaven he went to England to be ordained a clergyman in the Church of England, returning to be the first president of King's College (Columbia) in 1754.

The clergymen founders continued to work hand in glove with the legislature, and voted in 1716 to move the college from Saybrook to New Haven. However, a few students stayed on at Saybrook with the Reverend Azariah Mather, and a few others continued their studies at Wethersfield with tutor Elisha Williams. In 1717 four received their diplomas from the Collegiate School at the commencement in New Haven, while one received his degree at commencement held in Wethersfield. A year later the "dissatisfied party" (the group who disapproved the move to New Haven) graduated five at Wethersfield with the certificates being signed by the Reverend Mr. Woodbridge and the other ministers present.

About this time the famous clergyman Cotton Mather sent an appeal on behalf of the New Haven group to Elihu Yale, an employee of the East India Company who had worked his way up to become Governor of Madras. Elihu Yale came from a New Haven family and had become wealthy as a merchant. His favorable response with a gift of 800 pounds resulted in the Collegiate School being given the name of Yale College. Yale's gift plus an additional grant from the legislature made possible the construction of the famous building still known as Yale College.

As in the case of some other colonial colleges, nepotism prevailed in the early days. Rector Andrew was succeeded in 1719 by the Reverend Timothy Cutler, his son-in-law whom one of his successors, President Stiles, called an "excellent linguist, and a good Hebrician and Orientalist." During Cutler's three-year administration the legislature continued some grants, including amounts gained by the "impost on rum." One of his most famous students was Jonathan Edwards, who graduated at the head of his class in 1720. The students attended Sunday services in the Congregational Church; they paid a shilling a year for the seats reserved for them in the gallery.

Rector Cutler's fall from grace was due to his backsliding from true Congregational beliefs to the tenets of the Church of England. This so upset the trustees that they voted to "abolish the Reverend Mr. Cutler from all further services as Rector of Yale College." Shortly thereafter he sailed to England to take orders and returned to become Rector of Christ Church, Boston, until his death in 1765.

To avoid further defections the trustees voted that in the future all officers must "give satisfaction of the soundness of their faith and no Arminian and prelatical corruptions." For four years the college drifted along under tutors with no president, although four clergymen had been selected but had all declined to serve. In 1725 the trustees finally chose the Reverend Elisha Williams as rector. He had operated the part of the college at Wethersfield but various differences were forgotten and unanimous support of the board was given him. He was a graduate of Harvard and had studied law previous to his becoming the master at Wethersfield.

During his thirteen years of service Yale turned out some distinguished alumni, notably the four Livingstons who played such an important role in the history of their native state of New York; the Reverend Aaron Burr, who became the second of the three presidents Yale gave to the College of New Jersey (now Princeton); and the Reverend Eleazar Wheelock, the first president of Dartmouth College. The budget was balanced by the receipt of some important impost duties on rum and by raising the tuition to 50 shillings a year. The students were required to read the Scriptures each day so that "ye word of Christ may dwell in him ritchly. No student shall be absent from his study or appointed exercises in ye school except half an hour att breakfaste, and hour and a half att noon after dinner, and after ye evening prayer 'till nine of ye clock. . . . No student shall go into any tavern, victualling house, or inn to eat or Drink, except he shall be called by his parents, or some sufficient person, yt ye Rector or tutor thall except of." Present-day students would be further appalled at the thought of morning prayers at 6 A.M., and the requirement of "reading English into Greek" as well as turning "part of ye New Testament out of ye English or lattin into ye greek."

Gifts such as books and laboratory equipment continued to be received from England. One generous donor in London by the name of Daniel Turner sent over twenty-eight volumes and received at his request an honorary M.D. degree. Some local wag observed that this meant "Multum Donavit." On the other hand, a very sizable donation was made by the Reverend George Berkeley, a graduate of Trinity College in his native Dublin, Dean of Derry, and later the Bishop of Cloyne. He had been living at Newport, Rhode Island, since January 23, 1729, when he gave to the college his Rhode Island farm of 96 acres on July 26, 1732, shortly after his return to Europe. The income of this gift valued at about 3000 pounds was to be used for the expenses of students who had already graduated from college. Among the holders of the "Dean's bounty" were Eleazar Wheelock, the first president of Dartmouth; Aaron Burr, the second president of Princeton; William Samuel Johnson, the second president of Columbia; Presidents Naphtali Daggett and Timothy White of Yale; and the Reverend Abraham Baldwin, a signer of the Constitution from Georgia and first president of the University of Georgia.

When Rector Williams resigned in 1739 for health reasons he returned to his farm, served in the Connecticut legislature, having been chosen Speaker at once. Later he became a Superior Court judge. His successor was the Reverend Thomas Clap of Windham, also a Harvard graduate, the third and last of Yale's presidents to graduate from that institution. Thomas Clap served a total of twenty-seven years with remarkable success. In 1745 he engineered through the Assembly a new charter wherein the name of *Collegiate School* was changed to *Yale College*. Doubtless his most difficult problem was the quarrel which arose from the stir caused by a four-day visit to New Haven of that ecclesiastical stormy petrel, George Whitefield, whose activities we will note in relating the vicissitudes of other colonial colleges. Rector Clap entertained the itinerant evangelist at dinner and became his supporter for a season. Later he joined the group of "Old Lights," and soon engaged in a debate with Jonathan Edwards over Whitefield's activities. Feeling ran so high that a number of the "New Lights" were expelled from college for attending a "Separate meeting and refusing to make a public confession of wrong doing."

By the new charter the rector and trustees were to be called thereafter "president and fellows." Furthermore there were to be no qualifications concerning the election of the fellows. The record would indicate that this evidence of ecclesiastical concern was possibly due to the desire to get the charter through the legislature in the full expectation that the "fellows" would continue to look after the church interests in the proper manner. In a way this charter change puts further consideration of Yale outside the scope of this book, but the church influence continued to be so predominant that the record will be continued a little further.

Under his new title of president Thomas Clap continued strongly for a while in favor of the conservative religious party. On one occasion he called to task the Reverend Thomas Cooke, a member of the corporation, for his "New Light" beliefs, whereupon the latter resigned from the board. For a while the bitter contest continued with quite a war of pamphlets being carried on. The capable Philip Livingston of New York, father of the four Yale graduates, had endowed a professorship of divinity. Careful search was made for a suitable professor for the chair. He was found in the person of the Reverend Naphtali Daggett, a native of Massachusetts and a graduate of Yale in the class of 1748, the first president of the college from its own alumni body. When Daggett was installed on March 3, 1756, "he assented to the Westminster Catechism and confession of faith, the Nicene creed, the Saybrook Platform, Apostles and Athanasian Creeds, 9th of the 39 articles, i.e., on Original Sin, and presented five closely written pages of his confession. He then abjured all errors and heresies, which commonly go by the name of Arianism, Socinianism, Arminianism, Pelagianism, Antinomianism, and Enthusiasm."

The Yale students in the early days were subjected to strict rules. As has happened immemorially the freshmen were particularly subject to reproof from the upper classmen. Even the president of Yale was supposed to box the ears of a freshman in chapel when he deemed it necessary. All undergraduates were to be uncovered in the front yard of a president's or professor's house, and within ten rods of the person of the president, eight rods of the professor, and five rods of the tutors. The author remembers vividly, as a student at Johns Hopkins some fifty years ago, doffing his hat whenever he met a senior, a professor, or the president, Daniel Coit Gilman, a graduate of Yale of the class of 1852.

In those early days there was a system of fines for breaches of discipline. It is recorded that President Clap collected through this system about 172 pounds over a period of three years. If a student was absent from prayers it cost him one penny, if he was tardy it cost one-half penny, if he missed church it cost four pence. If he played cards he was fined two pence; for shooting dice, six pence;

for jumping out of a window or doing damage to the college, the fine was one shilling.

Other serious problems beset those early Yale boys. In 1764 a number of them became desperately ill when some Frenchman in New Haven put poison in their food. While the students were recovering from their narrow escape, Evangelist Whitefield came back to town and was again in such good graces of President Clap that he was invited to preach in Yale's new chapel. In his journal Whitefield exulted over the results of this experience: "The president came to me as I was going off in the chaise and informed me the students were so deeply impressed by the sermon that they were gone into the chapel and earnestly entreated me to give them one more quarter of an hour's exhortation. Not unto me, O Lord, not unto me, but unto Thy free and unmerited grace be all the glory."

During the American Revolution the college lived through a period of great confusion. The proximity of the British troops and the high cost of food supplies forced President Daggett to resign after turning over the buildings to the municipal officers of New Haven for a short while, the freshmen residing at Farmington, the sophomores and juniors at Glastonbury, and the seniors under tutor Timothy Dwight at Westersfield. Of course, many of the boys had joined the American Army. A twenty-one-year-old graduate of that period was Schoolmaster Nathan Hale who while carrying valuable information to General Washington was captured by the British and ignominiously hanged without trial. Famous is his final statement "I only regret that I have but one life to lose for my country."

During those parlous days the corporation selected as president the Reverend Ezra Stiles from the Yale class of 1746. The college continued to be operated after a fashion with no public commencements until 1781. Stiles accepted the presidency on condition that the corporation repeal their Act of 1753, which required religious tests of the faculty. He had the reputation of being such a scholar that it was said he could have been elected president of Harvard if he had been a graduate of that school. During the Stiles administration, which lasted eighteen years, there graduated many distinguished men who held prominent positions in church, state, and industry: many United States Senators; Supreme Court judges; Eli Whitney, inventor of the cotton gin; Noah Webster of dictionary fame; and several college presidents. Among the latter were the Reverend Azel Backus, the first president of Hamilton College; the Reverend Jeremiah Atwater, the first president of Middlebury College and later president of Dickinson College; the Reverend Edward Dorr Griffin, president of Williams College; the Reverend Jeremiah Day, another president of Yale College; the Reverend Ebenezer Fitch, first president of Williams College.

Curiously, the religious fervor inspired by the Whitefield visits soon died out under the influence of the French agnostics, Voltaire and Rousseau, so that by the time of the death of President Stiles on May 12, 1795, it was reported that there was but one student in the college who called himself a Christian. There was improvement in the religious atmosphere with the election of the Reverend Timothy Dwight as president in June 1795. He was a grandson of the famous Jonathan Edwards, had graduated from Yale in 1769, and had been a tutor there from 1771 to 1777, when he became a chaplain in the Revolutionary Army. He was pastor of the Congregational Church at Greenfield Hill, Connecticut, from 1783 to 1795. The faculty comprised one other professor and three tutors when he became president, but in four years the enrollment doubled and the faculty was increased accordingly. During his administration there graduated many distinguished Yale men, including the famous preacher, Lyman Beecher; the Reverend Bethel Judd, president of St. John's College in Maryland; the Reverend Henry Davis, president of Hamilton and later Middlebury College; the Reverend Daniel Haskell, president of Vermont University; William Maxwell, president of Hampden-Sydney College; the Reverend David A. Sherman, president of Eastern Tennessee College (later University of Tennessee); the Reverend Sereno E. Dwight, president of Hamilton College; the Reverend Horace Holley, president of Transylvania University; the Reverend Bennett Tyler, president of Dartmouth College; the Reverend Heman Humphrey, president of Amherst College; the Reverend Simeon Cotton, president of Mississippi College; Abraham B. Hasbrouck, president of Rutgers College; E. W. Baldwin, president of Wabash College; David B. Douglass, president of Kenyon

College; the Reverend Augustus H. Longstreet, president succes-
sively of Emory University (Georgia), Centenary College (Louisi-
ana), University of Mississippi and South Carolina College; the
Reverend Aratus Kent, president of Beloit College; the Reverend
George E. Pierce, president of Western Reserve College; the
Reverend Thomas M. Smith, president of Kenyon College; the
Reverend Nathaniel S. Wheaton, president of Trinity College.

Two of Dwight's graduates had more influence on shaping American history than all the rest: John C. Calhoun of South Carolina in
the class of 1804, and Samuel F. B. Morse, inventor of the telegraph,
of the class of 1810. Timothy Dwight's administration ended with his
death on January 11, 1817. He was universally considered an outstanding administrator and leader of men. He took initiative in
making Yale College a university by the establishment of professional schools in theology, law, and medicine.

Since our story is limited to the contribution of the church to the
four-year college, the further record of Yale must be greatly cur-
tailed. Dwight's immediate successor was the Reverend Jeremiah
Day who was president for twenty-nine years, the longest term in
the history of the college. His administration is noted for the increase
in the number of buildings, and in the finances of the institution,
and for the introduction of student athletics, college magazines, and
fraternities. Religion again asserted its primacy as indicated by
the "Illinois Band" composed of fourteen theological students who
went forth in 1828 to "Christianize that state." This group influenced
others to similar activities throughout the Northwest and thus to help
to make Yale an influential national institution.

President Day resigned in 1846 at the age of seventy-three but
lived twenty-one years longer. His immediate successor was the
Reverend Theodore D. Woolsey whose influence at Yale has been
considered unusually distinguished. He likewise held the presidency
a long while, twenty-five years, just four years less than the
Day regime. Woolsey's ministerial successors were the Reverend
Noah Porter, serving for fifteen years, and the Reverend Timothy
Dwight, the grandson of the earlier president Dwight. Under the
latter's administration the college continued to expand notably.

With the last ministerial president, this record of Yale College is concluded.

COLLEGE OF NEW JERSEY (PRINCETON UNIVERSITY)

The origin and the close connection with the Presbyterian Church of this colonial college can best be told by quoting the first two and one-half pages in the "history" section of the current issue of the Official Register of Princeton University:

PRINCETON UNIVERSITY is the child of the Great Awakening. It was during the third decade of the eighteenth century that Pietism, with its emphasis upon religious experience, gradually gained headway in the American colonies under the leadership of William Tennent, Sr., Theodore J. Frelinghuysen and other Calvinist leaders. It rose to a tidal wave a decade later when George Whitefield preached to immense assemblages in all the important colonial centers from Boston to Charleston. The evangelists won tens of thousands of ardent converts, but they also aroused resentment and bitterness because of their attacks upon the religion of faith and formalism.

It was chiefly because both Harvard and Yale denounced the movement and Yale actually expelled several students for joining in it, that the New Lights, as the revivalists called themselves, considered it necessary to found a new college, since an educated ministry was essential if the churches were to survive. Already several New Light academies were in existence, where some learned minister gathered a few young men around him for instruction in the classics, philosophy and theology. The most important of these was the academy of William Tennent, Sr., at Neshaminy, Pennsylvania, the famous Log College, which sent out a group of enthusiastic young preachers who exerted a powerful influence upon the Calvinistic groups in America.

But these isolated academies, with their lack of equipment and endowment, were unsatisfactory and William Tennent was becoming old and feeble, so that a group of New Jersey and New York New Lights "Concocted the plan and foundation of the college." The founders of Princeton were The Reverends Aaron Burr, Sr., Jonathan Dickinson, John Pierson, and Ebenezer Pemberton and three laymen—William Smith, Peter Van Brugh Livingston, and William Peartree Smith. To these men as trustees, the aged acting Governor of New Jersey, John Hamilton granted a charter on October 22, 1746. They at once secured the cooperation of their friends of the Log College by electing four of them—the Reverends Gilbert Tennent, William Tennent, Jr., Samuel Blair, and

Samuel Finley—together with Richard Treat, to the Board of Trustees. The original charter was lost, and for nearly two centuries historians searched for it in vain, but in 1945 a transcript was unearthed in the library of the Society for the Propagation of the Gospel, in London.

The College of New Jersey, as the institution was named, was not designed exclusively for educating ministers of the Gospel. "We hope it will be a means of raising up men that will be useful in other learned professions—ornaments of the State as well as the Church," declared the founders. "Therefore we propose to make the plan of education as extensive as our circumstances will admit." There were to be courses in the classics, divinity, philosophy and science comparable to those at Harvard and Yale and at the Scottish universities, and there was to be "free and equal liberty and advantage of education . . . any different sentiments on religion notwithstanding."

The Reverend Jonathan Dickinson was selected for the president, and in May, 1747, the first group of undergraduates, only eight or ten in number, assembled at Elizabeth, N.J., to report for work to this eminent divine. Thus opened the fourth college in the American colonies, and the first in the Middle Colonies. Since Dickinson had long conducted an academy of his own, it is probable that most of the students of the new college had already been under his instruction for one or more years. The only college building was the president's residence, the only library his collection of books on the classics and divinity. When, four and a half months after the opening, Dickinson died, the students moved to Newark and placed themselves under the learned, devout, affable young Aaron Burr, minister of the Presbyterian Church there.

In the meanwhile, doubts had arisen as to the validity of the charter, so that, on September 14, 1748, the trustees secured another from the new governor, Jonathan Belcher. The two charters are in substance the same, many paragraphs having identical wording, but the number of trustees was expanded to twenty-three and the Governor of New Jersey was made *ex-officio* a member of the Board.

The college prospered under Burr. It became obvious that funds must be raised for a building, however, so that the Reverends Gilbert Tennent and Samuel Davies crossed the Atlantic to tour England and Scotland appealing for aid. When news came back that they had several thousand pounds in hand, the trustees busied themselves with the plans for the college building and with selecting the proper site. At one time they had definitely fixed on New Brunswick, but when this town failed to meet all their conditions, they gave the prize to Princeton.

The plan for the new structure was made by the distinguished architect, Robert Smith, of Philadelphia, in collaboration with Dr. William Shippen. They decided upon a Georgian building of rough stone, with hipped roof, a cupola borrowed from the upper part of the cupola of St. Mary-le-Strand, London, a central facade with pediment, and a main doorway dominated by the head of Homer. On September 17, 1754, the cornerstone was laid in "the north westerly corner of the cellar," and in the fall of 1756 the students and tutors moved in. The trustees wished to call the building Belcher Hall, but the governor forbade it. May I ask "the favor of your naming the present building Nassau Hall," he said, "as expressing the honor we retain in this remote part of the globe to the immortal memory of the glorious King William III, who was a branch of the illustrious House of Nassau."

The direct influence of Scotch Presbyterianism is evidenced in the life of William Tennent, Sr. He was born in Ireland in 1673, graduated from the University of Edinburgh in 1695, and was ordained in 1706 in the Church of Ireland (Episcopal). He became a "dissenter" and migrated with his four sons in 1716 to Philadelphia where he came under the influence of the evangelist, George White-field, who seems to have had much influence on the origin of most of the colonial colleges.

The second president, the Reverend Aaron Burr, was the father of the notorious Aaron Burr whose fame and renown as a statesman turned to ill fame after his duel with Alexander Hamilton.

To the charter episode mentioned above can be added the fact that the application of the group for a charter was denied in 1745 by Royal Governor Morris who was opposed to any corporation not in sympathy with the Church of England. In the first group of twenty-three trustees authorized by the second charter there were twelve ministers, six of whom had graduated from Yale, three from Harvard, and three from the Log College. Of this original board all the members were Presbyterians (including Governor Belcher) except three, two of whom were members of the Society of Friends and one, a member of the Church of England.

The third president of the College of New Jersey was the famous divine and church philosopher, Jonathan Edwards. He succeeded his son-in-law, Aaron Burr. Edwards, in taking this appointment, responded to tremendous pressure to give up his work for the Indians in Stockbridge, Massachusetts. Within five weeks of his assumption of office he died from smallpox on March 22, 1758.

Like the three preceding presidents, the next two, also distinguished Presbyterian clergymen, died after short periods of service. Samuel Davies, who was reluctantly released by the Hanover Presbytery of Virginia, died from a severe cold on February 4, 1761, at the age of thirty-seven. Davies was succeeded by Samuel Finley, a native of Ireland, an alumnus of the Log College and founder of the Nottingham Academy in Northern Maryland, which for years has been prominent in the service of the church.

Again from Scotland came the next president whose influence on Princeton and the whole nation was remarkable. He was the Reverend Doctor John Witherspoon, a descendant of John Knox. Witherspoon arrived in this country at the age of forty-six. Immediately after taking office in 1768, he cast his influence with the Whigs who were soon to lead the colonies into the War of the Revolution. His leadership in the contest is indicated by his having been one of the signers of the Declaration of Independence.

During Witherspoon's presidency of twenty-six years he was able to bring back into the black the hopelessly muddled college finances by successful appeals to the public, by careful economy in operation, and also by a successful lottery. He was conspicuously influential in bringing about a reunion of the "new light" and "old side" Presbyterian groups.

In the General Assembly of the Presbyterian Church held in 1789 it was reported that 52 of the 188 member ministers had been pupils of Witherspoon. Among his clerical graduates were founders or early presidents of Brown University, Hampden-Sydney College, Union College, University of North Carolina, Washington and Jefferson College, and the University of Nashville, which later became George Peabody College for Teachers. Other students who became statesmen were James Madison, fourth President of the United States, Aaron Burr, Vice President of the United States, and Henry and Charles Lee of Virginia. Six of his other pupils were members of the Continental Congress, thirty-nine in the United States House of Representatives, twenty-one in the United States Senate, and ten became cabinet officers.

Witherspoon's successor in 1795 was the Reverend Samuel Stanhope Smith, his son-in-law. Smith had been the first president of Hampden-Sydney College in Virginia when he left to serve as vice president of the College of New Jersey while President Witherspoon was serving in the new United States Congress. For a short while during Witherspoon's administration the college was not in operation due to the occupancy of Nassau Hall by the British, who were run out on January 3, 1777, by George Washington's early morning suprise attack. A shot from one of Washington's men smashed the portrait of King George II, who had authorized the grant of the college charter. Appropriately, six and one-half years later the trustees voted to replace this portrait with one of Washington by the well-known artist Charles Willson Peale.

The College of New Jersey drifted along until the advent of another magnetic Scotch clergyman by the name of James McCosh. He became president in 1868, just one hundred years after Witherspoon's administration began. Like all other colleges Princeton had severe financial struggles during the panic years of 1819, 1837, and 1857.

Continuing under the policy of recruiting most of the trustees and faculty from the Presbyterian clergy, there developed at one period a serious situation when the trustees insisted on interfering with the faculty in matters of discipline, attendance on classes, oral examinations, and in other ways.

Of the presidents serving between Witherspoon and McCosh one was a strong Calvinist, Ashbel Green, who held office from 1792 to 1800. He was Chaplain of the United States while Congress was holding its sessions in Philadelphia. John Maclean, Jr., the first layman president, served from 1854 to 1868, and was on the faculty for a total of fifty years. Maclean had to contend with the second burning of Nassau Hall in 1855, the War Between the States, and the rising conflict between science and religion which became critical with the appearance of Darwin's *The Origin of the Species* in 1859. He continued the policy of electing Presbyterians to the faculty. He was able to increase the endowment by nearly $100,000 and to keep up the enrollment in spite of the war.

Although McCosh was fifty-seven when he took over the administration, he served for twenty years. He was accredited with inscrutable Scotch humor and an irresistible Scotch charm. He was responsible for the construction of some twelve important buildings now on Princeton's campus. He was particularly successful in hiring competent and distinguished scholars as members of his faculty.

At the 150th anniversary exercises of the College of New Jersey, McCosh's successor, President Francis Landey Patton, announced on October 22, 1896, that henceforth the College of New Jersey would be called Princeton University. This was caused partly by the addition over the years of the various professional schools, particularly the Graduate School. A chief address at the sesquicentennial exercises was entitled "Princeton In the Nation's Service," delivered by Professor Woodrow Wilson who later became President of Princeton, Governor of New Jersey, and twenty-eighth President of the United States. Both he and the present president, Harold Willis Dodds, who has shown conspicuous leadership, were sons of Presbyterian ministers.

College of Philadelphia (University of Pennsylvania)

According to the report of former President Thomas S. Gates in *The Encyclopedia Americana,* the University of Pennsylvania had its origins in the Charity School, established in Philadelphia in 1740. This observation has confirmation, with supporting data, in the definitive history of the University, written for its 1940 bicentennial by Edward P. Cheyney the well-known historian and professor of history for many years at the university. Other historians cast some doubt on this claim. They indicate that the Charity School did not carry on classes regularly and that the real start of the university was made in the organization of the Philadelphia Academy, January 7, 1751. The academy took over the Charity School building and in 1753 the trustees received a charter from Thomas and Richard Penn, "true and absolute proprietaries and governors in chief of the Province of Pennsylvania." The name given in the charter was "Academy and Charitable School in the Province of Pennsylvania." Benjamin Franklin had been elected in 1751 president of the board of trustees of the new academy.

The man responsible for the organization of the 1740 Charity

School was the Reverend George Whitefield, an ordained member of the clergy of the Church of England. He had been associated in the Holy Club while a student at Oxford University, 1732-36, with another Anglican clergyman, John Wesley. He was also an associate of Wesley in the early days of the Methodist movement and followed him to the United States. Whitefield became a flaming gospel evangelist, making repeated tours up and down the Atlantic seaboard, with regular stops at his Charity School in Philadelphia, in whose large auditorium he frequently preached. On one trip to Boston he caused a furor among the students and faculty of the staid old college erected in Cambridge a century earlier. Whitefield's eloquence was so powerful that even deistic Benjamin Franklin admits that once, when standing on the fringe of the outdoor multitude listening to Whitefield's appeal for his charity school in Savannah, Georgia, he was so stirred that he first decided to put in the collection plate the loose coppers in his pocket, then his silver and finally emptied his whole purse when the collector came along. Though poles apart in points of view, Franklin and Whitefield were close friends. In a letter to his brother, Franklin said of Whitefield: "He is a good man and I love him." Franklin printed Whitefield's *Journal* and sermons.

Appreciation of Whitefield's stimulus to improvement of higher education in Philadelphia is clearly noted in the erection of a monument to his honor and memory in a prominent location on the campus of the University of Pennsylvania. It bears these inscriptions on bronze tablets on three of the sides of its hexagonal granite base:

Zealous advocate and patron of higher education in the American Colonies. The Charity School of 1740, the beginning of the University of Pennsylvania, was a fruit of his ministry.

The University of Pennsylvania held its first sessions in a building erected for his congregations and was aided by his collections, guided by his counsel, inspired by his life.

I knew him intimately upwards of thirty years. His integrity, disinterestedness and indefatigable zeal in prosecuting every good work, I have never seen equalled, and shall never see excelled.

BENJAMIN FRANKLIN

In the "constitutions" of the new academy there is little mention of religion; the twenty-four trustees were chosen "without regard to difference of religious persuasion." The facts show, however, that three-fourths were members of the Church of England, two were Quakers, and one was a Presbyterian. Franklin himself was a pew-holder in Christ Church, of which several other trustees were vestrymen. The evidence is clear that the Anglican influence pre-dominated in the university until the Revolution. There was no financial or other support of any religious group or organization. The trustees of the academy did promise on taking over their build-ing to accept the religious implications of the Charity School, which was intended for the instruction of children of the poor "in useful literature and the knowledge of the Christian religion."

The trustees, notably Franklin, were avid to have their Philadel-phia Academy metamorphosed into a college. This desire was greatly enhanced by the energetic Reverend Doctor William Smith, who had joined the faculty in May 1754, to teach "Logick, Rhetorick, Ethicks and Natural Philosophy." Smith, a twenty-six-year-old alumnus of the University of Aberdeen, had come to America the previous year. He made a most favorable impression on Franklin by his brilliant essay, *Idea of the College of Mirania,* an imaginary institution where he put into effect his thoughts on an ideal cur-riculum and faculty. The head of this paper college he called *provost* or *principal.*

Smith was given the title of "provost" when he was made head of the new college in 1755, a title maintained until recently for the presiding officer of the University of Pennsylvania. Under urging of Professor William Smith of the academy and of the Reverend Richard Peters, Rector of the Charity School, maintained for the lower grades, the trustees sought and obtained promptly from the Penns in June 1755, a revised charter under the title "The Provost, Vice-Provost, and Professors of the College, Academy and Charitable School of Philadelphia in the Province of Pennsylvania."

Religious influence continued to prevail in the newly expanded institution. Provost William Smith had gone to England in 1754 to be ordained an Anglican priest. Vice-Provost Francis Alison, an Ulster Scotch-Irishman and graduate of the University of Glasgow, was an ordained Presbyterian minister. His great contributions to another early American college, the University of Delaware, are delineated in a later chapter.

Provost Smith was sent to England in 1764 to seek funds for the new college. Due to a long siege of illness and obstacles to be overcome in finding interested prospective donors, he stayed abroad nearly two and a half years. Through the friendship of the Archbishop of Canterbury and Thomas Penn, he met many distinguished persons, including William Pitt and King George III. The latter made a donation of 200 pounds to his fund. Early in his search for funds Smith met James Jay of New York, who was on a similar mission for King's College, and he wisely joined forces with him. To his chagrin the King gave twice as much to King's College for the reason that the college in New York had no rich patrons like the Penn family.

This cooperative attack on British philanthropy led Historian Cheyney to observe that Columbia and Pennsylvania Universities were better known in England then than at any time since, to which a dissent can be humbly offered. Smith was successful in his quest, even if he had to visit some of his prospects "twenty times" before securing a gift and had to hear repeatedly that his listeners were "harassed with an infinity of appeals." An eloquent sermon in Mayfair Chapel brought a gift of 100 pounds from Lady Curzon. The Penns gave him 500 pounds, the Princess Dowager of Wales, 100 pounds. He received innumerable smaller gifts from individuals like William Pitt and the Duke of Newcastle, from some Oxford Colleges and from several Baptist and Methodist congregations. He was even helped by the managers of the Drury Lane and Covent Garden theatres. He returned to Philadelphia with some 12,000 pounds. In 1771 this prototype of present-day college presidents brought back 1000 pounds from a begging trip to that other great American seaport of the time, Charleston, South Carolina. During Provost Smith's extensive travel in search of funds, the college paid part of its operating expenses from results of a lottery scheme set up by the trustees.

Soon after his productive trips, Smith became embroiled in debates with his former great friend and admirer, the clever politician Franklin who was seeking to have the proprietary governors ousted by appointees of the British Crown. Naturally Smith stood by his loyal and liberal friends, the Penns. Franklin was no longer chairman of the board of trustees. In line with the acrid type of pamphleteer debates then prevalent, Franklin let loose a blast against colleagues on the board "for Comfort of old Sinners that in Politics as well as in Religion Repentance and Amendment though late shall obtain Forgiveness . . . and P(eters) should preach your funeral Sermon and S(mith), the Poisoner of other's characters, embalm your Memory."

The quartering of Pennsylvania militia in the college buildings and its later use by the British as a hospital forced the college to suspend practically all of its activities during most of the years 1777-78. On the formation of the Commonwealth of Pennsylvania, the party that had come to power felt resentment at the "artistocrats" on the college board of trustees, some of whom actually were Tories, and passed a law on November 27, 1779, which replaced the old board with a new group of men not dominated by influential members of the Anglican Church. This was the culmination of a tendency that distressed the Archbishop of Canterbury who had written a ministerial colleague in Philadelphia as early as 1763, "That of fifteen teachers in the College all are Presbyterians except Dr. Smith and that they are endeavoring to destroy his influence and worm him out." And worm him out they did, by changing the title of the college to University of the State of Pennsylvania and electing as provost, the Reverend John Ewing, a Presbyterian minister who had served under Smith as professor of natural and experimental philosophy, a fancy name for the present-day chair of physics.

With this more social and political rather than economic metamorphosis, Provost Smith, himself accused of Tory leanings, was naturally reluctant to cooperate. After holding the keys and the seal of the college for about a year he relinquished them on receiving "legal process for his expulsion" and a promise by the trustees to pay monies due for his past services. The new trustees did include in their number a few ministers from the Presbyterian, Lutheran, and Roman Catholic persuasions, but there no longer lingered a distinct religious relationship.

The undaunted William Smith became rector of a parish in Chestertown, Maryland, in 1780 with a salary of 600 bushels of wheat per annum. In 1782 he was elected the first president of Washington College, this Maryland college being the first of several institutions of higher learning named for the nation's first President.

King's College (Columbia University)

King's College had its first session on July 17, 1754. During 1954 the two hundredth anniversary of this memorable event was celebrated by Columbia University, the name assumed by the college at the conclusion of the American Revolution. The Reverend Doctor Samuel Johnson met his first class of eight students in "the Vestry Room in the new School-House adjoining to Trinity-Church in New York, which the Gentlemen of the vestry are so good as to favour them with the Use of, in the interim, 'till a convenient Place may be built."

The temporary building was located on the site now occupied by the offices of the United States Steel Corporation. The new "convenient Place" was located in what is now Park Place, New York City, in 1760. There King's College remained until 1857 when it moved to 49th Street between Park and Madison Avenues. Forty years later in 1897 it moved to Morningside Heights, its present location.

As early as 1703 the rector and wardens of Trinity Church had plans for the establishment of a college in New York City. The proposal was revived when the royal governor of the colony gave his consent to the raising of a sum of 2250 pounds by a public lottery. Somewhat over a thousand pounds more were raised by individuals by November 1751, when ten trustees were selected for the proposed college. Seven of these were members of the Church of England, with some of them having been vestrymen of Trinity Church, two belonging to the Dutch Reformed Church, and one a Presbyterian. The latter, William Livingston, was decidedly opposed to connecting the college with any church. He was especially jealous of any connection with the Church of England.

In spite of Livingston's opposition, the charter of King's College was granted by King George II on October 31, 1754. Eleven months previously the trustees had invited to be president Samuel Johnson of Stratford Parish in Connecticut, who had served for thirty years as missionary for the Society of the Propagation of the Gospel. The salary was 250 pounds per annum, with the hint that the vestry of Trinity Church would make a considerable addition thereto, on the condition that he serve as assistant minister to the church. Dr. Johnson was fifty-eight years old at the time; he had graduated from Yale College in 1714; he had been a teacher there and later been ordained as a preacher of the Congregational Church; later had become a convert to the Church of England and taken holy orders in England in 1722. He had become a close friend of Bishop George Berkeley and was a leading exponent of the Berkeleian philosophy in the colonies.

The task of the new college named for George II was outlined by Dr. Johnson as follows:

. . . to instruct and perfect youth in the learned languages, and in the arts of reasoning exactly, of writing correctly and speaking eloquently; and in the arts of numbering and measuring, of surveying and navigation, of geography and history, of husbandry, commerce and government; and in the knowledge of all nature in the heavens above us, and in the air, water and earth around us . . . and finally to lead them from the study of nature to the knowledge of themselves, and of the God of nature, their duty to Him, themselves and one another.

When the vestry of Trinity Church gave the land for the original site of the college one condition of the gift was "that the president should *forever* be a member of or be in communion with the Church of England . . . and that the morning and evening service in the college should be the liturgy of the said church." However, the charter did explicitly insist that no person should be excluded from equal opportunities for education offered by the college. Further evidence of the liberality of the first board of governors is indicated by the fact that when the committee was appointed to prepare the seal of the college it included the ministers of the Dutch, Lutheran, and Presbyterian Churches who were then on the board.

Funds were obtained in England by the assistance of Dr. James Jay who happened to be there on business of his own. As recorded more extensively in the section on the College of Philadelphia, he teamed up with Provost William Smith of that college. President Johnson, frightened by an epidemic of smallpox, left the college in November 1757, to reside in Westchester, leaving the thirty students distributed among three classes under the care of Leonard Cutting, an alumnus of Pembroke Hall, Cambridge University, England. In March 1758, Johnson returned to his duties and on June 21, 1758, conferred the first Bachelor of Arts degrees upon eight students. A year later he was away again for six months because of another smallpox scare.

In the autumn of 1762 there came from England the Reverend Myles Cooper, a fellow of Queen's College, recommended by Archbishop Secker of Canterbury as a suitable assistant to Dr. Johnson.

The following April when Dr. Johnson resigned Cooper was elected the second president of the college. He was considered by some "the most elegant scholar that America ever saw." However, the role he played in the political controversies of the time and other prejudicial actions did indicate that this epithet was hardly appropriate. In Cooper's day there were some students who became famous during the Revolution and the early days of the nation like John Jay, Gouverneur Morris, Alexander Hamilton, the brothers William (first elected governor of New Jersey) and Robert R. Livingston, whose father had acted so cantankerously when the college was organized. In one political controversy the president who took the side of the British government was worsted by his pupil Alexander Hamilton, which event did not lessen Cooper's appreciation and respect for his brilliant student.

President Cooper continued boldly to write and speak for the Tory side in the colonial contest. This action resulted in his receiving a letter from Philadelphia hinting dire treatment if he continued as president. Warned by this and the urgency of one of his former pupils, he escaped in the nick of time on May 10, 1775, by jumping half-dressed over the college fence and running along the bank of the Hudson until he could find shelter in the home of his friend, Stuyvesant. Thence he took refuge on board a British ship that soon sailed for England. It is readily understood that there was no Commencement in 1775. In a few months the college was taken over for use by the American troops, with the library and other apparatus being deposited in the New York City Hall.

After a slumbering existence of eight years the college re-opened in 1784 with the receipt of a new charter on May 1st from the legislature of New York, reading "An Act for granting certain privileges to the college heretofore called King's College for altering the name and charter thereof and erecting an University within this state." This was the origin of the body known as the Regents of the University. They voted to call the revived institution *Columbia College*. In this charter twenty-nine gentlemen were named as trustees "who were to exercise their functions until their number should be reduced by death, resignation or removal from the state to twenty-four, after which all vacancies in their number were to be filled by their own choice."

This action removes Columbia from further consideration because of limitations in our plan. It is of interest to note that the new president elected on May 21, 1787, was William Samuel Johnson, LL.D., son of the first president, Samuel Johnson. Several of his successors continued to be Episcopal clergymen, one being Bishop Benjamin M. Moore who was president from 1801 to 1811. The transformation of the college into a university and the great influence it now wields does not fall within the scope of the present work. It should be added that its continued great progress has been made under the presidencies of church laymen Seth Low (later mayor of New York City), Nicholas Murray Butler, Dwight D. Eisenhower, and the present president, Grayson Kirk.

RHODE ISLAND COLLEGE (BROWN UNIVERSITY)

"The Great Awakening" of the eighteenth century stimulated a notable advance in religion and in the building of churches, and an interest in organizing educational institutions. Unlike the other early colleges which had indigenous roots, Brown University had its origin in the desire of the Baptist Churches scattered along the Atlantic seaboard to establish a college that would train ministers for the several church groups that firmly believed in separation of church and state. A movement in this direction came to a head in 1762 under the direction of the Baptist Association of Philadelphia.

It was decided to locate the college in Rhode Island, the state founded by the Baptist Roger Williams. There was to be no appeal made for donations by the state, as was the case with Yale and Harvard. Warren was chosen in 1764 as the location of the new institution chartered under the name of Rhode Island College. Although the charter definitely prohibited the use of religious tests and required that the college should open its doors to all denominations of Protestants, it did stipulate that of the 36 trustees, 22 must be Baptists, 5 Friends, 5 Episcopalians, and 4 Congregationalists. In the smaller Board of Fellows, 8 are to be "forever" Baptist and the other 4 may be members of any denomination. The charter also enjoined that the president shall "forever" be a member of the Baptist Church. The charter did advise the trustees to change the location of the college if a more suitable place were found, also to change the name if some benefactor were discovered who contributed considerable amounts for the welfare of the college.

In 1770 the college was moved from Warren to Providence in spite of spirited pleas from three other communities, notably Newport, the other capital of the colony.

James Manning, a New Jersey farmer's son and graduate in the class of 1762 of the College of New Jersey (now Princeton), was named by the trustees in September 1765, "president of the college, professor of languages and other branches of learning with full power to act in these capacities at Warren or elsewhere." He had come to Warren in February 1764, to open a Latin school and to serve as the local Baptist minister. The Latin school that he founded continued many years, taking later the name of University Grammar School.

Since the trustees were unwilling to seek funds from the state, they sent the Reverend Morgan Edwards in 1767-68 to England to secure subscriptions for the college. He had been born in Wales, ordained a minister in Ireland, and had served briefly as a preacher in England before coming to Pennsylvania.

Edwards had had previous success in obtaining subscriptions for the college from the Philadelphia churches. He had similar success in Ireland and England but failed to go to Scotland as he had been instructed by the trustees. The contributions he received were numerous but small. However they did total some 900 pounds which was to be used as an endowment for the president's salary. In a letter to President Manning, he commented on the generosity of the English, particularly of the residents of London, but indicated disgust at the boasting from America as announced in the British press concerning the great amount of cloth now being manufactured in the colonies. He added "this raises the indignation of the merchants and manufacturers. I have not only been denied by hundreds but also abused on that score. My patience, my feet, my assurance, are much impaired. I took a cold in November which stuck to me all winter, owing to my trampoosing the streets in all weathers."

As in the case of the College of Philadelphia, the Brown trustees were rewarded with a sizable gift from the South. A visit of Hezekiah Smith, Manning's classmate at Princeton, brought back some $2500 from South Carolina and Georgia.

While his financial emissaries were on the road, President Manning was tempted to try a lottery scheme to bolster the desperate financial status of the college. Unlike his distinguished colleagues at several other colonial colleges, mentioned in this chapter, President Manning did not yield to the temptation. He was bolstered in his faltering decision by a strong comment from the Reverend John Ryland of England for whose advice he had written. Ryland indicated that "lotteries were a cursed gambling . . . big with ten thousand evils."

The enrollment increased from one student in 1765 to 10 the next year, 21 in 1770, 35 in 1773, and 41 in 1775. The graduation of the first class in 1769 was an historic occasion; it established the earliest state holiday in the history of Rhode Island. The valedictorian of the class of seven was Charles Thompson, a chaplain of the Revolutionary army. Among the others were William Rogers, another chaplain of that Army, and James Mitchell Varnum, who became a Brigadier General in the American Army, a member of Congress from Rhode Island, and a judge in the Northwest Territory.

The Revolutionary War caused the college to close from 1776 to 1782. The buildings were used first as barracks by the American Army and later as a hospital for French soldiers. Although Manning had been elected in 1786 to represent Rhode Island in the Congress of the Confederation, he had great difficulty in obtaining favorable action from that body on claims for destruction of the college buildings during the Revolution. He finally obtained a total of $2000, although he had requested $5000.

Mindful of the permission granted in the charter, Manning tried to find wealthy friends in England who would lend their name to the college as had been the case of Yale in New Haven and Dartmouth in New Hampshire. Thomas Llewelyn failed to respond to the flattery indicated in Manning's letter: "Llewelyn College appears well when written, and sounds no less agreeably when spoken." Manning gradually gave more and more time to the college and less to his pastoral duties, but the strain continued unusually onerous. After serving for twenty-seven years as Brown's first president, he died on July 29, 1791.

Manning's successor was another Baptist clergyman by the name of Jonathan Maxcy. He took over the administration in 1792, also at the age of twenty-four. He was a graduate of Rhode Island College, had been a tutor there for four years, was ordained to preach in 1790 and had taken over Manning's church in 1791. He was reputed to be an accomplished orator. After serving ten years as president of Brown, he served two years as president of Union College in New York, and from 1804 to 1820 was the first president of South Carolina College, now University of South Carolina.

The next president was Asa Messer of the class of 1790 who served from 1802-26. He too was distinguished as a minister and orator. Early in his administration, September 6, 1804, came a letter from Nicholas Brown offering $5000 to endow a Chair of Oratory. In this letter, Brown, who was treasurer of the college, indicated that his interest was inspired by love for the institution from which he had graduated, as had his distinguished brother Moses. As suggested in this letter, the $5000 was allowed to accumulate until it totalled $10,000, which was turned over to the treasurer, another member of the Brown family, for endowment of the professorship. Forthwith the trustees voted to change the name of Rhode Island College to be known in all "future" time by the name of *Brown University in Providence, in the State of Rhode Island and Providence Plantations.* Later Nicholas Brown made further donations totalling more than $150,000.

Messer's successor was the Reverend Doctor Francis Wayland who held the presidency for twenty-nine years, 1826-55. On graduating from Union College at the age of seventeen, Wayland studied medicine for two and a half years under distinguished doctors in Troy, New York. In 1816 he responded to a call to the ministry and entered the Andover Seminary where he was greatly influenced by Moses Stuart who stimulated his interest in German, philology, and criticism. From 1821 to 1827 he became the pastor of the first Baptist Church in Boston. He was a modest man saying on occasion to a friend about a sermon he had preached before the annual meeting of the Boston Baptist Foreign Mission Society in 1823: "It was a complete failure. It fell perfectly dead." To his amazement the sermon was published with various editions being rapidly exhausted. As a disciplinarian and an administrator, he was to the manner born. He had a distinguished appearance and could hold unusually well any kind of audience, whether students or sophisticated alumni or other adults. He was noted also for his curriculum which, with its pronounced elective features, was far ahead of the colleges of his time.

On Wayland's resignation the trustees unanimously elected in 1855 the Reverend Barnas Sears. He had succeeded Horace Mann in 1848 as the second secretary of the Massachusetts Board of Education. He had graduated from Brown in 1825 and from the Theological Seminary at Newton in 1828. After two years as pastor of the Baptist Church in Hartford his health failed. He then assumed the heavy burden of being professor of ancient languages in Colgate University, then known as Hamilton Literary and Theological Institution. Since no class was immediately ready for him at Colgate, he went to study under several renowned classical scholars in Germany. His experience with the Massachusetts Board of Education and as a teacher and president brought him to the attention of George Peabody, who had set up in February 1867, a two million dollar trust fund "for promotion of education in the more destitute portions of the Southern and Southwestern states."

On May 9, 1867, Sears accepted the position of "General Agent" of the Peabody Fund and resigned the presidency of Brown. During his administration the college had accepted some land from the state through the operation of the Morrill Act for the establishment of a land-grant college. This arrangement was not happy and, after some debate and financial arrangements mutually satisfactory,

Brown University turned over its budding interest in a land-grant institution to the newly formed Rhode Island College of Agriculture, now known as the University of Rhode Island.

The Reverend Doctor Alexis Caswell succeeded Dr. Sears, heading the college in 1868 and serving only four years. He too was an alumnus of Brown and had held distinguished pastorates in various Baptist churches; he had taught part time in Columbian College, a Baptist institution in Washington, D. C., and had held a professorship at Brown University.

The next president of Brown served seventeen years from 1872 to 1889. He was the Reverend Doctor E. G. Robinson who came from the presidency of the Rochester Theological Seminary. He obtained his baccalaureate degree from Brown in 1838 under Francis Wayland and hoped to continue his regime and be as successful in administering his alma mater.

When Robinson resigned in 1889 he was succeeded by Elisha B. Andrews, then professor of political economy at Cornell University. However, he met all the charter requirements by having been a graduate of Brown in 1870 and the Newton Theological Seminary in 1874. After preaching for a year in Beverly, Massachusetts, he served as president of Denison University in Ohio from 1874 to 1879. The next three years he was professor at Newton Theological Seminary, and the following five years taught history and political economy at Brown before going to Cornell in 1888.

In 1899 Andrews resigned to become chancellor of the University of Nebraska. His successor, William Herbert Perry Faunce, another minister and an alumnus of the class of 1880, served for thirty years. His distinguished administration added luster to the renown of Brown. Another ministerial alumnus, Clarence A. Barbour, was president from 1929 to 1937.

The growth of the institution and its continuing drift from the primary task of educating clergymen brought about over the years gradually decreasing interest and support of the Baptists as an organization. The charter requirement of electing "forever" a president of the Baptist faith was abolished by legislative Act in 1926. In 1937 the trustees elected the present president, Henry M. Wriston, a son of a Methodist minister. Under President Wriston's direction, the prestige of Brown University has advanced notably.

In 1942 complete severance from Baptist control and influence became legal with another appropriate legislative amendment to the charter. Hereafter not only the president but also the trustees, faculty, and all other officers will be free of religious requirements.

Among the many distinguished alumni of Brown graduating from Wayland's day to the end of the nineteenth century, space permits the inclusion of only a very few. In addition to the alumni who became Brown presidents, already listed, mention can be made of James B. Angell (1849), who was president of the University of Vermont, the University of Michigan, later United States Minister to Turkey and China; Benjamin Ide Wheeler (1875), president of the University of California; Horace Mann (1819), first president of Antioch College, after serving as first secretary of the Massachusetts State Board of Education; Alexander Meiklejohn (1893), president of Amherst College; John D. Rockefeller, Jr. (1897), peerless philanthropist and churchman; John Hay (1858), private secretary to Abraham Lincoln and later United States Secretary of State; Charles Evans Hughes (1881), Governor of New York, United States Secretary of State, and Chief Justice of the Supreme Court. The influence of Brown became markedly international through the great work done for Christianity by Adoniram Judson (1807) in far-away Burma. His stature at home is recognized in the founding of Judson College in 1838 by the Baptists of Alabama.

Queen's College (Rutgers University)

Queen's College has advanced through a notable series of transformations. Although it received its first state charter on November 10, 1766, it did not open until November 1771, after receiving a second charter under date of March 20, 1770. It remained under the control of its organizers, the Dutch Reformed Church, up to 1920. It was given the name of Rutgers College in 1825. In 1864 the Scientific School of Rutgers was designated the Land Grant College of New Jersey when courses in agriculture and engineering were added to the curriculum. Rutgers College changed its name to Rutgers University in 1924, and in 1945 it became officially the *State University of New Jersey.*

The second charter was sought and obtained because the first had been lost, as well as minutes of trustee meetings, which had received newspaper announcements from time to time. In the amended charter there was dropped the distinction indicated between the residents and nonresidents of the state of New Jersey. According to tradition the requirement in the first charter that the Dutch language be the only one used was omitted in the second charter.

This illuminating excerpt from the charter approved by Governor William Franklin indicates the same sort of concern evinced by the founders of most of the colonial colleges:

Whereas our loving subjects being of the Protestant reformed religion, according to the constitution of the reformed churches in the United Provinces, and using the discipline of the said churches, as approved and instituted by the national synod of Dort in the year 1618-19, are in this and the neighboring provinces very numerous, consisting of many churches and religious assemblies, the ministers and elders of which having taken into serious consideration the manner in which the said churches might be properly supplied with an able, learned, and well-qualified ministry, and thinking it necessary, and being very desirous, that a college might be erected for that purpose within this our province of New Jersey, in which the learned languages and other branches of useful knowledge may be taught and degrees conferred, and especially that young men of suitable abilities may be instructed in divinity, preparing them for the ministry and supplying the necessity of the churches . . . inconveniences are manifold and the expenses heavy, in either being supplied with ministers of the gospel from foreign parts or sending young men abroad for education.

A perusal of this earnest and solemn reasoning for the founding of a college causes one to wonder if the same enthusiasm for religion still abides in the United States. Hope is supported by evidences of continuing interest, as indicated in later chapters.

The founders of Queen's College soon forgot their gratitude to the grantors of their ardently desired charter, "George the Third, by the grace of God, of Great Britain, France and Ireland, King, defender of the faith, etc.," and his appointed Governor of the Province of New Jersey, William Franklin. More animosity was really felt toward the latter, who remained an ardent Tory during the

Revolution, fleeing to Connecticut for asylum and later to England where he died in 1813. His unpatriotic actions caused estrangement from his famous father, Benjamin Franklin. They can be explained, doubtless, by his long residence abroad and his education at Oxford, where he received the Master of Arts degree in 1762.

Under the new charter for the college named in honor of Charlotte, the Queen Consort of George III, the trustees held their first meeting on May 7, 1771, at Hackensack. That town lost by a vote of ten to seven the permanent location of Queen's College because the citizens of New Brunswick claimed they had a more healthful location and were able to produce more funds. Another consideration might have been the nearer location to the German Reformed Churches of Pennsylvania, which, like the Dutch Reformed group, remained under the care of the *Classes* of Amsterdam.

Classes were begun in the fall of 1771 in an old New Brunswick tavern, The Sign of the Red Lion. Frederick Frelinghuysen comprised the faculty with the title of "tutor," which title was then held in higher esteem than "professor." Frelinghuysen was an honor graduate of Princeton in the class of 1770. He was a son of John Frelinghuysen and the step-son of Jacob Rutsen Hardenbergh, both distinguished divines and leaders in the Dutch Reformed Church and in the affairs of Queen's College. After two years as tutor, Frederick Frelinghuysen resigned to study and practice law. Evidence of his success in this field is his election to several important committees in the province, to the Continental Congress, and to the United States Senate in 1793. In his spare time he became a leader in the militia, rising through the ranks of captain, major, colonel, to general by the close of the Revolution.

Queen's College limped along without a president until 1786. The tutors, with the cooperation of a committee of local trustees, ran the college. One of these tutors was Colonel John Taylor who served about twenty years as its principal teacher, becoming a professor at Union College at its inception in 1796.

The nearness of the battle lines forced the college to leave New Brunswick several times during the Revolution, locating once at Millstone and on another occasion at North Branch. A quarrel between the Coetus and Conferentii Parties of the Reformed Church also tended to delay progress at the college.

By the close of the American Revolution the college had not graduated more than thirty young men. Matthew Leydt was the first graduate. He received the Bachelor of Arts degree at the 1774 Commencement, "who delivered Orations in Latin, Dutch and English" which were received "with high applause." A most distinguished person in this early group was Simeon DeWitt who delivered at the 1778 Commencement the Salutatory Oration in Latin and English. Serving with the American Army during the Revolution he was its "geographer" from 1780 to 1783. He was surveyor general of the State of New Jersey from 1784 to 1834, holding other important state offices to the time of his death.

Another outstanding graduate among the alumni soldiers of the Revolution was Jeremiah Smith of the class of 1780, who returned to his native state of New Hampshire to represent it for four terms in the United States Congress and to become its governor and later chief justice of its Supreme Court.

When the Revolutionary War had concluded and the conservative and liberal groups of the church had become reconciled, the trustees finally decided they needed a president, an office still considered a necessary nuisance in some academic circles. Lack of funds made it seem advisable to find a competent pastor of the local Reformed Church who could also serve as president of the college. The first so chosen was the Reverend Dirck Romeyn of Hackensack. He declined, moving soon afterward to Schenectady, New York, to become a founder of Union College. A similar offer was made to the Reverend Jacob Rutsen Hardenbergh, who accepted the dual position on February 9, 1786, remaining president of Queen's until his death, October 30, 1790. The loyalty of the Hardenberghs has long continued to abide. The first president had a son and several grandsons to graduate from the college. A great-great grandson, Henry Janeway Hardenbergh, served as architect for the college's Kirkpatrick Chapel in 1872 and for its renovation in 1916. This renovation was the gift of another great-great grandson, William P. Hardenbergh.

After a second vain attempt to persuade the synod to approve a union with Princeton, the trustees carried on the college with the aid of tutors until 1795. After the trustees were compelled by lack of finances to close their "collidge" they gave their chief attention to their flourishing Grammar School until 1807. At that time sufficient interest and support were obtained from the Reformed Synod so that the college could re-open. The pastor of the local church, Dr. Ira Condict, was made president *pro tempore*. He taught the senior class, his son Daniel was chosen as tutor, and Dr. Robert Adrian as professor of mathematics.

In 1810, Dr. John H. Livingston, the distinguished divine of the Reformed Church, was lured from his beloved New York to become president of the college. He had been recommended for president at its founding by the church authorities in Amsterdam and Utrecht. He had declined offers of the presidency made by the trustees in 1790 and 1808. He finally accepted at the age of sixty-four. In spite of attempts to raise funds through a legalized lottery scheme, finances became so low that the college again closed its doors in 1816. Dr. Livingston finally stimulated the local and the neighboring synods of New York and Albany to come to the rescue with gifts of over $50,000. Before Dr. Livingston could see the fruition of his plans he passed away on January 20, 1825.

That year became memorable in the history of the college; its name was legally changed to *Rutgers College* and the Reverend Doctor Philip Milledoler accepted its presidency. The latter, a trustee since 1815, was fifty years old, was a graduate of Columbia College in 1793, had preached from 1794 to 1800 in both German and English at the German Reformed Church, Nassau Street, New York, had served as minister of a Presbyterian Church in Philadelphia from 1800 to 1805 when he became minister of Rutgers Street Presbyterian Church in New York until 1813 when he shifted again his religious relations to become pastor of the Dutch Reformed Church of New York. In 1808 he served as moderator of the General Assembly of the Presbyterian Church.

Not relishing relics of royalty, the patriotic trustees were quite willing to drop the title of "Queen's" and approve the name of "Rutgers," in honor of an elder in Milledoler's New York Church. Henry Rutgers was descended from early Dutch settlers, had graduated from Kings College (Columbia) in 1766, was for many years a leading citizen in New York City. He had been active in public welfare and in the service of the church. He was known for his philanthropies in New York but the records fail to show that he gave more than $200 for the college bell, still in use, and $5000 for the endowment of the college. The latter was a conspicuously large gift for those days.

In 1839, after some years of committee study and synod debates, action was taken by the Reformed Synod whereby the trustees were allowed full control over the college without synodical supervision. No longer would the president be required to be one of the professors of theology, still a most important phase of the curriculum. The synod still retained title to the property. A year after the consummation of transfer of authority of administration, Philip Milledoler resigned as president, though continuing a year longer as professor of theology.

From 1840 to 1850 the presidency was held by Abraham Bruyn Hasbrouck, LL.D., a distinguished lawyer from Ulster County, New York. During his term of office much advance was made in new buildings, increased endowment and curricular offerings. It should be noted that this was most unusual for a layman to be elected president, especially since the covenant with the church demanded a clergyman as was still the general custom among all colleges.

The next president was the Honorable Theodore Frelinghuysen, LL.D., who served from 1850 to his death in 1861. He was the son of the first "tutor," General Frelinghuysen. He was educated in local schools, including the Queen's Grammar School, but went to Princeton for his college work, since the college department of Queen's College was closed at the time of his graduation in 1804. The new president was reputed to be an humble, zealous churchman; he became an elder in the Reformed Church and president of its Board of Foreign Missions; he attained distinction as a lawyer, becoming attorney-general of the state of New Jersey from 1817 to 1829 and United States Senator from 1829 to 1835. He was nominated by the Whigs in 1844 for the Vice-Presidency of the United States when Henry Clay was the candidate for the Presidency. From 1839 to 1850, the date of his election to the presidency of Queen's College, he was Chancellor of the University of the City of New York, now called New York University. While he was president of Rutgers the number of students increased notably and Peter Hertzog Hall was built.

Upon the death of President Frelinghuysen, the trustees naturally turned to the Reverend William Henry Campbell, D.D., LL.D., then professor in the theology department as his logical successor. Campbell was born in Baltimore in 1808, had graduated in 1828 from Dickinson College (then a Presbyterian school), and subsequently from the Princeton Theological Seminary. He promptly became a pastor of a small Dutch Reformed Church in upstate New York. After holding several Reformed Church pastorates and serving as principal of Erasmus Hall, Flatbush, Long Island, he presided over Albany Academy from 1848 to 1851. From 1851 to 1863 he was professor of Biblical literature in the Theological Seminary at New Brunswick. When he took over the presidency of Queen's College in 1863 he continued to teach in the Seminary while taking on the chair of moral philosophy and evidences of Christianity in the college.

During Campbell's presidency there occurred some revolutionary changes. The General Synod transferred in 1864 full title of grounds and buildings to the college trustees. On their part the trustees agreed that the property should ever be used for collegiate instruction and that the president, according to charter requirement, should "always be a member of the Reformed Dutch Church." The requirement still held that three fourths of the trustees be members of this church. Soon thereafter, by common agreement, this requirement was reduced to two thirds.

Further shift from predominance of church control occurred a year later, in 1865, when the Rutgers Scientific School, elevated from departmental status in 1863, was by the act of the New Jersey legislature made the New Jersey State Agricultural College, thus obtaining Federal grants through the operation of the Morrill Act.

When President Campbell resigned, the trustees again deviated from the policy of electing a clergyman by choosing as president Merrill Edward Gates who retired in September 1890, to become president of Amherst College. His successor was also a layman,

Austin Scott, "professor of history, political economy and constitutional law" on the Rutgers faculty from 1883.

The complete change from church to semi-independent and state control came during the term of the next president, a minister in the Dutch Reformed Church, William H. S. Demarest. He was a graduate of Rutgers of the class of 1883; after graduating from the New Brunswick Theological Seminary he had filled a number of pulpits in the Dutch Reformed Church; in 1901 he became professor of church history in the Seminary; and in 1905 was made acting president of Rutgers on resignation of President Scott who continued on the faculty for sixteen more years as professor of history and political science. Dr. Demarest served as president with distinction until 1924.

In 1925 he became president of the New Brunswick Theological Seminary for a ten year term. Dr. Demarest was the first alumnus to preside over the destinies of Rutgers.

The importance of Rutgers as a state university became more and more apparent so that in 1909 the General Synod of the Reformed Church in America cancelled the 1864 agreement with the trustees whereby two thirds of their number must be members of the Reformed Church. During President Demarest's administration great advances were made on all fronts. Noteworthy indeed was the progress in financial standing. In 1917 the Agricultural College of Rutgers became the State University of New Jersey. In 1920 the trustees abrogated the requirement that the Rutgers president must be a Dutch Reformed minister, so that now it is unreservedly a state university.

DARTMOUTH COLLEGE

The Royal Charter signed by King George III of England on December 13, 1769, establishing Dartmouth College includes as its reason for existence: "for the education and instruction of Youth of the Indian Tribes in this Land in reading, writing & all parts of Learning which shall appear necessary and expedient for civilizing & christianizing Children of Pagans as well as in all liberal Arts and Sciences; and also of English Youth and any others."

The Reverend Eleazar Wheelock was responsible for this charter.

His aim was to have a college suitably located to continue and expand the activity he started in Lebanon, Connecticut, in 1754 under the name of *Moor's Indian Charity School*. To be nearer the Indians he selected for the site of the new college a spot now known as Hanover, New Hampshire. *Vox clamantis in deserto*, chosen by Wheelock as the motto for his new college, seems most appropriate.

Funds totalling 11,000 pounds had been raised in England largely through the efforts of the Reverend Samson Occom, a distinguished Indian alumnus of Dr. Wheelock's Lebanon School. When Dr. Wheelock prepared to name his new college after the Royal Governor, John Wentworth, the latter tactfully suggested that it be called Dartmouth College in recognition of the sizeable gifts made in England by the second Earl of Dartmouth.

The original charter makes no church requirements for the Board of Trustees who were established as a self-perpetuating body of twelve members, at least seven of whom were to be laymen and seven to be natives of the state. With this clear evidence that there is to be no church domination or support, Dartmouth College can be considered to have the least church connection of any of the nine colonial colleges. Furthermore it was discovered in short order that the Indians of New England, like those in Virginia, were not avid for a forced education, religious or of any other sort. Soon Dartmouth College was devoted entirely to the education of non-Indians.

It should be noted, however, that the college was started under pious influences, even in addition to the ideal outlined in the royal charter. George Berkeley and George Whitefield, two Anglican divines different in their outlook had much to do with developing the aims and ideals of Eleazar Wheelock.

Bishop George Berkeley was a distinguished English philosopher who had become discouraged at social conditions in Europe. He looked hopefully toward the new continent of America and suggested the establishment of a college in Bermuda where the English and Indians both could be trained to become "ministers and missionaries of the new world." Due to skullduggery among high officials in the British government, the money for this project was not paid although it had been voted. Meanwhile the Bishop had come to Newport, Rhode Island, to live, giving the balance of the funds collected for the Bermuda venture to establish a foundation for graduate study at Yale College. Since Wheelock was the first one to hold the Berkeley scholarship at Yale the influence of Berkeley on the establishment of Dartmouth is patent.

After Wheelock had graduated from Yale in 1733 and had become a Congregational minister in 1735, he participated in "The Great Awakening" which had its origin in a spectacular revival at Northampton, Massachusetts under the local pastor Jonathan Edwards. In 1741 he is reputed to have preached some five hundred sermons but counseled wisely against "emotional extravagance." He had formed a close friendship with Evangelist George Whitefield, who was responsible for persuading him to educate Samson Occom, the Mohegan Indian, and later to send him to England and Scotland in quest of funds.

Whitefield continued his enthusiastic interest after he returned to England by stimulating gifts for Wheelock's new college. Among those responding were King George III who sent 200 pounds, the Marquis of Lothian who gave 150 pounds, and the Countess of Huntingdon who donated 100 pounds. The latter was a loyal friend and supporter of John Wesley's activities. Recognition of this fact is found in changing the name of the Methodist Woman's College of Alabama to Huntingdon College in 1935.

The influence of Whitefield on several other colleges, notably Yale, Harvard and Pennsylvania has been previously noted. Berkeley's influence also pervaded higher education in several other areas of the United States. Under the influence of his memorable aphorism "Westward the course of empire takes its way," Bishop Berkeley inspired the sturdy church groups that organized the College of California to name after him the community in which they planned to move the new college from its original crowded quarters in downtown Oakland just before the state took it over to make it the University of California.

As was the case in other colonial colleges, considerable rivalry arose among church bodies, which developed into a contest between the Federalist Congregationalists and Republican Presbyterians for the control of Dartmouth College. Other colonial colleges did have problems at times with state political factions, but these political groups fought hard and bitterly for the control of Dartmouth College. One faction was determined to make the school a state institution thus causing a quarrel that developed into the famous "Dartmouth College Case," which gave Daniel Webster national and international fame. The decision in favor of the anti-state faction by the United States Supreme Court has been of tremendous importance not only for struggling colleges but also for charitable foundations and other corporations. Chancellor Kent, the famous barrister, is reported to have commented on this case: "The decision in that case did more than any other single act proceeding from the authority of the United States to throw an impregnable barrier around all rights and franchises derived from the grant of government; and to give solidity and inviolability to the literary, charitable, religious, and commercial institutions of our country."

Funds from England ceased when the Revolutionary War began. The president failed in attempts to raise funds through a lottery and otherwise. The struggle told on the health of Eleazar Wheelock, who died in 1779, to be succeeded by his son John who had been appointed by his father, in accordance with a charter provision.

After he had maintained and even strengthened the college for thirty-six years, the second Wheelock was removed in 1815 from the presidency by his board of trustees because of his desire to cut loose from charter requirements and make the college a state institution.

When the trustees elected the Reverend Francis Brown of the class of 1805, the lawsuits began which resulted in the *Dartmouth College Case*. The Superior Court of New Hampshire, composed of three distinguished jurists, decreed in favor of the Wheelock faction. Two of them later became United States Senators and one a Justice of the United States Supreme Court. The case was next argued before the United States Supreme Court on March 10, 1818, with Josiah Hopkinson (author of "Hail Columbia") and Daniel Webster representing the college and with John Holmes and William Wirt, Attorney General of the United States, representing Dartmouth University, the name assumed by the other faction, by virtue of an act passed by the New Hampshire Legislature in 1816. The rest of the story which has become so important can best be told in two versions.

The eloquent lawyer, Rufus Choate of the class of 1819, writes in his Eulogy of Webster, that on addressing Chief Justice Marshall in concluding his famous five-hour address he said:

This sir, is my case. It is the case, not merely of that humble institution, it is the case of every college in our land. It is more. It is the case of every eleemosynary institution throughout our country, all of those great charities founded by the piety of our ancestors to alleviate human misery, and scatter blessings along the pathway of human life. It is more. It is, in some sense, the case of every man who has property of which he may be stripped,—for the question is simply this: Shall our State legislatures be allowed to take that which is not their own, to turn it from its original use, and apply it to such ends or purposes as they, in their discretion, shall see fit? Sir, you may destroy this little institution; it is weak; it is in your hands! I know it is one of the lesser lights in the literary horizon of our country. You may put it out; but if you do, you must carry through your work! You must extinguish, one after another, all those great lights of science which, for more than a century, have thrown their radiance over the land! It is, sir, as I have said, a small college, *and yet there are those that love it—*

Choate's eulogy continues:

Here the feelings which he had thus far succeeded in keeping down, broke forth. His lips quivered; his firm cheeks trembled with emotion; his eyes were filled with tears; his voice choked, and he seemed struggling to the utmost, simply to gain the mastery over himself which might save him from an unmanly burst of feeling. I will not attempt to give you the few broken words of tenderness in which he went on to speak of his attachment to the College. The whole seemed to be mingled with the recollections of father, mother, brother, and all the privations through which he had made his way into life. Every one saw that it was wholly unpremeditated,—a pressure on his heart which sought relief in words and tears.

The court-room during these two or three minutes presented an extraordinary spectacle. Chief Justice Marshall, with his tall, gaunt figure bent over as if to catch the slightest whisper, the deep furrows of his cheek expanded with emotion, and eyes suffused with tears; Mr. Justice Washington at his side, with his small and emaciated frame, and countenance more like marble than I ever saw on any other human being, leaning forward with an eager, troubled look; and the remainder of the court at the two extremities, pressing as it were, toward a single point, while the audience below were, wrapping themselves round in closer folds beneath the bench to catch each look, and every movement of the speaker's face. . . . There was not one among the strong-minded men of that assembly who could think it unmanly to weep, when he saw standing before him the man who had made such an argument melted into the tenderness of a child.

Mr. Webster, having recovered his composure and fixed his keen eye upon the Chief Justice, said, in that deep tone with which he sometimes thrilled the heart of an audience,—

"Sir, I know not how others may feel" (glancing at the opponents of the College before him, some of whom were its graduates), "but, for myself, when I see my alma mater surrounded, like Caesar in the senate house, by those who are reiterating stab upon stab, I would not for this right hand, have her turn to me and say, *Et tu quoque, mi fili!—And thou too, my son!*"

He sat down; there was a deathlike stillness throughout the room for some moments; every one seemed to be slowly recovering himself and coming gradually back to his ordinary range of thought and feeling.

Nearly a hundred years later the historian-philosopher Charles A. Beard presents a different and somewhat iconoclastic point of view:

By securing the boards of trustees of endowed educational institutions against political interference, the Dartmouth decision in effect decreed that a large part of the terrain of the higher learning should be forever occupied and controlled by private corporations composed of citizens empowered to select their own successors, collect and disburse money, choose presidents and professors, and more or less directly determine the letter and spirit of the curriculum.

In the story of that famous lawsuit are revealed entertaining phases of the economics and politics of the period. Dartmouth College was founded in the reign of King George III by a royal charter and was managed by a small self-perpetuating board of trustees, fashioned on the model of the trading corporation. In the natural course of things the board passed into the control of staunch Federalists who adhered to the ways of their party. But with the uprush of Jeffersonian Democracy discontent appeared in the state of New Hampshire and also in the college. Under the pressure of the new forces, a Democratic legislature and governor attempted a conquest of the college by changing it into a university, enlarging the board of trustees, adding a number of political appointees, and in effect transforming it into a state institution.

Not to be outdone by this Jeffersonian maneuver, the Federalist faction began to fight the state legislature through the courts of law, carrying the case finally to the Supreme Court at Washington, where that loyal Federalist, John Marshall, still held the wheel, with failing grip, it is true, but yet powerfully. Very astutely, the old board of trustees engaged as its counsel, Daniel Webster, that formidable opponent of everything Jeffersonian, to wage its judicial battle. When the case was tried at the state court in Exeter, Webster made the first of his sentimental speeches, introducing into a purely legal argument, as Rufus Choate said, a "pathos" that hardly seemed "in good taste."

Before the Supreme Court in Washington, Webster resorted to the same tactics, suffusing and crowning his legal argument with shrewd appeals to Federalist emotions and word-patterns, none of which was lost on Marshall, who hated Jefferson and all his works with an almost immeasurable intensity. Marshall was easily convinced, but at first, it appears, a majority of the Court, now coming steadily under current influence through judicious appointments, was against Webster and the old board of trustees. Discreet as well as valorous, Marshall postponed the decision until his colleagues could be brought around to his views. When at length the decision was reached, it was announced that the charter granted by King George to the college was a contract; that the obligation of the contract was transferred to the state at the time of the Revolution; and that under the federal Constitution the state legislature could not "impair" its binding force. In short, there was to be no political interference with educational companies.

The way was thus definitely cleared for the development of control over the higher learning in America. Private corporations—usually religious in origins,—for skeptics seldom endowed colleges—were free to go on with their historic mission secure from popular storms. Under the protection of the Dartmouth doctrine, established colleges, such as Harvard, Yale, and Princeton, continued, gathering in slowly, very slowly, gifts of money to augment their meager endowments. And under the same aegis, the religious sects, Methodists, Baptists, Presbyterians, and all the others, founded new colleges in the East and South—and all over the West as the frontier advanced toward the setting sun—small colleges usually, poorly endowed, mainly sustained by tuition fees and subscriptions of the faithful, theological in spirit, and generally managed by clergymen of the denomination, the most active and interested parties to the undertakings.*

It is interesting to note that Dartmouth College, independent of the church from the beginning, did elect as its first nine presidents distinguished clergymen with the exception of John Wheelock. Of these, seven clergymen who followed Eleazar Wheelock, five were Dartmouth alumni, Tyler was an alumnus of Yale and Lord of Bowdoin. The noteworthy contributions of these clergymen are sufficient to warrant the listing of their names: Francis Brown, Daniel Dana, Bennett Tyler, Nathan Lord, Asa Dodge Smith, Samuel Colcord Bartlett, and William Jewett Tucker.

* C. A. and M. R. Beard, *The Rise of American Civilization*, I, pp. 819-21. New York: Macmillan, 1927.

CHAPTER III

Baptist Colleges

Columbian College (now *George Washington University*). This was the first college organized by the Baptists after the United States became an independent nation. It received its charter from Congress on February 9, 1821. The leader in the movement for the establishment of Columbian College was Luther Rice, who was acting as an agent of the Triennial Baptist Convention meeting in Philadelphia in 1820. This group felt the need of a college primarily for the education of ministers, to serve the great increase in Baptist membership which came about largely from the "Second Awakening" which occurred early in the nineteenth century.

Luther Rice was born in Massachusetts in 1783, graduated from Williams College and was ordained a Congregational minister in 1812. The next year he sailed for India to become a missionary under the auspices of the Congregational Church. Like his closest friend, Adoniram Judson, Rice came under the influence of some English Baptists en route to the Far East; both were immersed while in India; shortly thereafter they resigned as agents of the Congregational Board of Foreign Missions, which had raised funds for their continued efforts in India and Burma.

The Baptists, like several other denominations in the early nineteenth century, relied on the zeal rather than the education of their ministers. In fact, the Baptists had such a prejudice against education that they favored the "lowly ministry of uneducated men." Rice and others seeing the necessity for better education among their ministers wrote and spoke continually on that subject. When Rice persuaded the group in Philadelphia to open the college in

Washington, he was made treasurer and financial agent. His standing as an educator is indicated by his having declined the presidency of Transylvania University in Kentucky in 1815 and the presidency of Georgetown College in Kentucky in 1832. The overoptimism of Rice resulted in a heavy debt at Columbian College which brought about quarrels with other leaders of the denomination. This led to the resignation in 1826 of the whole faculty, who called attention to the fact that the original charter stated clearly "that persons of every religious denomination shall be capable of being elected trustees," nor were faculty or students to be selected because of particular religious beliefs. Rice then traveled over the South urging his fellow members to organize schools and colleges for the better education of Baptist ministers. He died in 1836 in Edgefield, South Carolina, where he was buried. Luther Rice stands out in the annals of Baptist church history somewhat as does Francis Asbury in early Methodism.

Columbian College became *Columbian University* in 1873 by another Act of Congress. From 1898 to 1904 it was again fully under the control of the Baptist denomination. In 1904 by a third Act of the Congress its name was changed to George Washington University. This was most appropriate because Washington in his will had set aside fifty shares of stock of the Potomac (Canal) Company, later known as the Chesapeake and Ohio Canal, for the endowment of a university in the District of Columbia "to which the youth of fortune and talents from all parts thereof might be sent for the completion of their Education in all branches of polite literature;—in arts and Sciences,—in acquiring knowledge in the principles of Politics & good Government."

Here follows a list of the four-year colleges affiliated with the Board of Education and Publication of the American Baptist Convention:

Institution	Location	Date of Founding
Alderson-Broaddus College	Philippi, West Virginia	1871
Bates College	Lewiston, Maine	1863
Benedict College	Columbia, South Carolina	1870
Bethel College	St. Paul, Minnesota	1947

Institution	Location	Date of Founding
Bishop College	Marshall, Texas	1880
Bucknell University	Lewisburg, Pennsylvania	1846
Carleton College	Northfield, Minnesota	1866
Colby College	Waterville, Maine	1813
Denison University	Granville, Ohio	1832
Eastern Baptist College	St. David's, Pennsylvania	1932
Florida N & I Memorial College	St. Augustine, Florida	1892
Franklin College	Franklin, Indiana	1834
Hillsdale College	Hillsdale, Michigan	1844
Kalamazoo College	Kalamazoo, Michigan	1833
Keuka College	Keuka Park, New York	1892
Leland College	Baker, Louisiana	1870
Linfield College	McMinnville, Oregon	1857
Morehouse College	Atlanta, Georgia	1867
Ottawa University	Ottawa, Kansas	1865
Ricker College	Houlton, Maine	1847
Shaw University	Raleigh, North Carolina	1865
Shurtleff College	Alton, Illinois	1827
Sioux Falls College	Sioux Falls, South Dakota	1883
Spelman College	Atlanta, Georgia	1881
University of Chicago	Chicago, Illinois	1857
University of Redlands	Redlands, California	1907
Virginia Union University	Richmond, Virginia	1865
William Jewell College	Liberty, Missouri	1849

Bates College and *Hillsdale College* were originally affiliated with the Free Will Baptists. This group was an outgrowth of the "Great Awakening" and originally its members were more opposed to an educated ministry than the regular Baptists. They joined the Northern Baptists in 1911. There are a number of other Baptist sects, some nineteen in all, but only the four groups listed in this chapter maintain separate four-year colleges.

The following institutions had their origins under Baptist influence: Colgate University, University of Rochester, and Temple University.

On September 24, 1817, thirteen Baptists, six ministers, and seven laymen met in the home of Deacon Olmstead, Hamilton, New York, where still meet the trustees of *Colgate University,* to form the Baptist Educational Society of New York. The purpose of this society was to educate Baptist ministers. In 1819 they chartered the *Hamilton Literary and Theological Institute* with the Reverend Nathaniel Kindrick as president. In 1846 the school was rechartered under the name of *Madison University* with authority to grant degrees. It is interesting to note that previously their degrees were granted by Columbian College in the District of Columbia. In 1850 a rift occurred which resulted in several trustees, five professors, and some students leaving Madison University to organize another Baptist institution, the University of Rochester. In 1890 the new charter changed the name from Madison to Colgate which was done in appreciation of liberal support from the Colgate family.

In the catalog of the *University of Rochester* there appears a brief recognition of its Baptist origin, with a statement that the institution soon became nonsectarian. The Reverend Martin Brewer Anderson was its first president, serving from 1853 to 1888. Another distinguished Baptist clergyman, the Reverend Rush Rhees, was its president from 1900 to 1935.

Temple University was founded in 1888 largely under the leadership of the Reverend Russell H. Conwell. He turned over to the project more than one million dollars which he obtained through fees from the delivery of his famous address "Acres of Diamonds," which he gave more than six thousand times.

Central College, Pella, Iowa, now affiliated with the General Synod of the Reformed Church in America, started out under the auspices of the Baptist Convention of Iowa. It was chartered in 1853 as Central University of Iowa. In 1916 the Baptists turned over their charter, grounds, building, and equipment to the Reformed Church. The Baptists realized they did not have sufficient resources to continue to finance Central and Des Moines College, another college established by the Baptists in Iowa. Later they were obliged to abandon the latter institution also.

Rio Grande College, Rio Grande, Ohio, was organized by the Free Will Baptists and was for years affiliated with the Northern Baptist Convention. Recently the college severed this connection and is now nonsectarian.

The American Baptist Convention has currently developed a program of closer cooperation with its colleges. This action has resulted in strengthening the colleges and increasing support for them. Here is a summary of the program as outlined in a recent letter from the Secretary's office of their Department of Schools and Colleges:

Our function has been to provide certain services for the college that would strengthen it, deepen its Christian nature, and help it to sell its services and make its needs known to its church constituency. More specifically, we have majored in the following services:

1. Planning grants to assist in the initiation of creative projects that contribute either to the Christian witness on the campus or to the college's relationship to the churches.

2. Counsel and field service in the development and strengthening of Public Relations Departments. One of our strongest arms is a Department of Public Relations which works closely with many of our colleges in the selection of personnel, in the building of programs, in the production of literature, and in the actual raising of funds for both current and capital needs. The emphasis is on relationship with the church public, but carries over into the general area of public relations.

3. Assistance in locating qualified and dedicated personnel for college staffs. We operate the Educational Registry as an agency for the locating of qualified teachers and administrative personnel who stand among the best in American higher education, and who, in addition, are concerned for the Christian perspective in the work of their particular fields.

4. Educational and administrative counsel. The field service provided by our staff for college presidents, boards of trustees, curriculum committees, business managers, etc., has constantly grown. In all of these services the Christian emphasis and the church relationship have been constantly present.

5. Stimulation of the young people in our Baptist churches toward college attendance, and in particular, attendance at Baptist colleges. The major instrument in this direction has been a growing program of scholarships and other forms of student aid.

6. The general stimulation of denominational interest in higher education.

Here follow lists of four-year colleges operated under the auspices of other Baptist groups:

NATIONAL BAPTIST CONVENTION OF AMERICA

Institution	Location	Date of Founding
Arkansas Baptist College	Little Rock, Arkansas	1884
Butler College	Tyler, Texas	1905
Mary Allen College	Crockett, Texas	1944
Morris College	Sumter, South Carolina	1908

Bethel College, St. Paul, Minnesota, was transformed from a junior college, founded in 1931, to a four-year liberal arts college in 1947. It is "owned and operated by the Baptist General Conference of America." It is really an offshoot of the seminary department of the University of Chicago, founded in 1871.

Oakland City College, Oakland, Indiana, founded in 1885, states in its catalog that it "is administered by the General Baptist church," although "members of many communions are represented on the faculty."

SOUTHERN BAPTIST COLLEGES

Institution	Location	Date of Founding
Baylor University	Waco, Texas	1845
Bessie Tift College	Forsyth, Georgia	1849
Belmont College	Nashville, Tennessee	1952
Blue Mountain College	Blue Mountain, Mississippi	1873
Carson-Newman College	Jefferson City, Tennessee	1851
East Texas Baptist College	Marshall, Texas	1914
Furman University	Greenville, South Carolina	1826
Georgetown College	Georgetown, Kentucky	1829
Grand Canyon College	Prescott, Arizona	1949
Hardin-Simmons University	Abilene, Texas	1891
Howard College	Birmingham, Alabama	1842
Howard Payne College	Brownwood, Texas	1889
Judson College	Marion, Alabama	1838
Louisiana College	Pineville, Louisiana	1906
Mary Hardin-Baylor College	Belton, Texas	1845
Mercer University	Macon, Georgia	1833
Meredith College	Raleigh, North Carolina	1899
Mississippi College	Clinton, Mississippi	1826
Oklahoma Baptist University	Shawnee, Oklahoma	1911

SOUTHERN BAPTIST COLLEGES (*Continued*)

Institution	Location	Date of Founding
Ouachita Baptist College	Arkadelphia, Arkansas	1888
Shorter College	Rome, Georgia	1873
Stetson University	DeLand, Florida	1883
Union University	Jackson, Tennessee	1834
University of Corpus Christi	Corpus Christi, Texas	1941
University of Richmond	Richmond, Virginia	1830
Wake Forest College	Wake Forest, North Carolina	1834
Wayland College	Plainview, Texas	1909
William Carey College	Hattiesburg, Mississippi	1911
William Jewell College	Liberty, Missouri	1849

In 1845, shortly after the great schism of the Methodist Church, the Baptist Church was disrupted into the Northern and Southern branches. The conspicuous leader in the Southern area was Richard Furman, who as a child moved with his parents from New England to South Carolina. With little formal education, he was ordained a Baptist minister at the age of nineteen in 1774. His activities for the cause of the Colonies brought a price on his head by the British forces under Cornwallis so that he fled to the North until after the decisive battle at Yorktown in 1781. He became pastor of a prominent Baptist Church in Charleston, South Carolina. He was active in organizing the South Carolina Baptist State Convention in 1821. Later he took the lead in organizing an academy and theological school which came into existence about a year after his death in 1825. This academy evolved into the present Furman University located at Greenville, South Carolina. Furman's leadership extended throughout the Eastern seaboard; he was the first president of the Baptist Triennial Convention which was organized in Philadelphia in 1814; he was re-elected president in 1817. The address he gave at the time of his re-election stimulated the organization of Columbian College in Washington.

Like the Methodists who also came late into the field of higher education as compared to the Presbyterians, Congregationalists, and Episcopalians, the Baptists rapidly founded colleges throughout the country. In the South it was the aim of the church to concentrate on one strong college or university in each state.

In line with this policy the following three colleges founded by Baptists have recently become independent institutions: Coker College, in Hartsville, South Carolina, founded as a school in 1895, became a college in 1908; Hollins College, in Hollins, Virginia, established as a seminary in 1842, became a college in 1911; Limestone College, in Gaffney, South Carolina, established in 1845. All three are women's colleges.

SEVENTH DAY BAPTIST

Institution	Location	Date of Founding
Milton College	Milton, Wisconsin	1867
Salem College	Salem, West Virginia	1888

The first college of this group was *Alfred University,* Alfred, New York, founded in 1857 for the primary purpose of educating ministers. In 1900 Alfred added the New York State College of Ceramics which in 1948 became officially a unit of the State University of New York. Alfred is now an independent institution.

The Seventh Day Baptists established a number of churches in Rhode Island before 1800 but did not formally organize as a church until 1818.

CHAPTER IV

Congregational Church Colleges

THE Congregational Church prides itself on maintaining the policy of individual freedom in each church, quite unlike other churches such as the Episcopal, Methodist, and Presbyterian. Without any central authority, Congregational leaders have continued over the years to have a missionary spirit in developing and maintaining colleges and theological seminaries. This urge came directly and indirectly from the European heritage of the church. There continues in the group a strong feeling that colleges are needed to maintain and educate clerical and lay leadership.

In a fine spirit of brotherhood the Congregational group combined with their Calvinist brethren of the Presbyterian persuasion to form a Plan of Union in 1801 to cooperate in the founding of colleges in the areas opened up with the migrations to the Middle and Far West. During a period of harmonious cooperation the following colleges were established under this plan:

1. Beliot
2. Grinnell
3. Illinois
4. Knox
5. Milwaukee-Downer
6. Pacific University
7. Ripon
8. Rockford
9. University of California
10. Western Reserve

74

The Plan of Union was repudiated in 1852 at a Convention of the Congregational Church held in Albany, New York.

The Congregational Church has contributed largely to the founding and strengthening of many colleges, particularly those for Negroes, through its American Missionary Association. This association was a merger of the Almistad Committee (organized in 1836 to protect interests of a group of Africans who had mutinied and taken charge of a slave ship), the Union Missionary Society, The Committee for the West Indian Missions, and The Western Evangelical Missionary Society for Work Among the American Indians. The American Missionary Association is still effective in the support of a number of colleges in the South.

The colleges still maintaining affiliation with the Division of Christian Education of the Board of Home Missions of the Congregational Christian Churches follow:

Institution	Location	Date of Founding
Beliot College	Beloit, Wisconsin	1846
Carleton College	Northfield, Minnesota	1866
Defiance College	Defiance, Ohio	1884
Dillard University	New Orleans, Louisiana	1869
Doane College	Crete, Nebraska	1872
Drury College	Springfield, Missouri	1873
Elon College	Elon College, North Carolina	1889
Fisk University	Nashville, Tennessee	1866
Grinnell College	Grinnell, Iowa	1846
Huston-Tillotson College	Austin, Texas	1877
Illinois College	Jacksonville, Illinois	1829
Knox College	Galesburg, Illinois	1837
Lemoyne College	Memphis, Tennessee	1871
Marietta College	Marietta, Ohio	1830
Northland College	Ashland, Wisconsin	1907
Olivet College	Olivet, Michigan	1844
Pacific University	Forest Grove, Oregon	1849
Rockford College	Rockford, Illinois	1847
Rocky Mountain College	Billings, Montana	1878
Schauffler College	Cleveland, Ohio	1886
Talladega College	Talladega, Alabama	1867

Institution	Location	Date of Founding
Tougaloo Southern Christian College	Tougaloo, Mississippi	1869
Yankton College	Yankton, South Dakota	1881

Many other institutions were founded under the auspices of the Congregationalists. Some have gone out of existence and others no longer maintain a relationship to Congregational churches. The latter group comprises:

Institution	Location	Date of Founding
Amherst College	Amherst, Massachusetts	1821
Atlanta University	Atlanta, Georgia	1865
Bowdoin College	Brunswick, Maine	1794
Colorado College	Colorado Springs, Colorado	1874
Dartmouth College	Hanover, New Hampshire	1769
Hampton Institute	Hampton, Virginia	1868
Harvard University	Cambridge, Massachusetts	1636
Middlebury College	Middlebury, Vermont	1800
Milwaukee-Downer College	Milwaukee, Wisconsin	1851
Mount Holyoke College	South Hadley, Massachusetts	1836
Oberlin College	Oberlin, Ohio	1833
Pomona College	Claremont, California	1887
Ripon College	Ripon, Wisconsin	1851
Rollins College	Winter Park, Florida	1885
Scripps College	Claremont, California	1926
Smith College	Northampton, Massachusetts	1871
Washburn College	Topeka, Kansas	1865
Wellesley College	Wellesley, Massachusetts	1870
Western Reserve University	Cleveland, Ohio	1826
Whitman College	Walla Walla, Washington	1859
Williams College	Williamstown, Massachusetts	1793
Yale University	New Haven, Connecticut	1701

The following statement is found in *A Descriptive Bulletin of Congregational Christian Colleges and Junior Colleges,* published by the Department of Higher Education of the Division of Christian Education of the Board of Home Missions of the Congregational Christian Churches: "Faculties and administrations are religious, and, while there are wide differences in program, it can be confidently said that our colleges provide a wholesome environment. The emphasis is not sectarian, but there is a frank affirmation of Christian purpose and concern."

Elon College. Located in Elon College, North Carolina, this college was chartered in 1889. It was established by the O'Kellyites, who called themselves the Christian Church. This Christian Church should not be confused with the Church of the Disciples, frequently known as the Christian Church, founded by Alexander Campbell whose story will be outlined in some detail in the next chapter.

The Reverend James O'Kelly was an evangelistic Methodist preacher of Virginia who insisted that the Methodist Church should get along without bishops. Being outvoted by his colleagues, he and his friends withdrew and in 1794 established the Christian Church at a meeting held in Lebanon Church, Surry County, Virginia. The church organized other educational units such as the Southern Union College, a junior college at Wadley, Alabama.

Dillard University, New Orleans, Louisiana, is a merger of New Orleans University (Methodist) and of Straight College (Congregational).

Rocky Mountain College, Billings, Montana, is a merger of the College of Montana (Presbyterian), Montana Wesleyan College (Methodist), and Billings Polytechnic Institute (Congregational).

Tillotson College, Austin, Texas, and *Sam Huston College* (Methodist) merged in September 1954.

Berea College. This college is the outgrowth of antislavery agitation in eastern Kentucky, with the Reverend John G. Fee as the prime mover. He was an alumnus of Augusta College, Kentucky, had become a Presbyterian minister but withdrew from that church because of its attitude on slavery. In 1854 he established the Berea Union Church around which the college grew. He remained pastor of the church some forty years and was a trustee of the college all that time. His activity against slavery was supported by the famous Kentucky abolitionist, Cassius M. Clay.

The American Missionary Association paid part of Fee's salary for thirty-four years, thus becoming in a sense one of the founders of the school. The society also contributed to the salaries of other teachers but never had a part in the management of the college. Most of the early teachers were Oberlin graduates and most of the presidents were ministers, the last of this group having been William J. Hutchins, the father of the present president, Francis S. Hutchins, and of Robert M. Hutchins, former president of the University of Chicago.

The Articles of Incorporation contain this statement: "This college shall be under an influence strictly Christian, and as such, opposed to sectarianism, slaveholding, caste, and every other wrong institution or practice." From the beginning manual labor has been required of all students. No student pays full fees: he not only does some work towards his expenses but also has scholarship or loan help.

CHAPTER V

Disciples of Christ Colleges

DISCIPLES OF CHRIST is the only religious denomination indigenous to the United States. To be sure, the Methodist Church was established as an independent denomination in Baltimore in 1784, but the leaders of the organizing conference were followers of John Wesley who had been known as a Methodist since his student days in the Holy Club of Oxford University, when he, his brother Charles Wesley, and George Whitefield became leaders of an evangelistic movement in the Church of England. The Church of England itself was metamorphosed into the Protestant Episcopal Church in the United States of America in 1789.

There are many smaller sects that are native to the United States. The Baptists have about nineteen separate divisions; the Presbyterians and Methodists half a dozen each or more; and the Disciples group have an offshoot known as the Church of Christ. Since the limitations of this book will not permit a separate chapter devoted to denominations having less than fifteen affiliated colleges, those colleges operating under the aegis of the Church of Christ are included in Chapter X. The Disciples of Christ, sometimes known as Christians or Campbellites, have more than a million members, while the membership of the Churches of Christ is approaching a million.

The Disciples of Christ was a church resulting from a "restoration movement" whereby all creeds are renounced "in favor of the Bible as the only guide in faith and practice interpreted by the individual conscience." The founders of this Church were Alexander Campbell and his father, Thomas Campbell. They were both born

79

in Ireland and educated at Glasgow University in Scotland. The father was a Presbyterian clergyman of Ireland who operated a school to eke out a living salary. He belonged to a "Seceder Group" known as Anti-Burgher Presbyterians. When he settled in Washington, Pennsylvania, in 1807, he got into hot water by inviting Presbyterians of any creed to join his church. Two years later he and his followers, then popularly known as Campbellites, formed the Christian Association of Washington, Pennsylvania, and issued a *Declaration and Address* which became the most important document for the Church of the Disciples. When the son, Alexander, arrived in America, he and his father accepted the doctrine of immersion and joined the Baptist Church, in which church the Campbells and their followers held nominal membership until 1830.

Alexander Campbell soon realized the necessity of an educated clerical and lay leadership. He postponed establishing a college under the auspices of the church until after the demise of Bacon College, Kentucky, in 1839. The history of this college, which evolved into the University of Kentucky, is told briefly in Chapter X.

In 1840 Alexander Campbell obtained a charter from the Virginia legislature for the establishment of Bethany College to be located on his property in Bethany, now West Virginia, which he had inherited from his father-in-law, John Brown. In appealing to his friends for help in the venture, he outlined this interesting educational philosophy:

Men, and not brick and mortar, make colleges, and these colleges make men. These men make books, and these books make the living world in which we individually live, and move, and have our being. How all-important then, that our colleges should understand and teach the true philosophy of man! They create the men that furnish the teachers of men —the men that fill the pulpit, the legislative halls, the senators, the judges and the governors of the earth. Do we expect to fill these high stations by merely voting or praying for men? Or shall we choose empirics, charlatans, mountebanks, and every pretender to eminent claims upon the suffrages of the people? Forbid it, reason, conscience, and Heaven!

President Campbell boasted that when Bethany College was opened in 1840 there was no other "literary college" in America or elsewhere in the civilized world that had a regular department of

Sacred History and Biblical Literature as a component part of a college education. Like in all the other colonial and early church-related colleges, the Bible was read publicly by the students. Alexander Campbell continued as president of Bethany College from 1840 until his death in 1866. He was succeeded by President William Kimbrough Pendleton, who was president from 1866 to 1886. Pendleton had married successively two of Alexander Campbell's daughters.

The list of four-year colleges cooperating with the Board of Education of the Disciples of Christ includes:

Institution	Location	Date of Founding
Atlantic Christian College	Wilson, North Carolina	1902
Bethany College	Bethany, West Virginia	1840
Butler University	Indianapolis, Indiana	1850
Chapman College	Los Angeles, California	1861
Culver-Stockton College	Canton, Missouri	1853
Drake University	Des Moines, Iowa	1881
Eureka College	Eureka, Illinois	1855
Hiram College	Hiram, Ohio	1849
Jarvis Christian College	Hawkins, Texas	1912
Lynchburg College	Lynchburg, Virginia	1903
Northwest Christian College	Eugene, Oregon	1895
Phillips University	Enid, Oklahoma	1906
Texas Christian University	Fort Worth, Texas	1873
Tougaloo Southern Christian College	Tougaloo, Mississippi	1869
Transylvania College	Lexington, Kentucky	1780

The followers of Alexander Campbell were filled with zeal for the establishment of colleges. With great enthusiasm they founded colleges throughout the South, Middle and Far West, many of which were established on such insecure bases that they were obliged to close their doors after short periods of existence. In other instances discretion was shown in the combinations of a number of struggling institutions: some of the stronger colleges that resulted from these combinations are indicated below.

Butler University received its charter as Northwestern Christian University in 1850. In recognition of the generous gifts of time and money by Ovid Butler, the name was changed to Butler University in February, 1877.

Chapman College. This college was known in the beginning as Hesperian College, opened for students at Woodland, Yolo County, California, on March 4, 1861. In 1874 Pierce Christian College started under similar auspices at College City, Colusa County. Hesperian and Pierce Christian Colleges united in 1896, moved to Berkeley, thence to San Francisco under the name of Berkeley Bible Seminary. The name was again changed to California School of Christianity and moved in the fall of 1920 to Los Angeles. A year later the name was changed to California Christian College and in 1934 it was renamed Chapman College, which still operates under the provisions of the charter granted to Hesperian College, seventy-three years previously.

Culver-Stockton College had its beginnings under the name of Christian University, which was changed to its present name in 1917 in recognition of generous benefactors.

Hiram College. The original name of this college was Western Reserve Eclectic Institute, with the assumption of the present name in 1867. One of its early presidents was James A. Garfield, later president of the United States.

Phillips University began under the name of Oklahoma Christian University in 1906. In recognition of the largesse of T. W. Phillips of Butler, Pennsylvania, it received its present name in 1913.

Texas Christian University was founded as Add Ran College at Thorp Springs, Texas, some twenty miles from Fort Worth, in 1873. The odd name in the title was given as a compliment to Addison and Randolph Clark, brothers who were pioneer educators and distinguished preachers of the Church of the Disciples. In 1895 the institution was moved to Waco, Texas, with the present name having been assumed in 1902. In 1910 a disastrous fire made it advisable for the church to move the university to Fort Worth.

Tougaloo Southern Christian College is a liberal arts college for Negroes, operated under the joint sponsorship of the American Missionary Association Division of the Congregational Christian Churches and the United Christian Missionary Society of the Disciples of Christ.

CHAPTER VI

Lutheran Colleges

IN HIS most ecstatic moments Martin Luther never dreamed, when he nailed his famous Ninety-five Theses on Wittenberg's church door in 1517, that one day he would be considered the founder of the largest Protestant Church in the world. Nor could he have imagined that his action would have resulted in the establishment of over thirty accredited four-year colleges in the United States plus theological seminaries, junior colleges, and innumerable parochial schools.

Of the eighty million adherents of the Lutheran Church throughout the world more than one-tenth, or about eight million, are in the United States, thus making this church the third in size among the Protestant groups in this country. The evolution of Lutheran colleges became particularly noticeable after the great number of German emigrants came to the United States in the 1830's, most of them settling in the Middle West.

UNITED LUTHERAN

Institution	Location	Date of Founding
Carthage College	Carthage, Illinois	1846
Gettysburg College	Gettysburg, Pennsylvania	1832
Hartwick College	Oneonta, New York	1928
Lenoir Rhyne College	Hickory, North Carolina	1891
Midland College	Fremont, Nebraska	1887
Muhlenberg College	Allentown, Pennsylvania	1848
Newberry College	Newberry, South Carolina	1856

UNITED LUTHERAN (*Continued*)

Institution	Location	Date of Founding
Roanoke College	Salem, Virginia	1842
Susquehanna University	Selinsgrove, Pennsylvania	1858
Thiel College	Greenville, Pennsylvania	1866
Wagner College	Staten Island, New York	1883
Wittenberg College	Springfield, Ohio	1842

Gettysburg College was the first in this group of Lutheran Colleges to be established. It was chartered in 1832 as *Pennsylvania College* with the primary purpose of preparing men for the Lutheran Theological Seminary on an adjacent campus. The name was changed to Gettysburg College in 1921. The college became coeducational in 1935.

Carthage College started out as Hillsboro College in Hillsboro, Illinois, in 1846. In 1852 it moved to Springfield, Illinois, and assumed the name of Illinois State University. It was rechartered as Carthage College in 1870 when it moved to Carthage, Illinois.

AMERICAN LUTHERAN

Institution	Location	Date of Founding
Capital University	Columbus, Ohio	1830
Texas Lutheran College	Seguin, Texas	1891
Wartburg College	Waverly, Iowa	1852

The metamorphoses of *Wartburg College* are outlined in the current catalog of the school:

WARTBURG COLLEGE is a combination and continuation of five midwestern educational institutions founded and operated by the church bodies which merged in 1930 to form the American Lutheran Church. The origin of the College itself dates back to 1852. Wartburg Normal College, begun in Andrew, Iowa, in 1878 and moved to Waverly the following year, was merged with the College in 1885, but was separated again in 1894. Martin Luther Academy, founded in Sterling, Nebraska in 1909, was merged with Wartburg Normal College in 1924. St. Paul-Luther College, founded in Afton, Minnesota in 1885, was relocated in St. Paul, Minnesota eight years later. It was merged in 1933 with

Eureka Lutheran College, opened in Eureka, South Dakota in 1910. Wartburg College was again merged with Wartburg Normal College at Clinton in 1933, and in 1935 with St. Paul-Luther College at Waverly.

Texas Lutheran College, like Wartburg College, received the inspiration for its founding from Pastor Wilhelm Loehe of Neuendettelsau in Bavaria. He raised funds and sent teachers to help in the establishment of schools and colleges. He had a missionary zeal for serving the un-churched Lutherans who had migrated to the Midwest area of the United States.

AUGUSTANA LUTHERAN

Institution	Location	Date of Founding
Augustana College	Rock Island, Illinois	1860
Bethany College	Lindsborg, Kansas	1881
Gustavus Adolphus College	St. Peter, Minnesota	1862
Upsala College	East Orange, New Jersey	1893

EVANGELICAL LUTHERAN (NORWEGIAN)

Augustana College	Sioux Falls, South Dakota	1860
Concordia College	Moorhead, Minnesota	1890
Luther College	Decorah, Iowa	1861
Pacific Lutheran College	Parkland, Washington	1894
St. Olaf College	Northfield, Minnesota	1874

LUTHERAN FREE CHURCH (NORWEGIAN)

Augsburg College	Minneapolis, Minnesota	1869

LUTHERAN MISSOURI SYNOD

Concordia Teachers College	River Forest, Illinois	1864
Concordia Teachers College	Seward, Nebraska	1894
Valparaiso University	Valparaiso, Indiana	1859

Valparaiso University was opened on September 21, 1859, at Valparaiso, Indiana, under the name of Valparaiso Male and Female College. Reverses resulting from the War Between the States caused suspension of classes in 1869. On September 16, 1873, the college was reopened under the name of Northern Indiana Normal School and Business Institute as a private business venture. The owners changed the name to Valparaiso College in 1900 and to Valparaiso

University in 1907. They did hold up the ideals of character training and education in both the liberal arts and prevocational subjects. The college has made a remarkable growth since its purchase in 1925 by the Evangelical Lutheran Synodical Conference of North America.

LUTHERAN WISCONSIN SYNOD

Institution	Location	Date of Founding
Northwestern College	Watertown, Wisconsin	1865

UNITED EVANGELICAL LUTHERAN (DANISH)

Dana College	Blair, Nebraska	1884

CHAPTER VII

Methodist Colleges

We recognize as related to the Methodist Church all educational institutions which were founded under the auspices of the Church or by some agency or member thereof, or have come under the aegis of the Church through later agreement, and which have maintained a vital, organic or cooperative relation to the Church."

The criteria for the assemblage of the following list are outlined in the above statement from the General Board of Education of the Methodist Church:

Institution	Location	Date of Founding
Adrian College	Adrian, Michigan	1845
Albion College	Albion Michigan	1835
Allegheny College	Meadville, Pennsylvania	1815
American University	Washington, D. C.	1893
Athens College	Athens, Alabama	1842
Baker University	Baldwin, Kansas	1858
Baldwin-Wallace College	Berea, Ohio	1845
Bennett College	Greensboro, North Carolina	1873
Bethune-Cookman College	Daytona Beach, Florida	1904
Birmingham-Southern College	Birmingham, Alabama	1856
Boston University	Boston, Massachusetts	1839
Centenary College of Louisiana	Shreveport, Louisiana	1825
Central College	Fayette, Missouri	1854
Claflin College	Orangeburg, South Carolina	1869
Clark College	Atlanta, Georgia	1869

Institution	Location	Date of Founding
College of The Pacific	Stockton, California	1851
College of Puget Sound	Tacoma, Washington	1888
Columbia College	Columbia, South Carolina	1854
Cornell College	Mount Vernon, Iowa	1853
Dakota Wesleyan University	Mitchell, South Dakota	1885
De Pauw University	Greencastle, Indiana	1837
Dickinson College	Carlisle, Pennsylvania	1773
Dillard University	New Orleans, Louisiana	1930
Drew University	Madison, New Jersey	1867
Duke University	Durham, North Carolina	1838
Emory and Henry College	Emory, Virginia	1836
Emory University	Emory University, Georgia	1836
Evansville College	Evansville, Indiana	1854
Florida Southern College	Lakeland, Florida	1885
Greensboro College	Greensboro, North Carolina	1838
Hamline University	St. Paul, Minnesota	1854
Hendrix College	Conway, Arkansas	1884
High Point College	High Point, North Carolina	1924
Huntingdon College	Montgomery, Alabama	1854
Illinois Wesleyan University	Bloomington, Illinois	1850
Iowa Wesleyan College	Mount Pleasant, Iowa	1842
Kansas Wesleyan University	Salina, Kansas	1885
Kentucky Wesleyan College	Owensboro, Kentucky	1866
LaGrange College	LaGrange, Georgia	1831
Lambuth College	Jackson, Tennessee	1924
Lawrence College	Appleton, Wisconsin	1847
Lycoming College	Williamsport, Pennsylvania	1947
MacMurray College	Jacksonville, Illinois	1846
McKendree College	Lebanon, Illinois	1834
McMurry College	Abilene, Texas	1923
Millsaps College	Jackson, Mississippi	1892
Morningside College	Sioux City, Iowa	1899
Mount Union College	Alliance, Ohio	1846
Nebraska Wesleyan University	Lincoln, Nebraska	1887
Northwestern University	Evanston, Illinois	1851
Ohio Northern University	Ada, Ohio	1871
Ohio Wesleyan University	Delaware, Ohio	1842
Oklahoma City University	Oklahoma City, Oklahoma	1889

Institution	Location	Date of Founding
Philander Smith College	Little Rock, Arkansas	1868
Randolph-Macon College	Ashland, Virginia	1830
Randolph-Macon Woman's College	Lynchburg, Virginia	1893
Rust College	Holly Springs, Mississippi	1866
Scarritt College	Nashville, Tennessee	1924
Simpson College	Indianola, Iowa	1860
Southern Methodist University	Dallas, Texas	1911
Southwestern College	Winfield, Kansas	1885
Southwestern University	Georgetown, Texas	1840
Syracuse University	Syracuse, New York	1870
Tennessee Wesleyan College	Athens, Tennessee	1866
Texas Wesleyan College	Fort Worth, Texas	1891
Union College	Barbourville, Kentucky	1879
University of Chattanooga	Chattanooga, Tennessee	1886
University of Denver	Denver, Colorado	1864
University of Southern California	Los Angeles, California	1880
Wesley College	Grand Forks, North Dakota	1891
Wesleyan College	Macon, Georgia	1836
Wesleyan University	Middletown, Connecticut	1831
West Virginia Wesleyan College	Buckhannon, West Virginia	1890
Western Maryland College	Westminster, Maryland	1867
Wiley College	Marshall, Texas	1873
Willamette University	Salem, Oregon	1842
Wofford College	Spartanburg, South Carolina	1854

HISTORICAL BACKGROUND

The famous historical ten-day Christmas Conference that resulted in the founding of the Methodist Church was convened in Lovely Lane Chapel, Baltimore, on December 24, 1784. Sixty-six of the eighty-one ministers of the Gospel, mostly young men, who were carrying on the religious movement initiated in Great Britain by John Wesley had assembled to take stock of their future. They had gained many members and much support throughout the colonies in spite of the handicap brought on by Wesley's support of the Crown during the Revolution.

After organizing as the Methodist Episcopal Church separate from the Church of England in which Wesley continued as an ordained minister, these independent and ambitious young clergymen proposed the immediate founding of a college for the advancement of religion in America. They were not content with an academy like the Kingswood School established near Bristol, England, by John Wesley.

The ambitious venture was named *Cokesbury College,* the title being compounded from Coke and Asbury, the names of the first two Bishops of the Methodist Church, Thomas Coke and Francis Asbury, who had been elected at the organizing conference. The college building was begun in 1785 and two years later the college was opened for students. After operating more or less successfully for eight years the building burned down, an indication to Bishop Asbury that his mentor John Wesley was right when, in his last letter to Asbury dated September 20, 1788, he had this comment on the founding of Cokesbury: "But in one point, my dear brother, I am a little afraid both the Doctor and you differ from me. I study to be little: you study to be great. I creep, you strut along. I found a school: you a college! Nay, and call it after your own names. O beware, do not seek to be something! Let me be nothing, and 'Christ be all in all!'"

Cokesbury College was located at Abingdon some twenty miles north of Baltimore, Maryland, in which state about one-third of all Methodists were then residing. Regulations for the Cokesbury students were even more rigorous than those in vogue at other colonial colleges. They were supposed to arise at 5 A.M., to assemble for prayers at six, to breakfast at seven, and "were closely kept" at their studies from eight until noon. After a one o'clock dinner they had a recreation period until three with the rest of the afternoon and evening devoted to study. Their recreation consisted of "gardening, walking, riding, and bathing, without doors; and the carpenter's, joiner's, cabinet maker's, or turner's business, within doors." Further rigorism was evidenced in requirements that the students should not take part in anything "which the world calls play," nor should they enjoy the luxury of sleeping on feather beds.

Since the new Methodist Episcopal Church had no well-educated clergymen, they selected as the first teacher of the college Freeman Marsh, a Quaker who had the reputation of being a good Latin scholar and, what was more important, an excellent disciplinarian. John Wesley finally gave sanction to the institution by recommending for the presidency the Reverend Mr. Heath who had been formerly the master of an English grammar school. He arrived with his wife and "two lovely daughters" to assume the presidency at the dedication of the college in 1787. Twenty-five students were enrolled.

Undaunted by the disastrous fire of 1795, the Methodists started a college in Baltimore in a brick building adjacent to their church on Light Street. This second attempt also met with a disastrous fire in December 1796. The Light Street Church was consumed in this fire, which conflagration caused rugged old Asbury to write in his journal: "I conclude God loveth the people of Baltimore, and will keep them poor in order to keep them pure."

In 1816 a third unsuccessful trial was made to establish a Methodist college by a group of Baltimoreans under the name of Asbury College. A successful physician and local preacher by the name of Dr. Samuel K. Jennings became its president. The charter was secured in 1818. After a few years of apparent prosperity the college folded up "for want of money" and because "of a mongrel religion," a Methodist comment on the fact that most of the teachers were not of their faith.

These three futile attempts at maintaining a college were made in spite of the fact that the first Book of Discipline of the new Methodist Church, issued in 1784, emphasized the saving of souls over the gaining of knowledge. Like some other contemporary churches its leaders felt that zeal and enthusiasm are much more important than education. The "Great Awakening" of the early part of the eighteenth century and the "Second Awakening" of the latter part brought many accessions to the Methodist membership. Then the General Conference of the Methodist Episcopal Church came to realize that the Christian college is the bulwark of the Church and at their 1824 meeting passed this recommendation: "That each Annual Conference establish a seminary of learning under its own regulations and patronage." However, previous to this formal action of the governing body of the Church, Augusta College was established in 1822 in Augusta, Kentucky, under the joint auspices of the Ohio and Kentucky Methodist Conferences. This college faded out of the picture by combining with Transylvania University in 1841 when the Kentucky Conference took over Transylvania. Professor Henry B. Bascom of the Augusta faculty became the president of Transylvania University. During its short period of existence Augusta College graduated the distinguished Methodist bishop Randolph S. Foster.

Early Colleges

Madison College was established in 1826 at Uniontown, Pennsylvania, by the Pittsburgh Conference. Its first president was the Henry B. Bascom mentioned above. The college opened in 1827 with sixty-three students and six teachers. In spite of heroic efforts by President Bascom, who had received fine letters of encouragement from ex-President James Madison and other statesmen of the era, including the Roman Catholic Charles Carroll for whom he planned to establish the Carroll Institute of Agriculture, he was forced by financial pressure to abandon the enterprise in 1829.

Henry Clay stated that Bascom was the greatest orator he had ever listened to. His most distinguished student was Matthew Simpson, who walked from his Ohio homestead to become student and tutor at Madison College and later a famous bishop of the Methodist Episcopal Church.

La Grange College. This was another Methodist institution that had a short and brilliant career discussed in Chapter X, which tells the story of its alteration into a state-owned college.

Randolph-Macon College was the first existing Methodist college to receive a charter. This was granted by the General Assembly of Virginia, February 3, 1830. The college was first located at Boydton, Virginia, near the boundary line of North Carolina with the hope of enticing patronage from both states. However, it did not begin operations until October 1832. Its first president was the Reverend Stephen Olin, a Northerner who had gone South for his health and had for a while been a member of the faculty of Franklin College of the University of Georgia. He was valedictorian of the class of

1820 at Middlebury College. He had owned slaves while in the South. As a member of the Methodist General Conference of 1844 he argued valiantly against the motion that brought about the schism resulting in the Northern and Southern branches of Methodism, though in the end he voted for the motion. In 1839 Olin resigned to become the second president of Wesleyan University in Connecticut in 1842, after a three-year trip abroad for the sake of his health. The second president of Randolph-Macon was Landon C. Garland, who later became president of the University of Alabama and the first chancellor of Vanderbilt University.

Wesleyan University. This institution was chartered and opened its doors for students in 1831: thus it was really the first surviving college to begin operations under Methodist auspices. The Reverend Wilbur Fisk was the first president. Originally he was fearful that education would be harmful to preachers. During its first forty years one third of Wesleyan's graduates became Methodist preachers. Due to differences of opinion between a strong-minded Bishop and a strong-minded chairman of its board of trustees, the university some years ago had its charter altered so that henceforth the New England Methodist Conference would have no responsibility in approving persons selected to serve as trustees.

Although Methodism had a late start in the founding of colleges, it established thirty-six "permanent" colleges in the three decades from the founding of Randolph-Macon until the beginning of the War Between the States. From the beginning most of these colleges had some or all of their trustees approved by the various conferences. Emory University founded in 1836 and Duke University founded in 1852 still hold this relationship to the Southeastern Jurisdiction of the Methodist Church.

The two present-day Methodist colleges established before 1830 are *Allegheny* and *Dickinson*. Their vicissitudes and struggles merit separate paragraphs.

Allegheny College. Timothy Alden, a Presbyterian minister of the family made famous by the poet Longfellow, founded Allegheny College. After a fight against tremendous economic conditions from 1815 to 1831, Alden took a Presbyterian pulpit in the suburbs of

Pittsburgh. The college then became the home of bats and owls for two years. This melancholy status was partially due doubtless to competition for funds and patronage with two older Presbyterian colleges in Western Pennsylvania: Washington college, chartered in 1806, and Jefferson College in nearby Canonsburg, chartered in 1802. Both had been "Academies," Washington having received its charter in 1787 and Jefferson in 1794.

In 1833 the Pittsburgh Conference of the Methodist Episcopal Church re-opened the college with the full approval of the surviving trustees. The new president was Martin Ruter, a restless, roving, eloquent preacher who had come in as an itinerant evangelist to serve what was then Pittsburgh's largest Methodist church. Ruter was a self-educated New Englander who had attained distinction as a preacher. He had served on the committee of Methodists that obtained a charter on December 7, 1822, from the state of Kentucky for the founding of Augusta College, while he was serving in Cincinnati, Ohio, as the Western Agent of the "Methodist Book Concern"; he had accepted with reluctance the presidency of Augusta College in 1827.

Martin Ruter became pastor of the Smithfield Methodist Church in Pittsburgh in 1832, after leading a notable "revivalist" movement there. He had to have two assistant pastors to care for the enlarged membership. Again he reluctantly became a college president when his clerical brethren persuaded him to lead in re-establishing Allegheny College in 1833. Among his students during his quadrennium there was the Reverend Cyrus Nott, who became an early president of Indiana University; on his faculty was Matthew Simpson, who later became a Methodist bishop and for whom a well-known college in Iowa was named.

While a delegate to the Methodist General Conference in Cincinnati in May 1836, Ruter felt again an irresistible urge for missionary service by the inspiration of the opportunities in the new state of Texas, then being wrested from Mexico. A year later he resigned the Allegheny presidency to become the head of the first Methodist Mission in Texas. But the primitive conditions there were too severe for him, and in 1838, at the age of fifty-three, he succumbed to typhoid pneumonia after but one year in the Lone Star

State. He made such an impression in so short a time that a town was named for him, Rutersville, and Ruter College was established in 1840. The latter was amalgamated later with three other Methodist colleges to become Southwestern University, in Georgetown, Texas.

The author came to know intimately the story of this rugged pioneer, first as a member of the Allegheny College faculty for thirteen years where daily he passed Ruter Hall, and later, while president of Birmingham-Southern College, as a close friend of Martin Ruter's aged grandson and granddaughter. He helped write the wills of the latter and shortly thereafter had charge of their obsequies.

Dickinson College. The chief founder of Dickinson College was Dr. Benjamin Rush, a graduate of Princeton in the class of 1750, a signer of the Declaration of Independence, a professor of chemistry in the College of Philadelphia, an active and public-spirited citizen who gave hearty encouragement to the founders of Franklin and Marshall College. Rush persuaded the Presbyterian founders of the new college to name it for his friend John Dickinson "in memory of the great and important services rendered to his country" by the patriotic fervor he stirred up in the colonies, through his letters "from a farmer in Pennsylvania to the inhabitants of the British colonies." Dickinson had been a general in the Revolutionary War, and a signer of the Constitution from Pennsylvania.

The Reverend Charles Nisbet, a Presbyterian minister from Scotland, was elected the first president of Dickinson College. His long term of service was beset with worrisome economic problems and more worrisome quarrels among the church factions. The economic and social conditions resulted in the college going through a period of hibernation from 1816 to 1821. During Nisbet's administration there was graduated in 1809, James Buchanan, the fifteenth President of the United States; in 1795, Roger Brooke Taney, Chief Justice of the United States Supreme Court from 1836 to 1864.

The college again suspended operations in 1832 for a period of about one year. The Baltimore Conference of the Methodist Church had been seeking for several years a college to serve its interests, and in 1833 it persuaded the Philadelphia Conference of the Methodist Church to join in proposing to the Presbyterian trustees to re-open Dickinson College. This proposal was accepted and the property transferred to the Methodists, with the election of Bishop John Emory as the first president of the new board of trustees. Another distinguished member of this new board was United States Supreme Court Justice John McLean.

Bishop Emory was an important influence in Methodist higher education: Emory University in Georgia and Emory and Henry College in Virginia were named for him. He was born in 1789 on the Eastern Shore of Maryland and he died from an accident in 1835 after serving as bishop for only three years. His college education was obtained at Washington College (Maryland), whose president was the Reverend William Smith, previously the first provost of the College of Philadelphia. Bishop Emory had also participated in the founding of Wesleyan and New York Universities; he had been elected the first president of Randolph-Macon College in 1831 but declined to serve.

American University is unique in the group in that it is wholly under the control of the General Conference of the Methodist Church. It was chartered in 1893, primarily as a post-graduate institution. When it added an undergraduate college in 1925 it found itself without a supporting conference and thus with no financial support from the Methodist body. In 1948 the General Conference of the Methodist Church appointed a committee of nine, with the author as secretary, to study the responsibilities and opportunities of Methodism in the capital of the nation. In 1952, the General Conference meeting in San Francisco gave approval to the recommendation of this committee that American University become the property of the church, which was legally effected shortly thereafter.

Asbury College, Wilmore, Kentucky, was founded in 1890 by a member of the Kentucky Conference of the Southern Methodist Church. Although it is named for one of the two first Methodist bishops and is operated "according to doctrinal standards set up and taught by John Wesley and his immediate followers," the college is governed by a self-perpetuating board of trustees who consider the institution fully interdenominational.

Taylor University, Upland, Indiana, began operations in 1846 at

Fort Wayne, Indiana, under the auspices of the Indiana Conference of the Methodist Episcopal Church. In 1890 Fort Wayne College, as it was then called, came under the control of the National Association of Local Preachers of the Methodist Episcopal Church. The name was then changed to Taylor University in honor of Bishop William Taylor, distinguished for his success in the mission fields of Africa, and a hearty supporter of the college by his assistance with influence and personal means. The college was removed in 1893 to its present location. In 1921 the control was turned over to an independent board of trustees which still emphasize "world evangelism, and the spreading of Scriptural Holiness—which were the motivating passions of Bishop William Taylor."

Goucher College was incorporated on January 26, 1885, as the Woman's College of Baltimore under the auspices of the Baltimore Conference of the Methodist Episcopal Church. In 1910 the charter was amended so as to change the name to Goucher College in honor of the Reverend Doctor and Mrs. John Franklin Goucher who were among the founders and were generous benefactors. Dr. Goucher was president for eighteen years. As in the case of Wesleyan University, friction between strong-minded Methodist leaders resulted in an amended charter which brought about complete severance of Methodist relationships.

Vanderbilt University. This institution was opened under Methodist control in 1875. It was not only the first university organized by the Southern Methodists with their first Theological School, but in a sense, with its six divisions, including also law, medicine, dentistry, it was the first real university to be established in the South. Although all the Southern Conferences were supporting the appeals for funds, the project became a reality when Cornelius Vanderbilt responded with a gift of $1,000,000 to the supplication of his brother-in-law, a Southern Methodist bishop, Holland N. McTyeire. A generation later another bishop, on elevation to that office from the Vanderbilt Theological faculty, interfered so greatly with the operation of the university that the trustees had the charter changed by the State of Tennessee so as to sever all connections with the church; the severance was made effective only after long legal battles. Two Southern Methodist families came to the support of the church by sharing large fortunes made in Coca Cola and tobacco: the Candlers gave large sums to expand Emory College into Emory University; the Dukes did likewise to make Trinity College into the well-known Duke University.

In the list of Methodist colleges are to be found several that were organized by the Methodist Protestant Church which joined in 1939 with the Methodist Episcopal Church and the Methodist Episcopal Church, South, to become the present Methodist Church. These colleges include Adrian, High Point, and Western Maryland Colleges.

Adrian College had its genesis as Marshall College, Leoni, Michigan. It received its first charter on April 6, 1839, with the Wesleyan Methodists as the founders. It later moved to Marshall, Michigan, and took the name of Michigan Union College. In 1859 its location was changed to Adrian, Michigan, where control shifted in 1868 to the Methodist Protestant Church under which group it operated until 1939. West Lafayette College, Ohio, founded in 1899 by the Muskingum Conference (Ohio) of the Methodist Protestant Church, was consolidated with Adrian College in 1916.

In 1939 Adrian College automatically came under the jurisdiction of the Methodist Church, when it was formed by the union of the Methodist Episcopal Church, the Methodist Episcopal Church, South, and the Methodist Protestant Church.

AFRICAN METHODIST EPISCOPAL CHURCH

Institution	Location	Date of Founding
Allen University	Columbia, South Carolina	1870
Morris Brown College	Atlanta, Georgia	1881
Paul Quinn College	Waco, Texas	1872
Wilberforce University	Wilberforce, Ohio	1856

The African Methodist Episcopal Church is the next largest and one of the oldest branches of the Methodist family, having a membership of about one million, with seventy-five hundred ministers, and nearly six thousand churches with property valued at one million dollars. Its work extends beyond the United States into West and South Africa, the Dominican Republic, and the West Indian Islands.

Richard Allen, a friend of Francis Asbury, and a slave who purchased his freedom with money saved while preaching to other Negroes, was the founder of this church in 1816. The origin of the establishment of the church dates from an incident that occurred several years previous in old St. George's Church in Philadelphia, when Allen and four other Negroes were ejected from the church because they declined to go to the gallery to participate in the religious services. Allen continued to be a close friend of Bishop Asbury, who consecrated him as the first bishop in the new church "which adhered strictly to Wesleyan heritage."

AFRICAN METHODIST EPISCOPAL CHURCH ZION

Institution	Location	Date of Founding
Livingstone College	Salisbury, North Carolina	1879

This branch of the Methodist Church had an origin similar to the one described in the previous section. Its original group broke away from another strict old Methodist church, the John Street Church of New York City. It became a separate organization in 1820 with the present membership numbering three quarters of a million. The church has established home missions in the South and in foreign lands like Africa and British Guiana. W. J. Trent has been president of Livingstone College for over twenty-nine years. His son, W. J. Trent, Jr., also a graduate of Livingstone College, has for a number of years been the executive officer of the United Negro Fund.

CENTRAL METHODIST EPISCOPAL CHURCH

Institution	Location	Date of Founding
Lane College	Jackson, Tennessee	1882
Miles College	Birmingham, Alabama	1905
Mississippi Industrial College	Holly Springs, Mississippi	1905
Paine College	Augusta, Georgia	1883
Texas College	Tyler, Texas	1894

The Central Methodist Episcopal Church founded in 1870 has nearly 400,000 members and 2500 churches. Until a few months ago it was called the Colored Methodist Church. It was established by the Methodist Episcopal Church, South, shortly after the War Between the States, to take care of the Negroes who had worshipped in the galleries of the Southern Methodist Churches attended by their owners. A leader in the origin of this church was Bishop Robert Paine, organizer and first president of La Grange College in Alabama. He and Bishop McTyeire, the chief founder of Vanderbilt University, ordained two Negro preachers as the first bishops of this church.

FREE METHODIST CHURCH

Institution	Location	Date of Founding
Greenville College	Greenville, Illinois	1892
Roberts Wesleyan College	North Chili, New York	1866
Seattle Pacific College	Seattle, Washington	1891

The Free Methodist Church was organized at Pekin, New York, in 1860 by the Reverend B. T. Roberts and other ministers who were considered too conservative to continue affiliations as members of the Genesee Methodist Conference. This group believes in utmost simplicity of worship and the "full inspiration" of the Scriptures. Its members opposed the use of musical instruments and choirs until very recently. They hold in taboo secret societies, and the use of tobacco and alcohol. The church has a strong missionary program: it is a member of the National Holiness Association.

WESLEYAN METHODIST CHURCH

Institution	Location	Date of Founding
Houghton College	Houghton, New York	1883
Marion College	Marion, Indiana	1920

The Wesleyan Methodist Church was organized in 1843 at Utica, New York, in protest against the lack of firmness against slavery then prevalent in the Methodist Episcopal Church. Furthermore, the founders dispensed with bishops and insisted on lay participation in church government.

There must have been many debates and hot-headed debaters

in the Methodist Episcopal Church around 1840, for in that year the Methodist Protestant Church was organized over the same question of domination by the bishops, though its leaders took no definite stand on slavery to the disappointment of the Wesleyan group. With the secession of the Southern Church in 1844, there were four Methodist churches in a period of four years, due to the division of opinion over slavery and lay participation in church control. Like the Free Methodists the Wesleyan group is rigid in its membership tests, which include the prohibition of alcohol, tobacco, and membership in secret societies. Also like the Free Methodists the Wesleyan Methodists are mostly tithers.

Wheaton College, Wheaton, Illinois, was established by the Wesleyan Methodists as the Illinois Institute in 1853. It was re-organized by a Congregational group as Wheaton College in 1860. The leader in this organization was the Reverend Dr. Jonathan Blanchard who had been for twelve years president of Knox College. After twenty-two years as president of Wheaton he was succeeded in 1882 by his son, the Reverend Dr. Charles A. Blanchard, who held office for forty-three years until his death in 1925. Wheaton College is now interdenominational and under private control.

CHAPTER VIII

Presbyterian Colleges

BELOW is the list of four-year colleges that have been endorsed by the General Assembly of the Presbyterian Church in the United States of America. All of the colleges on this list have a defined relationship to the Presbyterian Church in the U.S.A. Each accepts the Set of Standards for Presbyterian colleges as approved by the General Assembly. The endorsement of a college by the Board of Christian Education and its inclusion in the list indicate that its program and policies are in substantial accord with sound educational procedures and an effective Christian approach.

COLLEGES RELATED TO THE PRESBYTERIAN CHURCH, U.S.A.

Institution	Location	Year Organized
Alma College	Alma, Michigan	1886
Beaver College	Jenkintown, Pennsylvania	1853
Blackburn College	Carlinville, Illinois	1857
Buena Vista College	Storm Lake, Iowa	1891
Carroll College	Waukesha, Wisconsin	1846
Centre College	Danville, Kentucky	1819
Coe College	Cedar Rapids, Iowa	1851
Davis and Elkins College	Elkins, West Virginia	1904
Dubuque, The University of	Dubuque, Iowa	1852
Emporia, The College of	Emporia, Kansas	1882
Grove City College	Grove City, Pennsylvania	1876
Hanover College	Hanover, Indiana	1827
Hastings College	Hastings, Nebraska	1882
Huron College	Huron, South Dakota	1883

COLLEGES RELATED TO THE PRESBYTERIAN CHURCH, U.S.A. (*Continued*)

Institution	Location	Year Organized
Idaho, The College of	Caldwell, Idaho	1891
Illinois College	Jacksonville, Illinois	1829
Jamestown College	Jamestown, North Dakota	1883
Johnson C. Smith University	Charlotte, North Carolina	1867
Lafayette College	Easton, Pennsylvania	1826
Lake Forest College	Lake Forest, Illinois	1857
Lewis and Clark College	Portland, Oregon	1866
Lindenwood College	St. Charles, Missouri	1827
Macalester College	St. Paul, Minnesota	1885
Maryville College	Maryville, Tennessee	1819
Millikin University	Decatur, Illinois	1901
Missouri Valley College	Marshall, Missouri	1889
Occidental College	Los Angeles, California	1887
Ozarks, The College of	Clarksville, Arkansas	1891
Park College	Parkville, Missouri	1875
Parsons College	Fairfield, Iowa	1875
Rocky Mountain College	Billings, Montana	1883
Trinity University	San Antonio, Texas	1869
Tulsa, The University of	Tulsa, Oklahoma	1894
Tusculum College	Greeneville, Tennessee	1794
Waynesburg College	Waynesburg, Pennsylvania	1849
Westminster College	Fulton, Missouri	1853
Westminster College	Salt Lake City, Utah	1875
Whitworth College	Spokane, Washington	1890
Wilson College	Chambersburg, Pennsylvania	1869
Wooster, The College of	Wooster, Ohio	1886

The colleges in the above list accept the following Set of Standards, approved by the Presbyterian General Assembly after adoption by the Board of Christian Education, Presbyterian Church, U.S.A. on April 28, 1943:

(1) The college shall adopt a statement of purpose clearly defining its status as a Christian college. This statement of purpose shall be included in the statement of institutional purpose in the official college catalogue and shall furthermore indicate that the college is affiliated with the Presbyterian Church, U.S.A.

(2) It shall be declared policy of the college to employ as regular members of the faculty only men and women who are active members in good standing of some evangelical Christian church which affirms its loyalty to Jesus Christ as the Divine Lord and Savior.

(3) The college shall provide courses in Biblical studies and shall require at least one such course for graduation.

(4) The college shall submit annually to the Board of Christian Education complete financial information for the year on forms supplied by the Board, and shall have an annual audit made by a certified public accountant. It is further recommended that the statements contained in the accountant's report shall conform with the accounting principles applicable to institutions of higher education.

(5) The college shall be officially and fully accredited by the regional accrediting agency. If not so accredited, it shall be specifically approved by the Board of Christian Education upon recommendation of an examining committee consisting of the President of the Presbyterian College Union, two other members of the Presbyterian College Union, elected by the Nexus Committee of that body, three members of the Board of Christian Education, and the Director of the Department of Colleges.

The Presbyterian Church, U.S.A. was responsible for the establishment of many other colleges whose alumni contributed greatly to the cultural advancement of the United States. Some of them evolved into well-known state institutions, such as the Universities of California, Delaware, and Kentucky. Some became fully independent. Some languished for a while and re-opened under other auspices, such as Allegheny and Dickinson Colleges in Pennsylvania, both of which were revived under Methodist auspices. Others served well their day, then yielded to insolvable social, economic, and occasionally political conditions and passed into oblivion. It is hoped a later study can soon be published that will summarize the heroic struggles and notable contributions of this last group.

The remarkable contribution rendered the educational program of the Presbyterian Church, U.S.A. by Princeton University has been partially detailed in the chapter on colonial colleges. According to the records, sixteen of the early colleges were founded by Princeton alumni and 127 of these alumni have become college and university presidents.

Here is a list of present-day accredited independent colleges which had their beginnings under the aegis of the Presbyterian Church of the U.S.A.

Institution	Location	Year Organized
Allegheny College	Meadville, Penna.	1815
College of California	Berkeley, California	1855
Dickinson College	Carlisle, Penna.	1773
Elmira College	Elmira, New York	1855
Hamilton College	Clinton, New York	1812
Knox College	Galesburg, Illinois	1837
Lincoln University	Lincoln University, Penna.	1854
New York University	New York, New York	1831
Pennsylvania College for Women	Pittsburgh, Penna.	1869
Princeton University	Princeton, New Jersey	1746
University of Delaware	Newark, Delaware	1833
University of Kentucky	Lexington, Kentucky	1783
Wabash College	Crawfordsville, Indiana	1832
Washington and Jefferson College	Washington, Penna.	1802
Western College	Oxford, Ohio	1894

Economic conditions were largely responsible for the abandonment of Allegheny and Dickinson Colleges by the Presbyterians, the former in 1831 and the latter in 1832. Both were re-opened in 1833 with Methodist control and support: these transformations are outlined briefly in Chapter VII.

Union College, Schenectady, New York, can lay claim to inclusion in the group of colleges once under the aegis of the Presbyterian Church of the United States of America. Union College was founded in 1795 by three church groups: the Presbyterians, the Dutch Reformed, and the Congregationalists, thus accounting for its appropriate appellation. For some years previous to its founding, all three of these church groups were considering the establishment of a college in upstate New York. The Reverend Dirck Romeyn, minister of the Dutch Reformed Church, mentioned in the Queen's College section of Chapter II, was chairman of the committee that obtained the charter. He had founded the Schenectady Academy in 1785 and had acted as its principal while continuing to hold his pastorate. On the establishment of the college the consistory of the Dutch Reformed Church donated for its main building the structure that housed the handsome academy.

By request of the founding group, the charter stipulated that the majority of the trustees should never be from one sect, further that the president should not hold a pastorate while in office. The first president chosen was the Reverend Doctor John Blair Smith, who had been for ten years president of Hampden-Sydney College in Virginia in succession to his brother, Samuel Stanhope Smith, who had gone to Princeton to succeed his father-in-law, John Wither-spoon, as president there. The succeeding presidents at Union until 1929 were ordained ministers, most of them of the Presbyterian connection. Eliphalet Nott served as president from 1804 to 1866, the longest term in the history of American colleges. He had been minister of the Albany Presbyterian Church. This great president gave the college a "strong religious and theological tone."

Pennsylvania College for Women. The officers and members of the Shadyside Presbyterian Church in Pittsburgh acted with consummate daring but with faith and vision in founding Pennsylvania College for Women. They were determined to have a convenient college for their daughters to match the nearby Western University of Pennsylvania (now the University of Pittsburgh), limited to male students.

Other Colleges. It is worthy of note that Centre, Davis and Elkins, and Westminster Colleges operate under the aegis of both of the largest Presbyterian groups. When the cornerstone of Westminster (Missouri) was laid on July 4, 1853, it was announced that fully two-thirds of all colleges in the United States were then directly or indirectly under the control of the Presbyterian Church.

COLLEGES AFFILIATED WITH THE PRESBYTERIAN CHURCH IN THE UNITED STATES

Institution	Location	Year Organized
Agnes Scott College	Decatur, Georgia	1889
Arkansas College	Batesville, Arkansas	1872
Austin College	Sherman, Texas	1849

COLLEGES AFFILIATED WITH THE PRESBYTERIAN CHURCH
IN THE UNITED STATES (*Continued*)

Institution	Location	Year Organized
Belhaven College	Jackson, Mississippi	1894
Centre College	Danville, Kentucky	1819
Davidson College	Davidson, North Carolina	1836
Davis and Elkins College	Elkins, West Virginia	1904
Flora MacDonald College	Red Springs, North Carolina	1896
Hampden-Sydney College	Hampden-Sydney, Virginia	1775
King College	Bristol, Tennessee	1867
Mary Baldwin College	Staunton, Virginia	1842
Montreat College	Montreat, North Carolina	1916
Presbyterian College	Clinton, South Carolina	1880
Queens College	Charlotte, North Carolina	1857
Southwestern	Memphis, Tennessee	1848
Stillman College	Tuscaloosa, Alabama	1876
Westminster College	Fulton, Missouri	1851

All the colleges in the above list except Agnes Scott and Mary Baldwin have their trustees elected subject to the approval of the respective Presbyterian Church bodies that contribute to their support.

Hampden-Sydney College. The oldest member of the group, *Hampden-Sydney College,* was chartered as Hampden-Sydney Academy in 1775 and incorporated as Hampden-Sydney College in 1783 by the General Assembly of Virginia. In 1919 its charter was again amended so as to transfer its ownership to the Presbyterian Synod of Virginia.

Hampden-Sydney College wielded great influence throughout the whole Presbyterian Church for many years up to the time of the schism over the question of slavery into Presbyterian Church, United States of America, and Presbyterian Church in the United States. It was the child of the Presbytery of Hanover founded in 1755 and which encompassed the states of Virginia, North Carolina, South Carolina, and a large part of the territory that later became the state of Ohio. The chief organizer of the Presbyterian Church in this vast area was the Reverend Samuel Davies of Delaware, who succeeded Jonathan Edwards as president of the College of New Jersey (Princeton). When the Academy was established in 1775 its first president was the Reverend Samuel Stanhope Smith, who in 1779 transferred to the faculty of Princeton where he later succeeded the famous John Witherspoon as its president.

The institution was known as Hampden-Sydney Academy until 1783, when it was granted a charter by the Virginia House of Delegates under the title of Hampden-Sydney College. Although it is claimed that work of collegiate grade was offered from the beginning, Hampden-Sydney is not generally included among the nine well-known colonial colleges whose establishment as colleges preceded and survived the American Revolution.

The record does clearly indicate that Hampden-Sydney was not narrowly sectarian for at one time Thomas Jefferson seriously considered the college for the location of his life-cherished plan of a state university. It also received grants of land in 1784 and 1794 from the Commonwealth of Virginia.

James Madison and Patrick Henry were on its first board of trustees. William Henry Harrison, ninth president of the United States, was an early alumnus.

When Samuel Stanhope Smith joined the faculty at Princeton in 1779, he was succeeded as president of Hampden-Sydney by his brother, the Reverend John Blair Smith. After ten years in this office he became the first president of Union College, Schenectady, New York. Later there was evidence of a fair exchange between North and South when a distinguished Episcopal layman, Jonathan P. Cushing, a Dartmouth alumnus, became president of Hampden-Sydney in 1821, to serve with significant success for fourteen years. Early in the Cushing era the Department of Divinity of the college evolved into the Union Theological Seminary, which continued on the Hampden-Sydney campus until 1898 when it was moved to Richmond.

Hampden-Sydney's far-flung influence throughout the world is illustrated magnificently in the career of John Leighton Stuart of the class of 1896. In 1919 he was elected the first president of Yenching University, Peiping, China. He retired from this office in 1946 to become United States Ambassador to the Republic of China which post he had to relinquish when Chiang Kai-shek was driven out by Mao Tse-tung's Communist government.

Davidson College. Another college in this group to become the alma mater of a President of the United States is Davidson College. His name is Woodrow Wilson, known as Thomas Woodrow Wilson, and affectionately called "Tommy," while a student at Davidson, who became the twenty-eighth president, after having served as president of Princeton University and Governor of New Jersey. His father, Joseph R. Wilson, was professor of Theology from 1885 to 1892 at another member of this group, Southwestern at Memphis.

Oglethorpe College, Atlanta, Georgia, had its beginnings under the auspices of the Presbyterian Church, United States, being chartered in 1835.

Washington and Lee University. Another Virginia college that had its origin under Presbyterian influences is Washington and Lee University. It began as Augusta Academy in 1749; was known as Liberty Hall from 1776-82 while under control of the Hanover Presbytery; received its first charter in 1782 under the name of Liberty Hall Academy; changed its name to Washington Academy in 1798 on receipt of a gift of $50,000 by George Washington's will; became known as Washington College in 1813; and in 1871 took its present name to recognize Robert E. Lee, who was its president from 1865-70. Under the 1782 charter the trustees became a self-perpetuating body, however the Presbyterian influence continued to be felt for years as most of the presidents were Presbyterian ministers and laymen.

FOUR-YEAR COLLEGES UNDER THE AUSPICES OF THE
UNITED PRESBYTERIAN CHURCH OF NORTH AMERICA

College	Location	Year Founded
Knoxville College	Knoxville, Tennessee	1875
Monmouth College	Monmouth, Illinois	1853
Muskingum College	New Concord, Ohio,	1836
Sterling College	Sterling, Kansas	1887
Tarkio College	Tarkio, Missouri	1883
Westminster College	New Wilmington, Pennsylvania	1852

Muskingum College. The oldest college of this group, Muskingum College, began under the auspices of a board composed of local citizens of New Concord, Ohio, men of opposite politics and Christians of different denominations. They were awarded a charter on March 8, 1837. In 1877 control was transferred to the United Presbyterian Presbyteries of Muskingum and Mansfield. In 1888 these Presbyteries turned over the control of the college to the United Presbyterian Synod of Ohio, thus enlarging the college's constituency while offering equal advantages to all groups irrespective of denominational affiliation.

Sterling College was originally called Cooper College, though located in Sterling, Kansas.

Westminster College. In 1852, at New Wilmington, Pennsylvania, Westminster College was opened under the auspices of the Associate Presbyterian Church "to promote principles of Protestant Christianity." In 1858 the Associate Church joined the Associate Reformed Church to become the United Presbyterian Church. Westminster was then placed under the care of the First Synod of the West. It thus became actually the first college to come under the control of the United Presbyterian Church.

CUMBERLAND PRESBYTERIAN CHURCH

The Cumberland Presbyterian Church now maintains and supports one institution of higher learning, *Bethel College*, McKenzie, Tennessee, founded in 1842. As a result of an historical evangelistic "revival" movement in the "Cumberland country" of newly settled sections in Kentucky and Tennessee, there developed a dissidence on the part of many in this area with some of the tenets of the Presbyterian Church, resulting in the formation in 1810 of a new sect, the Cumberland Presbyterian Church. This group, anxious to educate ministers and laymen with the proper educational and religious point of view, organized a number of academies and colleges. These included:

Cumberland College, Princeton, Kentucky, founded 1825. Ceased to operate in 1858.

College of the Ozarks, Clarksville, Arkansas, started as Cane Hill College, Cane Hill, Arkansas in 1834. Moved to Clarksville in 1891 and named Arkansas Cumberland College. In 1920 present name was adopted, the college having affiliated with the Presbyterian Church, U.S.A., in 1906.

Cumberland University, Lebanon, Tennessee, founded in 1842. Passed under control of Presbyterian Church, U.S.A., in 1906. Operated by Baptists 1945-51. Liberal arts school discontinued 1951. Law school still in operation. Institution now independent.

Bethel College, McKenzie, Tennessee, founded as Bethel Seminary at McLemoresville, Tennessee, 1842. Chartered as Bethel College 1847. Moved to McKenzie 1872. Still operated by Cumberland Presbyterian Church.

Waynesburg College, Waynesburg, Pennsylvania, founded 1851. Passed under control of Presbyterian Church, U.S.A., 1906.

Lincoln University, Lincoln, Illinois, founded in 1866. Passed to control of Presbyterian Church, U.S.A., 1906. Now operated as Lincoln College, a junior college.

Trinity University, founded 1869 at Tehuacana, Texas, 1869. Moved to Waxahachie 1902. Passed to control of Presbyterian Church, U.S.A. in 1906. Moved to San Antonio, Texas, 1942.

Missouri Valley College, Marshall, Missouri, founded in 1888. Passed to control of Presbyterian Church, U.S.A., 1906.

James Milliken University, Decatur, Illinois, founded 1903. Passed to control of Presbyterian Church, U.S.A., 1906.

When most of the members and official groups of the Cumberland Presbyterian Church voted in 1906 to return to the parent church, a small group held out for the original tenets of the church. This group continued to maintain Bethel College, which is fully owned by the church.

Cumberland College. This college was established at Princeton, Kentucky, in 1826 by the Cumberland Presbyterian Synod of Kentucky. All students were required to work at least two hours a day on the college farm. Doubtless it was the first college to include manual labor as part of each student's program. Later, many other colleges tried this plan with the same lack of success. By this plan the total expenses for a student were kept down to $80 a year. Soon the control of Cumberland College was taken over by the General Assembly of the church when the Reverend Doctor F. R. Cossitt took charge as president. He was a native of New Hampshire and an alumnus of Middlebury College. In 1842 the Cumberland Presbyterian patronage was transferred to the new Cumberland University, Lebanon, Tennessee, with Cossitt continuing as president. Control of Cumberland College reverted to the local synod, which abandoned the enterprise in 1858. Whereupon Princeton citizens carried it on for a while as a high school which it had really become on the organization of Cumberland University in 1842. This Cumberland College should not be confused with another of the same name which evolved in 1806 from Davidson Academy founded in 1786 in Nashville, Tennessee. The latter expanded into the University of Nashville in 1825 which became Peabody Normal College in 1875 and George Peabody College for Teachers in 1905.

Cumberland University flourished for some sixty years until economic conditions forced the transfer of all its assets to the Southern Baptist Convention of Tennessee in 1946. This latter group, desirous of strengthening its program for higher education in Tennessee deserted Cumberland University in 1951 to concentrate their college activities in the newly acquired commodious plant of Ward-Belmont College, formerly a well-known junior college that had flourished in Nashville for many years, and is now known as *Belmont College*.

Cumberland University amply justified its existence by the number of distinguished alumni who rendered conspicuous service as laymen and clergymen. Among them were a number of college professors and presidents, noted lawyers and judges of state and federal courts, state governors, United States Congressmen and Senators, and Cordell Hull, an outstanding United States Secretary of State.

To *Trinity University* was given outright by the Southwest Texas Conference of the Methodist Church, the campus and equipment of the University of San Antonio at the time of its removal in 1942 from Waxahachie to San Antonio. Shortly before that time the University of San Antonio had its origin in the amalgamation of San Antonio Female College and Westmoreland College, the latter a junior college which had operated successfully for a number of years. At the time of the Methodist wise and judicious donation of their new struggling four-year college, the University of San Antonio, to the Presbyterians, it was facetiously reported that the only return to the Methodists was an honorary doctorate to a prominent churchman who had taken a leading part in the merger—nor had he expected such a generous reward.

Waynesburg College. An outgrowth of Greene Academy, Carmichaels Boro, Greene County, Pennsylvania (a school of Cumberland Presbyterian leanings), and Madison College in Uniontown, Pennsylvania, Waynesburg College was founded by the Methodist Church in 1826. It was turned over by them to the Cumberland Presbyterians in 1838, after being closed for a while. In 1906 the college became affiliated with the Presbyterian Church, U.S.A., when most of the Cumberland Presbyterian Churches returned to the fold of the parent church.

ASSOCIATED REFORMED PRESBYTERIAN CHURCH

The Associate Reformed Presbyterian Church maintains one college, *Erskine College* in Due West, South Carolina. This college was established in 1839. The same church organized Due West Female College (later called Women's College of Due West) about 1860 and the Erskine Theological Seminary about 1842. These three institutions were merged during 1923-25 as Erskine College, with separate deans for the Woman's College and for the Seminary.

The church also organized and operated for several years Bryson College, Fayetteville, Tennessee.

REFORMED PRESBYTERIAN CHURCH

The Reformed Presbyterian Church maintains *Geneva College,* Beaver Falls, Pennsylvania, as the college under its auspices. It was chartered and opened in 1848. It is the only college in the world operated by this branch of the Presbyterian Church which is also called the "Covenanter Church." This group does have one academy, approximating a junior college in curricular strength; it is located at Larnaca on the island of Cyprus in the Mediterranean Sea.

The College began in Northwood, Ohio, as Geneva Hall. Its primary purpose was to educate "Covenanter" preachers. It is hard to realize in these days, when tuition charges run as high as $1000 per annum, that the forty-two students, mostly boys, who enrolled ambitiously in Geneva Hall had to pay only $8.00 per semester for tuition and $1.00 per week for board in nearby village homes. In 1873 the title of the school was changed to Geneva College. The college was strongly "abolitionist" in its views and activities but strangely admitted none of its few Negro students to either of the two literary societies that had a controlling influence in the life and progress of the institution. In 1883 the college was moved to its present location, Beaver Falls, Pennsylvania, primarily to cash in on promised local and Presbyterian support. In the new location Negroes were freely admitted to membership in the literary societies.

The new 1853 charter granted to Geneva Hall by the Ohio legislature required that it should "be and remain forever under the direction of the persons known and acknowledged members of the Reformed Presbyterian Church." As in the case of other colleges previously described, the word "forever" was treated somewhat like "never" in Gilbert and Sullivan's comic opera where it was interpreted to mean "hardly ever." The newer and present charter, granted by the Beaver County Court of Pennsylvania, June 18, 1883, provides that non-Covenanters can be elected to the board of trustees, though affirming that the title to the property remain vested in the Reformed Presbyterian Synod.

CHAPTER IX

Roman Catholic Colleges

THE Roman Catholics were responsible for the establishment of Maryland, one of the original thirteen states. King Charles I gave a charter to George Calvert, the first Lord Baltimore, which gave him proprietary rights over the colony. The first settlement was made in 1634 by two small shiploads of colonists, part Catholic and part Protestant. In spite of the Act of Toleration passed by the colonists in 1649 to save the Catholic settlers from persecution, the Puritans soon seized control. However, in 1658 Lord Baltimore regained his proprietorship for some twenty-five years. Later Maryland became a royal province with the Church of England as the established church.

The above-listed conflicts must have had much to do with the lateness of the Catholic Church in establishing colleges in the United States. The first of the Catholic group was *Georgetown University*, founded in the District of Columbia in 1789 under the leadership of the Reverend John Carroll, later the first Archbishop of Baltimore.

The Jesuits had established a school in Newtown, Maryland, as early as 1677 which was closed about 1699. Some fifty years later the Jesuits were operating a school at Bohemia Manor, at which institution were educated John Carroll and his distinguished cousin, Charles Carroll of Carrollton, a Maryland signer of the Declaration of Independence.

When the Society of Jesus was reorganized in Maryland in 1805 it took over Georgetown College, established by John Carroll, as previously indicated. The college received its power to confer degrees by an Act of the United States Congress dated March 1, 1815, and signed by President James Madison. The Holy See on March 30, 1833, empowered the college to confer "in its name" degrees of philosophy and theology.

The Society of Jesus founded by Ignatius Loyola in 1534 has maintained throughout the years a high grade of liberal education. Over the years it has established in Europe hundreds of schools and colleges "for the Christian education of youth." As early as 1750 it was administering 669 schools throughout the world and 176 theological seminaries. There are at present twenty-seven Jesuit colleges in the United States, a list of which is given later in this chapter.

The next oldest Jesuit college is *Spring Hill College,* located near Mobile, Alabama. It opened for classes in November 1831, under the leadership of Bishop Michael Portier. In 1836 the legislature of Alabama gave the college its charter, thus making it one of the oldest colleges in the South. One of the early presidents of Spring Hill College was called to be the Bishop of Dubuque, Iowa, for whom Loras College was named. Because of limited personnel available, Bishop Portier transferred his college to the Fathers of Mercy, a French congregation that had been organized by early settlers in Mobile. Probably due to lack of experience, these missionaries gave up the task after two years. The Eudists then undertook to operate the college but soon were forced to suspend operations. After a suspension of two years the Lyons Province of the Society of Jesus was persuaded to take over the college in 1847. Although beset with many vicissitudes the Jesuits have gradually increased the prestige of Spring Hill College so that it is now a well-known center of liberal culture. The history of Spring Hill College indicates that the Roman Catholic colleges have faced terrific struggles like the colleges established under other church auspices. They too have been obliged to let some of their enterprises lapse or transfer them to other groups.

The oldest college for women established by the Roman Catholics is *St. Joseph's College,* Emmitsburg, Maryland. It was founded in 1809 and has maintained a distinguished record under the control of the Daughters of Charity of St. Vincent de Paul.

The Order of St. Benedict (Benedictines) is the oldest of the Roman Catholic groups founding and operating colleges. This order was established in 529 A.D. in Italy by St. Benedict of Nursia. The order has supported a number of colleges throughout the United States, as indicated by the list which follows.

In addition to colleges operated by Diocesan priests and clerical members of the various orders, there is another group of strong colleges founded and conducted by the Christian Brothers. The patron saint and organizer of this group was John Baptist de la Salle. The members of this order are not ordained. The Order was the first that was devoted exclusively to Christian education.

The list of colleges and universities that follows was assembled by the Reverend James F. Whelan, S. J., of the Loyola University faculty in New Orleans. He is Secretary of the Committee on Membership of the College and University Department of the National Catholic Educational Association. The list was issued in 1954.

LIST OF FOUR-YEAR COLLEGES OWNED AND OPERATED
BY CATHOLIC GROUPS

Group and Institution	Location	Date of Founding
Assumptionist Fathers		
Assumption College	Worcester, Massachusetts	1917
Augustinian Fathers		
Merrimack College	Andover, Massachusetts	1947
Villanova College	Villanova, Pennsylvania	1842
Basilian Fathers		
St. John Fisher	Rochester, New York	1951
University of St. Thomas	Houston, Texas	1947
Benedictine Fathers		
Belmont Abbey College	Belmont, North Carolina	1878
St. Anselm's College	Manchester, New Hamp.	1889
St. Benedict's College	Atchison, Kansas	1859
St. John's University	Collegeville, Minnesota	1857
St. Martin's College	Olympia, Washington	1895
St. Procopius College	Lisle, Illinois	1885
St. Vincent College	Latrobe, Pennsylvania	1846

LIST OF FOUR-YEAR COLLEGES OWNED AND OPERATED
BY CATHOLIC GROUPS (*Continued*)

Group and Institution	Location	Date of Founding
Benedictine Sisters		
Benedictine Heights College	Guthrie, Oklahoma	1917
College of St. Benedict	St. Joseph, Minnesota,	1913
College of St. Scholastica	Duluth, Minnesota	1912
Mount Angel Women's College	St. Benedict, Oregon	1917
Mount St. Scholastica College	Atchison, Kansas	1926
Brothers of the Christian Schools		
La Salle College	Philadelphia, Pennsylvania	1863
Manhattan College	New York, New York	1853
St. Mary's College	St. Mary's College, Calif.	1863
St. Mary's College	Winona, Minnesota	1913
St. Michael's College	Santa Fe, New Mexico	1947
Brothers of the Congregation of Holy Cross		
St. Edward's University	Austin, Texas	1885
Canons Regular of Premontre		
St. Norbert College	West De Pere, Wisconsin	1898
Catholic Laymen		
Lewis College of Science and Technology	Lockport, Illinois	1930
Christian Brothers of Ireland		
Iona College	New Rochelle, New York	1940
Clerics of St. Viator		
Fournier Institute of Technology	Lemont, Illinois	1947
Congregation of the Mission		
De Paul University	Chicago, Illinois	1898
Niagara University	Niagara University, N. Y.	1856
St. John's University	Brooklyn, New York	1870
Congregation of the Sisters of Charity of the Incarnate Word		
Incarnate Word College	San Antonio, Texas	1881
Congregation of the Sisters of the Third Order of St. Francis of the Perpetual Adoration		
Viterbo College	La Crosse, Wisconsin	1931

LIST OF FOUR-YEAR COLLEGES OWNED AND OPERATED
BY CATHOLIC GROUPS (*Continued*)

Group and Institution	Location	Date of Founding
Congregation of the Sisters of the Holy Cross		
College of St. Mary-of-the-Wasatch	Salt Lake City, Utah	1926
Dunbarton College of Holy Cross	Washington, D.C.	1935
St. Mary's College	Notre Dame, Indiana	1844
Congregation of the Sisters of the Third Order of St. Francis		
Marian College	Indianapolis, Indiana	1937
Congregation of the Third Order of St. Francis of Mary Immaculate		
College of St. Francis	Joliet, Illinois	1925
Daughters of Charity of St. Vincent de Paul		
St. Joseph's College	Emmitsburg, Maryland	1809
Daughters of the Holy Ghost		
Annhurst College	Putnam, Connecticut	1941
Diocese, Archdiocese, the Bishop or Secular Priest		
Bellarmine College	Louisville, Kentucky	1950
Carroll College	Helena, Montana	1909
College of St. Thomas	St. Paul, Minnesota	1885
Loras College	Dubuque, Iowa	1839
Mount St. Mary's College	Emmitsburg, Maryland	1808
St. Ambrose College	Davenport, Iowa	1882
St. Basil's College	Stamford, Connecticut	1939
St. John College	Cleveland, Ohio	1928
St. Mary's College	Orchard Lake, Michigan	1885
Seton Hall College	South Orange, New Jersey	1856
Villa Madonna College	Covington, Kentucky	1921
Dominican Sisters		
Albertus Magnus College	New Haven, Connecticut	1925
Aquinas College	Grand Rapids, Michigan	1923
Barry College	Miami, Florida	1940
Caldwell College for Women	Caldwell, New Jersey	1939
Dominican College	Racine, Wisconsin	1935
Dominican College	San Rafael, California	1891

LIST OF FOUR-YEAR COLLEGES OWNED AND OPERATED
BY CATHOLIC GROUPS (*Continued*)

Group and Institution	Location	Date of Founding
College of St. Mary of the Springs	Columbus, Ohio	1925
Edgewood College of the Sacred Heart	Madison, Wisconsin	1927
Queen of the Holy Rosary College	Los Angeles, California	1930
Rosary College	River Forest, Illinois	1901
St. Mary's Dominican College	New Orleans, Louisiana	1910
Sacred Heart Dominican College	Houston, Texas	1946
Siena College	Memphis, Tennessee	1923
Siena Heights College	Adrian, Michigan	1919
Felician Sisters		
Madonna College	Livonia, Michigan	1937
Franciscan Brothers of Brooklyn		
St. Francis College	Brooklyn, New York	1858
Franciscan Fathers		
Quincy College	Quincy, Illinois	1860
St. Bernardine of Siena College	Loudonville, New York	1937
St. Bonaventure University	St. Bonaventure, New York	1856
St. Francis College	Burlington, Wisconsin	1931
Franciscan Sisters of Christian Charity		
Holy Family College	Manitowoc, Wisconsin	1939
Grey Nuns of the Sacred Heart		
D'Youville College	Buffalo, New York	1908
Holy Ghost Fathers		
Duquesne University	Pittsburgh, Pennsylvania	1881
Holy See and the Hierarchy of the United States		
Catholic University of America	Washington, D.C.	1887
Jesuit Fathers		
Boston College	Chestnut Hill, Massachusetts	1863
Canisius College	Buffalo, New York	1870
College of the Holy Cross	Worcester, Massachusetts	1843

LIST OF FOUR-YEAR COLLEGES OWNED AND OPERATED
BY CATHOLIC GROUPS (*Continued*)

Group and Institution	Location	Date of Founding
Creighton University	Omaha, Nebraska	1878
Fairfield University	Fairfield, Connecticut	1942
Fordham University	New York, New York	1841
Georgetown University	Washington, D.C.	1789
Gonzaga University	Spokane, Washington	1887
John Carroll University	Cleveland, Ohio	1886
Lemoyne College	Syracuse, New York	1946
Loyola University of Los Angeles	Los Angeles, California	1911
Loyola University	Chicago, Illinois	1870
Loyola University	New Orleans, Louisiana	1912
Loyola College	Baltimore, Maryland	1852
Marquette University	Milwaukee, Wisconsin	1864
Regis College	Denver, Colorado	1888
Rockhurst College	Kansas City, Missouri	1910
St. Joseph's College	Philadelphia, Pennsylvania	1851
St. Louis University	St. Louis, Missouri	1818
St. Peters College	Jersey City, New Jersey	1872
Seattle University	Seattle, Washington	1891
Spring Hill College	Spring Hill, Alabama	1830
University of Detroit	Detroit, Michigan	1877
University of Santa Clara	Santa Clara, California	1851
University of San Francisco	San Francisco, California	1855
University of Scranton	Scranton, Pennsylvania	1888
Xavier University	Cincinnati, Ohio	1831

Maryknoll Sisters

Maryknoll Teachers College	Maryknoll, New York	1942

Order of Preachers

Providence College	Providence, Rhode Island	1917

Poor Sisters of St. Francis Seraph of the Perpetual Adoration

St. Francis College	Fort Wayne, Indiana	1937

Priests of the Congregation of Holy Cross

King's College	Wilkes-Barre, Pennsylvania	1946
Stonehill College	North Easton, Massachusetts	1948
University of Notre Dame	Notre Dame, Indiana	1842
University of Portland	Portland, Oregon	1901

LIST OF FOUR-YEAR COLLEGES OWNED AND OPERATED
BY CATHOLIC GROUPS (*Continued*)

Group and Institution	Location	Date of Founding
Religious of the Sacred Heart of Mary		
Marymount College	Los Angeles, California	1934
School Sisters of Notre Dame		
College of Notre Dame of Maryland	Baltimore, Maryland	1873
Mount Mary College	Milwaukee, Wisconsin	1915
School Sisters of St. Francis		
Alverno College	Milwaukee, Wisconsin	1936
Sisters of Charity of Leavenworth, Kansas		
St. Mary College	Xavier, Kansas	1923
Sisters of Charity of Nazareth		
Nazareth College	Louisville, Kentucky	1920
Sisters of Charity of Providence		
College of Great Falls	Great Falls, Montana	1932
Sisters of Charity of St. Vincent De Paul		
College of Mount Saint Joseph-on-the-Ohio	Mt. St. Joseph, Ohio	1854
College of Mount St. Vincent	New York, New York	1910
College of St. Elizabeth	Convent Station, New Jersey	1899
Mount St. Vincent College	Halifax, Nova Scotia	1925
Seton Hill College	Greensburg, Pennsylvania	1883
Sisters of Charity of the Blessed Virgin Mary		
Clarke College	Dubuque, Iowa	1843
Mundelein College	Chicago, Illinois	1925
Sisters of Divine Providence of San Antonio, Texas		
Our Lady of the Lake College	San Antonio, Texas	1896
Sisters of Loretto at Foot of the Cross		
Loretto Heights College	Loretto, Colorado	1918
Webster College	Webster Groves, Missouri	1915
Sisters of Mercy		
College of Our Lady of Mercy	Portland, Maine	1915
Georgian Court College	Lakewood, New Jersey	1908
Mount Mercy College	Pittsburgh, Pennsylvania	1929
Mount St. Mary's College	Hooksett, New Hampshire	1934

LIST OF FOUR-YEAR COLLEGES OWNED AND OPERATED
BY CATHOLIC GROUPS (*Continued*)

Group and Institution	Location	Date of Founding
St. Joseph's College	West Hartford, Connecticut	1932
Trinity College	Burlington, Vermont	1925
Sisters of Mercy of the Union in the United States of America		
College Misericordia	Dallas, Pennsylvania	1923
College of St. Mary	Omaha, Nebraska	1923
Mercy College	Detroit, Michigan	1941
Mercyhurst College	Erie, Pennsylvania	1926
Mount St. Agnes College	Baltimore, Maryland	1867
Our Lady of Cincinnati	Cincinnati, Ohio	1935
Salve Regina College	Newport, Rhode Island	1934
St. Francis Xavier College	Chicago, Illinois	1912
Sisters of Notre Dame		
Notre Dame College	South Euclid, Ohio	1922
Sisters of Notre Dame de Namur		
College of Notre Dame	Belmont, California	1863
Emmanuel College	Boston, Massachusetts	1919
Trinity College	Washington, D.C.	1897
Sisters of Providence of Saint Mary-of-the-Woods, Indiana		
Saint Mary-of-the-Woods College	St. Mary of the Woods, Ind.	1840
Sisters of St. Ann		
Anna Maria College	Paxton, Massachusetts	1946
Sisters of St. Francis of Penance and Christian Charity		
Rosary Hill College	Buffalo, New York	1947
Sisters of St. Francis of the Holy Family		
Briar Cliff College	Sioux City, Iowa	1930
Sisters of St. Joseph		
Chestnut Hill College	Chestnut Hill, Pennsylvania	1871
College of Our Lady of the Elms	Chicopee, Massachusetts	1928
Marymount College	Salina, Kansas	1922
Nazareth College	Nazareth, Michigan	1897
Nazareth College	Rochester, New York	1924
Regis College	Weston, Massachusetts	1927
St. Joseph's College for Women	Brooklyn, New York	1916
Villa Maria College	Erie, Pennsylvania	1925

LIST OF FOUR-YEAR COLLEGES OWNED AND OPERATED
BY CATHOLIC GROUPS (*Continued*)

Group and Institution	Location	Date of Founding
Sisters of St. Joseph of Carondelet		
College of St. Catherine	St. Paul, Minnesota	1905
College of St. Rose	Albany, New York	1920
College of St. Teresa	Kansas City, Missouri	1940
Fontbonne College	St. Louis, Missouri	1923
Mount St. Mary's College	Los Angeles, California	1925
Sisters of St. Mary of Namur		
Our Lady of Victory College	Fort Worth, Texas	1930
Sisters of the California Institute of the Most Holy and Immaculate Heart of the Blessed Virgin Mary		
Immaculate Heart College	Los Angeles, California	1916
Sisters of the Congregation de Notre Dame		
Notre Dame College of Staten Island	Grymes Hill, Staten Island, New York	1933
Sisters of the Congregation of St. Agnes		
Marian College	Fond du Lac, Wisconsin	1936
Sisters of the Divine Compassion		
Good Counsel College	White Plains, New York	1923
Sisters of the Holy Names of Jesus and Mary		
College of the Holy Names	Oakland, California	1890
Holy Names College	Spokane, Washington	1907
Marylhurst College	Marylhurst, Oregon	1930
Sisters of the Presentation of Mary		
Rivier College	Nashua, New Hampshire	1933
Sisters of the Third Order of St. Francis Assisi		
Cardinal Stritch College	Milwaukee, Wisconsin	1932
Sisters of the Third Order Regular of St. Francis of the Congregation of Our Lady of Lourdes		
College of St. Teresa	Winona, Minnesota	1907
Sisters, Servants of the Immaculate Heart of Mary		
Immaculata College	Immaculata, Pennsylvania	1920
Marygrove College	Detroit, Michigan	1910
Marywood College	Scranton, Pennsylvania	1915

LIST OF FOUR-YEAR COLLEGES OWNED AND OPERATED
BY CATHOLIC GROUPS (*Continued*)

Group and Institution	Location	Date of Founding
Society of Mary		
St. Mary's University	San Antonio, Texas	1852
University of Dayton	Dayton, Ohio	1850
Society of Saint Edmund		
St. Michael's College	Winooski Park, Vermont	1904
Society of the Holy Child Jesus		
Rosemont College	Rosemont, Pennsylvania	1921
Society of the Precious Blood		
St. Joseph's College	Collegeville, Indiana	1889
Society of the Sacred Heart		
Barat College of the Sacred Heart	Lake Forest, Illinois	1919
College of the Sacred Heart	Grand Coteau, Louisiana	1939
College of Sacred Heart	Santurce, Puerto Rico	1935
Duchesne College	Omaha, Nebraska	1881
Manhattanville College of the Sacred Heart	Purchase, New York	1841
Maryville College of the Sacred Heart	St. Louis, Missouri	1872
Newton College of the Sacred Heart	Newton, Massachusetts	1946
San Diego College for Women	San Diego, California	1952
San Francisco College for Women	San Francisco, California	1930
The Sisters of the Blessed Sacrament for Indians and Colored People		
Xavier University	New Orleans, Louisiana	1925
Third Order Regular of St. Francis		
College of Steubenville	Steubenville, Ohio	1946
St. Francis College	Loretto, Pennsylvania	1847
Ursuline Nuns (Roman Union)		
College of New Rochelle	New Rochelle, New York	1904
Ursuline Nuns of the Congregation of Paris		
Mary Manse College	Toledo, Ohio	1922
Ursuline College	Louisville, Kentucky	1938
Ursuline College for Women	Cleveland, Ohio	1888

CHAPTER X

Other Church Colleges

LIBERAL arts colleges sponsored by church groups that have not been included in previous chapters are listed here. Separate chapters are devoted to denominations with whom fifteen or more colleges are affiliated. Comment is limited to matters of unusual import or that which is needed for clarification of relationships. In many instances the dates indicate time of organization of the college as an academy or an institute from which the college evolved. Dates in parentheses show when the colleges were chartered as four-year institutions.

ADVENT CHRISTIAN CHURCH

Institution	Location	Date of Founding
Aurora College	Aurora, Illinois	1893 (1899)

Aurora College was founded and is controlled and supported by members of the Advent Christian Church in America who desire a liberal arts college in which their young people may secure an effective higher education and crystallize character into its mature patterns under the influence of competent teachers who are convinced of the co-ordinate importance of spiritual and intellectual values in building effective personalities and successful lives.

BRETHREN CHURCH

Institution	Location	Date of Founding
Ashland College	Ashland, Ohio	1878

BRETHREN IN CHRIST

Institution	Location	Date of Founding
Messiah College	Grantham, Pennsylvania	1909
Upland College	Upland, California	1920

This group is a branch of the Mennonite Church. President D. D. Eisenhower's family have been among the chief supporters of Messiah College, his uncle and aunt giving over $40,000 to the institution.

CHURCH OF THE BRETHREN

Institution	Location	Date of Founding
Bridgewater College	Bridgewater, Virginia	1880 (1889)
Elizabethtown College	Elizabethtown, Pennsylvania	1899
Juniata College	Huntingdon, Pennsylvania	1876 (1878)
La Verne College	La Verne, California	1891
Manchester College	North Manchester, Indiana	1889
McPherson College	McPherson, Kansas	1887

Three other four-year colleges that were founded by the Church of the Brethren are no longer in operation. Mount Morris College, Mount Morris, Illinois, merged with Manchester College in 1932. Blue Ridge College was founded as Maryland Collegiate Institute at Union Bridge, Maryland, in 1899; it moved to New Windsor, Maryland, and renamed Blue Ridge College in 1910. Later, the college became affiliated with Bridgewater College and was reduced to a junior college status. About 1937, it was sold to a non-Brethren group who did not operate the school very long. In 1945, the property was purchased by the Brethren Service Committee and the plant is now used for the Brethren Service Center. Daleville College, Daleville, Virginia, also became affiliated with Bridgewater College and operated for a time as an academy, closing in 1937.

Ashland College was founded by the Church of the Brethren in 1879 at Ashland, Ohio. When the division of the church came in the early 1880's, this school was taken over by the Progressive Brethren and is still in operation under their church auspices.

CHURCH OF CHRIST SCIENTIST

The Principia. This college, located in Elsah, Illinois, is not under the control of the church but it does limit its student body to members or the children of Christian Scientists. However, in its curriculum the subjects are not interpreted for the student from the standpoint of religious convictions. In other words, the college clearly recognizes that it has no right to teach Christian Science through the medium of history, physics, chemistry, etc.

CHURCH OF CHRIST

Institution	Location	Date of Founding
Abilene Christian College	Abilene, Texas,	1906
David Lipscomb College	Nashville, Tennessee	1891
George Pepperdine College	Los Angeles, California	1937
Harding College	Searcy, Arkansas	1924

Members of the Church of Christ claim to be followers of Alexander Campbell, the acknowledged founder of the Church of the Disciples. They also received inspiration from the Reverend Barton W. Stone, a famous evangelist who contributed to the "Second Awakening" of the early nineteenth century. The revival inspired by Barton W. Stone at Cane Ridge, Kentucky, was largely responsible for the movement resulting in the Cumberland Presbyterian Church. Like the Campbells he pleaded for "restoration" of New Testament Christianity. His followers called themselves Christians and logically joined with the Campbellites in 1832.

When the "Foreign Christian Missionary Society" was formed in 1875, a group of "Christians" under the leadership of Fanning Talbott and David Lipscomb of Nashville, Tennessee, took the lead in a conservative movement which considered such a missionary organization as non-Scriptural and that it usurped the work and authority of the local Church. This conservative group also had positive convictions against the employment of musical instruments in church worship. From this it is manifest that each college supported by the Churches of Christ is really a "private enterprise," with no claim on the churches as a group except the claim of common interest.

In all probability the attitude against missionary activities has resulted in the hasty organization and early demise of a considerable number of colleges organized by individual Churches of Christ. There are several recently organized junior colleges in this group which plan early development into four-year colleges, notably Florida Christian College, founded near Tampa, Florida, in 1946, and Central Christian College, founded in 1949 in Bartlesville, Oklahoma.

CHURCH OF JESUS CHRIST OF LATTER-DAY SAINTS (MORMON)

Institution	Location	Date of Founding
Brigham Young University	Provo, Utah	1875
Ricks College	Rexburg, Idaho	1898

Here are the "objectives" of these two colleges as outlined in the catalog of Brigham Young University:

I. To train students for leadership in professional, vocational, church and other civic activities.
II. To provide a university society in which all Latter-day Saints may participate.
III. To lead students to know and live Latter-day Saint ideals and to enable them to realize their greatest intellectual and spiritual potentialities by creating testimonies of the divinity of our Lord Jesus Christ.

The first paragraph in the current catalog of Brigham Young University concerning its founding gives this *raison d'être*:

Brigham Young University, originally Brigham Young Academy, was founded to teach not only the learning of men, but also the revealed word of God—therefore, the sum total of human knowledge rather than the limited knowledge of secular education, which often leads to disbelief in God. It was established, pursuant to a deed of trust executed by Brigham Young, President of the Church of Jesus Christ of Latter-day Saints, on October 16, 1875. That deed expressly set forth that the "pupils shall be instructed in . . . such branches as are usually taught in an academy of learning," and also "in the Old and New Testaments, the Book of Mormon and the Book of Doctrine and Covenants."

CHURCH OF GOD

Institution	Location	Date of Founding
Anderson College	Anderson, Indiana	1917
Findlay College	Findlay, Ohio	1882
Pacific Bible College	Portland, Oregon	1937

Anderson College is, according to its catalog, "a Christian college. It seeks to give the student a unified philosophy of education and an over-all view of human life and destiny. It holds that the central factor of unification is theological and that true education must proceed in harmony with the Christian revelation."

Findlay College, which was established by and serving the General Eldership of the Churches of God in North America, has as its objective: "To develop character through the presentation of the omnipotence of God and of personal salvation through His Son, the Lord Jesus Christ."

CHURCH OF THE NAZARENE

Institution	Location	Date of Founding
Bethany-Peniel College	Bethany, Oklahoma	1899
Eastern Nazarene College	Wollaston, Massachusetts	1900 (1918)
Northwest Nazarene College	Nampa, Idaho	1915
Olivet Nazarene College	Kankakee, Illinois	1907 (1909)
Pasadena College	Pasadena, California	1910
Trevecca Nazarene College	Nashville, Tennessee	1901

The objectives of this group are well outlined in this quotation from the current catalog of *Eastern Nazarene College*:

As a college of liberal arts, Eastern Nazarene College is committed to the long-range view of education. It aims to keep alive in a world of unrest a faith in the spiritual and enduring values as superior to the material and merely contemporary.

As a college of the Church of the Nazarene, it purposes to serve the church by supplying an educated, thinking ministry and laity loyal to the ideals of the church, particularly the Wesleyan doctrine of Christian perfection; it aims to assist its young people to realize the highest possible measure and quality of development in all areas of personality and living.

Bethany-Peniel College is the result of the merger of several educational institutions united to form the present college, as follows:

Institution	Founded	Location	United to form Bethany-Peniel College
Peniel University	1899	Peniel, Texas	1920
Arkansas Holiness College	1900	Vilonia, Arkansas	1931
Bresee College	1905	Hutchinson, Kansas	1940
Beulah Heights College	1906	Oklahoma City, Oklahoma	1909
Oklahoma Holiness College	1909	Bethany, Oklahoma	1920
Central Nazarene University	1910	Hamlin, Texas	1929

These various educational institutions were founded by men and women who felt the urgent need for trained Christian leadership, both lay and ministerial, in the respective areas where the newly organized Holiness groups came into being.

Olivet Nazarene College in its peregrination from town to town and from school to Holiness University to College has its present home on the campus of what was once St. Viator College, a Roman Catholic institution.

CHURCH OF THE NEW JERUSALEM

Institution	Location	Date of Founding
Academy of the New Church	Bryn Athyn, Pennsylvania	1876

The General Church of the New Jerusalem is a religious body evolving from the teachings of Emmanuel Swedenborg which established its first American unit in Baltimore in 1792. "Baptism into the New Church is required prior to admission to any of the schools."

EVANGELICAL AND REFORMED

Institution	Location	Date of Founding
Catawba College	Salisbury, North Carolina	1851
Cedar Crest College	Allentown, Pennsylvania	1868
Elmhurst College	Elmhurst, Illinois	1865
Franklin and Marshall College	Lancaster, Pennsylvania	1787
Heidelberg College	Tiffin, Ohio	1850
Hood College	Frederick, Maryland	1839
Mission House College	Plymouth, Wisconsin	1862
Ursinus College	Collegeville, Pennsylvania	1832

All the colleges in the above list were founded under the auspices of the German Reformed Church except *Elmhurst College,* which was organized by that branch of the Evangelical Church which combined with the Reformed Church at a uniting conference held in Cleveland, Ohio, in 1934.

Franklin and Marshall College was formed in 1853 when Franklin College, founded in 1787 in Lancaster, Pennsylvania, and named for Benjamin Franklin, was joined by Marshall College. Marshall College had been established in 1836 in Mercersburg, Pennsylvania, and named for John Marshall, late Chief Justice of the Supreme Court of the United States. The first president of the board of trustees of the consolidated college was James Buchanan, later fifteenth President of the United States.

EVANGELICAL UNITED BRETHREN

Institution	Location	Date of Founding
Albright College	Reading, Pennsylvania	1856
Indiana Central College	Indianapolis, Indiana	1902
Lebanon Valley College	Annville, Pennsylvania	1866
North Central College	Naperville, Illinois	1861
Otterbein College	Westerville, Ohio	1847
Westmar College	LeMars, Iowa	1900
York College	York, Nebraska	1890

Of the above group *Albright, North Central* and *Westmar* were organized by that branch of the Evangelical Church which combined with the United Brethren Church on November 16, 1946, at a conference held in Johnstown, Pennsylvania.

FIVE-YEAR MEETING OF FRIENDS

Institution	Location	Date of Founding
Earlham College	Richmond, Indiana	1847 (1859)
Guilford College	Guilford College, N. C.	1834 (1889)
Whittier College	Whittier, California	1891
William Penn College	Oskaloosa, Iowa	1873
Wilmington College	Wilmington, Ohio	1863

SOCIETY OF FRIENDS

Institution	Location	Date of Founding
Friends University	Wichita, Kansas	1888
George Fox College	Newburg, Oregon	1891
Haverford College	Haverford, Pennsylvania	1833
Swarthmore College	Swarthmore, Pennsylvania	1864

Bryn Mawr College, Bryn Mawr, Pennsylvania, was organized in 1880 by a group of members of the Society of Friends.

HEBREW COLLEGES

Institution	Location	Date of Founding
Brandeis University	Waltham, Massachusetts	1948
Yeshiva University	New York, New York	1886

Yeshiva University is the result of a merger of Rabbi Isaac Elchanan Theological Seminary, organized in 1896, with Etz Chaim Yeshiva (founded in 1886), the oldest Orthodox Jewish Theological Seminary in the United States. All twenty-one members of the self-perpetuating board of trustees must be Orthodox Jewish.

MENNONITE

Institution	Location	Date of Founding
Bethel College	North Newton, Kansas	1882
Bluffton College	Bluffton, Ohio	1900
Eastern Mennonite College	Harrisonburg, Virginia	1917
Goshen College	Goshen, Indiana	1894
Tabor College	Hillsboro, Kansas	1908

MORAVIAN

Moravian College	Bethlehem, Pennsylvania	1807
Moravian College for Women	Bethlehem, Pennsylvania	1742
Salem College	Winston-Salem, N. C.	1772 (1866)

PROTESTANT EPISCOPAL

Bard College	Annandale, New York	1860
Hobart College	Geneva, New York	1822
Kenyon College	Gambier, Ohio	1824
St. Augustine's College	Raleigh, North Carolina	1867

Institution	Location	Date of Founding
Trinity College	Hartford, Connecticut	1823
University of the South	Sewanee, Tennessee	1857
William Smith College	Geneva, New York	1908

As indicated in Chapter I, the Episcopalians were actually the founders of William and Mary, the second oldest "permanent" college in the United States and of King's College (Columbia University), the fifth oldest. They were justifiably credited with supporting and controlling in the early days The College of Philadelphia (University of Pennsylvania).

Kenyon College was established by the Right Reverend Philander Chase. He was born in New Hampshire and graduated from Dartmouth College in 1796. He converted his family of fourteen older brothers and sisters and his father and mother from the Congregational faith to the Protestant Episcopal faith. This missionary effort must have inspired him to become a loyal missionary of the Episcopal Church in the Middle West, where he established numerous parishes. In 1818 he gathered together a number of parishes to form the Diocese of Ohio, at which time he was elected Bishop. Finding no support in the East for his proposal to establish a college in that remote area, he sailed to England where he soon collected $30,000 to found his first college. He named it for Lord Kenyon in a new town named for Lord Gambier, both of whom had responded favorably to his request for funds for the college.

In 1831 he resigned from the Bishopric of Ohio because of the strong objection to his arbitrary rule on the part of faculty and clergy under his supervision. After a brief sojourn in Michigan he established the new Episcopal diocese of Illinois in 1835 and became its first Bishop. Again he had the urge to organize a college and went to England in search of funds. Meeting no success there he made a trip to the South where he obtained enough money to encourage him to establish, in 1839, *Jubilee College*, a few miles west of Peoria, Illinois. This college did not survive long but a fine old building still stands near the cemetery where the Bishop lies buried: it is now maintained as a part of an Illinois State Park. The Bishop was elected Presiding Bishop of his church in 1843 and came to an untimely end in 1852 through a carriage accident. His numerous peregrinations did not subject him to the far greater dangers of present modes of transportation—railways, automobiles, and airplanes.

Trinity College. The original impetus for Trinity College took place at a meeting of a group of eighteen clergymen at the home of Bishop Brownell in New Haven. It received its first charter in 1823 under the name of Washington College. Since Washington College had been chosen as the name of several other institutions, its name was changed to Trinity College in 1845. It seems somewhat ironic that there probably are as many or more Trinity Colleges organized since then as there are Washington Colleges. The Trinity students of the early days had to be on time for class at 5 A.M. in summer and 6 A.M. in winter, nor could they play musical instruments on Sunday.

REFORMED CHURCH IN AMERICA

Institution	Location	Date of Founding
Central College	Pella, Iowa	1853
Hope College	Holland, Michigan	1862

As indicated in Chapter I, the Reformed Church in America made a great contribution in establishing *Rutgers University*. In Chapter VIII reference is made as to how this same church had a most important part in the organizing of Union College in Schenectady, New York.

Central College was originally Baptist. Its evolution is related in Chapter II.

CHRISTIAN REFORMED CHURCH

Institution	Location	Date of Founding
Calvin College	Grand Rapids, Michigan	1876

Calvin College in its current catalog indicates the following as part of its "aim":

According to the constitution all instruction given must be in harmony with Reformed truth. The various branches of study, therefore, are considered from the standpoint of faith and in the light of Calvinism as a life and world view. The aim of the college is to give young people an education that is Christian, in the larger and deeper sense that all the class work, all the students' intellectual, emotional, and imaginative activities shall be permeated with the spirit and teaching of Christianity.

SEVENTH DAY ADVENTIST

Institution	Location	Date of Founding
Atlantic Union College	South Lancaster, Massachusetts	1882
Emmanuel Missionary College	Berrien Springs, Michigan	1901
La Sierra College	Arlington, California	1922
Oakwood College	Huntsville, Alabama	1896
Pacific Union College	Angwin, California	1882
Southern Missionary College	Collegedale, Tennessee	1919
Union College	Lincoln, Nebraska	1891
Walla Walla College	College Park, Washington	1892
Washington Missionary College	Takoma Park, Washington, D.C.	1904

UNITED BRETHREN IN CHRIST

Huntington College	Huntington, Indiana	1897

YOUNG MEN'S CHRISTIAN ASSOCIATION

The Young Men's Christian Association is largely responsible for the genesis of the following colleges:

Institution	Location	Date of Founding
George Williams College	Chicago, Illinois	1890
Golden Gate College	San Francisco, California	1923
Roosevelt University	Chicago, Illinois	1945
Springfield College	Springfield, Massachusetts	1910
Youngstown College	Youngstown, Ohio	1908

Two other colleges had their beginnings under Church influence: *American International College,* Springfield, Massachusetts, was established in 1885 at Lowell as French Protestant College; it moved to Springfield in 1888, changing its name in 1894 to French American College, and in 1905 to its present name.

Cascade College, Portland, Oregon, lists itself as interdenominational, having been established in 1918 under the name of North Pacific Evangelistic Institute; its name was changed to Portland Bible Institute in 1930 and in 1939 to its present title.

CHAPTER XI

Church Colleges That Became State Colleges

THE church maintained a monopoly in the establishment of colleges for 149 years, from the founding of Harvard in 1636 to 1785 when the University of Georgia received a charter from the state. For the record it should be noted that while the University of North Carolina did not receive its charter until 1787, it opened its doors to students in the fall of 1795, whereas instruction was not given before 1801 at the University of Georgia.

There were probably two reasons for the long delay in the development of state institutions of higher learning in the United States. The example of the mother country with its reliance for advanced study on the great colleges grouped at the university centers of Cambridge and Oxford must have been the chief reason for a long while. In the second place there was felt no need of spending large sums for plant and operation of state colleges in competition with well-established church colleges concerned primarily, if not solely, in educating leaders for "church" and "state." Gradually there developed a climate of opinion that the dominant leaders of the colleges established and fostered by the church were not sufficiently broad in their outlook and sympathies. The chief protagonist of this point of view was Thomas Jefferson, who felt also that the colleges were ignoring the poor boys and continuously catered to the sons of the rich. The results of his agitation bore fruition in the chartering of the University of Virginia in 1819, although it was not opened for students until 1825. It will be recalled that Jefferson rejoiced that his chief contributions to posterity were the founding of the University of Virginia and the writing of the Declaration of Independence.

Great impetus toward organization of state universities was given by the Ordinances of 1785 and 1787 concerning the Northwest Territory passed by the Congress of the Confederation before our Federal Constitution became operative in 1789. In the Ordinance of 1785 there was made a reservation of section sixteen of every township for the maintenance of public schools. The new Ordinance of 1787 reasserted this policy with a more definite statement: "Religion, morality and knowledge, being necessary to good government and the happiness of mankind, schools and the means of education shall forever be encouraged."

The states carved from the Northwest Territory chartered their universities in the following order: University of Michigan, 1817; Indiana University, 1820; University of Wisconsin, 1848; University of Minnesota, 1851; University of Illinois, 1867; Ohio State University, 1870.

On June 2, 1862, in the midst of fratricidal strife when the very existence of the Union was most seriously threatened, Congress passed a law proposed by Congressman Justin Smith Morrill (later Senator) of Vermont that did most to expedite the development of state-supported colleges in the United States. Through the Morrill Act the federal government made to the states additional grants of lands for the endowment and support of institutions, "to promote the liberal and practical education of the industrial classes in the several pursuits and professions in life." It is encouraging to observe that the vocational aim of this act does not overlook the importance of the liberal arts and sciences.

The Church was indifferent to the necessity of educating competent persons for the teaching profession, although it has continuously been concerned about aid to schools for advanced education in other areas, notably law and medicine, in addition, of course, to theology. Predominant was the influence of Horace Mann in the proliferation of normal schools throughout the nation. He rendered conspicuous service in this field as the first secretary of the State Board of Education of Massachusetts, the first state to have such a board. Serving in this post from 1837 to 1849 he was elected to the United States Congress as an antislavery Whig. In 1853 he became the first president of Antioch College, where he was also Professor of Philosophy and Theology until his death in 1859.

Over the years the two-year normal schools have evolved into four-year state teachers colleges. Recently, many of them have become state colleges, with an increase of offerings in the humanities and a corresponding reduction in "methods" courses required for the baccalaureate degree. As indicated later in this chapter, several of these excellent institutions were the outgrowth of fine old colleges established by some church group which could not keep up sufficient financial support for their survival.

The occasional evolution of a church college into a state institution is by no means a presage of what the future holds for higher education in the United States. It certainly does not indicate the fulfillment of the dire prophecy of the President's Report on Higher Education issued in 1948, where it was surmised that the days of the independent colleges may be numbered. Such a catastrophe will spell the doom of free enterprise and of our nation as a free democracy. Nothing will remain but the socialized state if the independent colleges lose their independence by seeking and obtaining federal aid.

A summary of the evolution of church colleges into state institutions follows, arranged alphabetically by states.

ALABAMA

Alabama Polytechnic Institute. In an early section of the current catalog of the Alabama Polytechnic Institute is to be found this statement:

> The State Legislature, by an act approved February 26, 1872, accepted an offer of the Alabama Conference of the Methodist Episcopal Church, South, to donate to the State the college building, land, equipment, and good will of the East Alabama Male College and located the Alabama Agricultural and Mechanical College at Auburn. An Act passed by the Alabama legislature on January 27, 1899 changed the official name to Alabama Polytechnic Institute.

The East Alabama Male College was established by the Methodists at Auburn in 1859. Two years previously the same Methodist group opened Southern University at Greensboro, Alabama. Since the Alabama Conference of the Methodist Church was not strong numerically or financially, it was well-nigh axiomatic that one or both of its colleges founded simultaneously would sooner or later "give up the ghost" or be taken over by another institution. Southern University amalgamated in 1918 with Birmingham College, an institution founded by the North Alabama Conference of the Methodist Episcopal Church, South, in 1898 to make what is now known as Birmingham-Southern College.

The inspiration for the founding of East Alabama Male College came from a suggestion made by a commission, appointed by the Alabama Methodist Conference in 1854, that the community raising $100,000 should have the location of the Conference College. When the next Conference was held in 1855, the commission reported an offer of $100,000 from the citizens of Auburn in east-central Alabama and one of $300,000 from a group at Greensboro in the west-central part of the state. Naturally the delegates voted for the location of their church college at Greensboro. With more enthusiasm than wisdom, the ambitious, and somewhat hotheaded group at Auburn went ahead with their plans for a four-year college.

Southern University was incorporated on January 25, 1856, by the General Assembly of Alabama. East Alabama Male College received its charter a little later. Both colleges began operations in the fall of 1859, both were closed by war conditions from about 1862 to 1866. Like the poet's "poor" the annals of East Alabama Male College were "short and simple."

During the first year it enrolled 80 in the college and 100 in the preparatory department; in 1860-61, the second year, there was an increase of 10 in the college and 30 in the preparatory school; in 1869-70 there were enrolled 90 college students and 40 preparatory students. A total of nearly 1000 students, including college and preparatory, were enrolled during the life of East Alabama Male College. Because of its suspension during 1862-66, it graduated only six classes, with a total of thirty-five degrees awarded before its transformation into the Alabama Polytechnic Institute.

With a small faculty of good preparation and some distinction, the students were educated and inspired to become ministers, teachers, doctors, lawyers, merchants, and farmers. Several attained considerable distinction as ministers, teachers, and statesmen. After service in the Confederate Army, Wilbur Fisk Glenn, of the class of 1860, held important posts as a Methodist minister for forty-four years and for ten more years was editor of the Alabama *Christian Advocate*. James F. Dowdell of the class of 1867, after teaching, practicing law, and serving as circuit judge, spent his later years as Justice of the Supreme Court of Alabama. William F. Samford who left college before graduation to join the Confederate Army became Governor of Alabama in 1900.

Alabama State Teachers College at Florence. This institution was founded as *La Grange College* in 1830. The name was changed to Florence Wesleyan University in 1855. It was taken over by the State of Alabama and established as a normal school in 1872.

La Grange College received its charter from the General Assembly of Alabama on January 19, 1830. It had begun operations eight days previously. The college was established by the Tennessee and Mississippi Conferences of the Methodist Church. These two conferences covered the Alabama area before the organization of the Alabama Conference. Slender indeed were the resources available at the inception of La Grange College—$10,000 in subscriptions from the citizens of the town and surrounding community, plus an additional subscription of $3000 made by the ministers belonging to the two controlling conferences.

La Grange was located about ten miles from Florence on a spur of the Cumberland Mountains with a magnificent view of the Tennessee River and Valley. It owed its name to the famous estate of the great Lafayette who had visited Alabama some six years previously: Three towns in the state are named for him, La Fayette, Fayette, and Fayetteville. The town thrived for a while because of the mineral springs there and of the "fame of its pure atmosphere," all of which attracted nearby wealthy planters to spend their summers there. In addition to the scenery, pure atmosphere, and healthful water, parents were enticed to send their sons to this college because the village could "offer few temptations to vice, and no concealment for dissipation."

Since the University of Alabama did not open its doors to students until 1831 (though chartered in 1820), La Grange was the first college to begin operations in Alabama. Its opening antedated that of Randolph-Macon College by two years and of Wesleyan University in Connecticut by a year. The former was chartered in 1830 and the latter in 1831. Stephen Olin was the first president of Randolph-Macon, going from the Virginia College in 1842 to become the second president of Wesleyan.

During its first twenty-five years, La Grange College attracted many young men from Alabama and nearby states. In 1851 it enrolled as many as 250 students. Its graduates included several who became prominent in Alabama and in the Old South. Among them were Governors David P. Lewis and Edward A. O'Neal of Alabama, United States Senator Jeremiah Clemens of Alabama, Bishop William R. Nicholson of the Reformed Episcopal Church, and William M. Byrd, an Alabama Supreme Court Justice.

La Grange College had as its first president, Robert Paine, a thirty-year-old Methodist minister from Nashville, Tennessee. In addition to raising funds, constructing college buildings, and finding students, the young zealot was professor of moral science and belles-lettres, which department embraced the subjects of "Moral and Intellectual Philosophy, Political Economy, Rhetoric, Evidences of Christianity, and Logic." He found time also to teach courses in geology and mineralogy, made attractive by the excellent opportunities for practical study in the area surrounding La Grange.

In the first faculty, William Hudson, an alumnus of Yale was professor of mathematics and modern languages and Edward D. Sims, a graduate of the University of North Carolina was professor of the ancient languages. Thus it was manifest that this triumvirate were able to administer the formalized classical curriculum then prevalent throughout the country. In 1834 the faculty had increased from three to five.

Robert Paine continued as president until 1846, when he was elected the first Bishop of the new Southern Methodist Church, continuing in this office until his death in 1882. Four years previously he had been awarded the honorary doctorate of divinity by Wesleyan University in Connecticut. During his presidency, La Grange College was a leading college in the South, and probably the foremost college of the Methodist Church at the time of its division into the Northern and Southern branches at its 1844 General Conference. At this historical gathering President Paine was chairman of the committee that prepared the Plan of Separation which provided for a peaceable division of the property holdings of the Methodist Church.

Bishop Paine was active in organizing the former slaves, who sat in the balconies or rear sections of the Methodist Churches before 1865, into the Colored Methodist Episcopal Church in 1870. In recognition and appreciation, the leaders of this church—which has become numerous and strong—named their first institution of higher education Paine College, established in 1883 at Augusta, Georgia.

When it was apparent that heroic faith, a most modest income, and tuition fees from the dwindling number of students were insufficient to cover even a minimum of operating expenses, the trustees accepted alluring offers from the citizens of nearby Florence to move the college to that growing city in the winter of 1855. Over the governor's veto the Alabama legislature granted the college a new charter under the name of Florence Wesleyan University. Richard H. Rivers had just accepted the presidency of La Grange when the agitation began that resulted in the removal of the college to Florence. Shortly thereafter he departed to become the first president of Athens College in Alabama.

Trustees opposed to the moving of the college to Florence tried to maintain a college and an academy on the original campus. In 1860 it was called the La Grange Military Academy. On April 28, 1863, the *coup de grace* was given when a federal cavalry detachment burned the buildings. Nothing now remains but the old site as the inaccessibility of the location and changes in modes of summer recreation left La Grange quite uninviting for residents.

In musing on the fate of such a college founded with so great enthusiasm and faith but with so little assets, one must conclude it was eminently worth the efforts of all concerned, particularly of the energetic president and his earnest colleagues. Its existence was certainly justified by the record of the distinguished alumni mentioned previously, as well as by the beneficent influence of the many unheralded graduates and former students of La Grange College. The same accolade can be given East Alabama Male College, even with its shorter span of existence.

ARKANSAS

Henderson State Teachers College in Arkadelphia evolved in 1929 as a state-controlled and supported institution from Henderson-Brown College, which had been operating under the aegis of the Southern Methodist Church for nearly forty years. It was chartered in 1890 and began operation the same year under the name of Arkadelphia Methodist College. In 1904 the name was changed to Henderson College in recognition of benefactions made to the college by Captain C. C. Henderson, a member of the board of trustees. In 1911 the name was changed again to Henderson-Brown College, in appreciation of financial support given by W. W. Brown.

The Methodists were finding it increasingly difficult to maintain three colleges—Galloway Woman's College at Searcy, Hendrix at Conway, and Henderson-Brown at Arkadelphia. Under the pressure of continuing financial problems the trustees of Henderson-Brown avoided extinction of their college by turning over in 1929 their campus and buildings to the city, which in turn transferred them to the state for the establishment of a second State Teachers College, the one at Conway having been chartered in 1907. The alumni records and other Methodist interests were transferred to Hendrix College, established by the Southern Methodist Church at Conway in 1884 through purchase of Central Collegiate Institute founded in 1876.

Among the many distinguished graduates of the institution when operated by the Methodists, mention can be made of the following: Matt L. Ellis, President of Hendrix College; Farrar Newberry, President, Woodmen of the World; the late Charles W. Pipkin, Dean, Graduate School, Louisiana State University; John R. Steelman, formerly Assistant to the President of the United States and Conciliator of Labor, Department of Labor; Rupert B. Vance, Professor of Sociology, University of North Carolina; James W. Workman, formerly President of Henderson-Brown College and later Associate Secretary of the General Board of Lay Activities, the Methodist Church.

CALIFORNIA

The University of California had its origin in the College of California, incorporated on April 13, 1855. It was an outgrowth of Contra Costa Academy located in Oakland. The Academy came into existence on May 10, 1853, at a joint meeting, held in Nevada City, California, of the Presbytery of San Francisco and of the Congregational Association of California. This occurred during the heyday of the American Home Missionary Society, a project under the joint auspices of the New School Presbyterians and the Congregationalists. The organizers made it clear that they did not desire a narrow denominational institution but rather a college or university that would include all Christian groups, more or less federated as a state university. Before these men could realize their goal the Methodists had established California Wesleyan College, now College of the Pacific, and the Catholics had opened Santa Clara College.

Due to financial difficulties the College of California was not opened for class work until 1860. On its first faculty were two professors who later became presidents of the University of California: the Reverend Henry Durant, A.M., professor of Latin and Greek languages; and the Reverend Martin Kellogg, A.M., professor of mathematics. Both were Yale graduates and had been ministers in the Congregational Church, although Durant became a Presbyterian minister shortly after arriving in California in May 1853.

When Durant became the first president of the new university in 1870, Martin Kellogg was made professor of ancient languages, which post he held for many years, including part of the time he served as seventh president, 1893-99. It is interesting to note that the second president, Daniel Coit Gilman, was also a Yale alumnus and had once toyed with the notion of becoming a Congregational minister. After only three years as president, Gilman became the head of the new Johns Hopkins University in Baltimore.

By a sudden shift in the political control of the state during the public agitation over the need for a university, the recently elected governor used his influence to have selected General George B. McClellan as first president of the new university. McClellan had attained fame as the one-time Commander-in-Chief of the Union Army and as candidate for President of the United States in 1864, when he was defeated by Abraham Lincoln. Fortunately, McClellan declined and the scholarly Henry Durant was elected, though already sixty-eight years old. He served as president from 1870 to 1872.

Dissatisfied with the cramped quarters in Oakland, the trustees of the College of California had bought property somewhat north of the town at a suitable location which later received the name of Berkeley, in honor of the British bishop, scholar, philosopher, and poet. On October 9, 1867, these same trustees voted to donate their buildings and lands, both in Oakland and in Berkeley, to the state on condition that California organize a university rather than a single college of agricultural and mechanical arts, made possible by the recent passage of the Morrill Act by the United States Congress.

The state accepted the offer and on March 23, 1868, granted the charter for the University of California. In accordance with the stipulation in the gift, the university was established on the grounds in Berkeley, donated to the state by the College of California. However, the college classes were continued for a while in Oakland. The class of 1873 was the first to hold its commencement on the Berkeley campus, at the time its first buildings were opened.

The degrees of the College of California were recognized by the University of California. President Martin Kellogg affirmed that the quality of the work of the College of California was equal to the best and that it had never been hampered by a preparatory department.

COLORADO

Colorado School of Mines. Strange as it may seem, this college evolved from an institution known as Episcopal University. The Right Reverend George M. Randall, Bishop of Colorado, was its founder. He had raised sufficient funds from his friends in the East and from business men in the Territory of Colorado to begin operations in the autumn of 1869. The plant was located in what is now known as Golden, some 12 miles west of Denver and 40 miles east of the main range of the Rocky Mountains.

When laying the cornerstone of Jarvis Hall, the first college building in Colorado, on the afternoon of August 23, 1869, Bishop Randall made this significant utterance:

This is the inception of an institution which, in the name of Christianity, rising from the foundation, shall honor God while it elevates man. The laying of the cornerstone of the first collegiate building in Colorado marks an epoch in the history of the Territory. I trust that this event will be but the beginning of an educational progress which will render this whole land more distinguished for its wealth of good learning than for its mines of precious metals.

Obtaining additional funds from friends and a grant of $3,872.45 from the Colorado Territorial Legislature, Bishop Randall built in 1870-71 another edifice known as the School of Mines Building. The Bishop had included in his original university plans a School of Mines, so appropriate for the area. The first professor of this school was a New York chemist, E. J. Mallet, who was responsible for the test that proved that Colorado coal was suitable for fuel, not so considered up to that time.

The good bishop, finding that time involved in shepherding souls prevented him from continuing to find necessary funds for his university, turned it over to the Territory of Colorado on February 6, 1874, when Governor Elbert signed the appropriation bill for $5000 to finance the School of Mines. Since that date it has attained both a national and an international reputation in its special field of educational endeavor.

Delaware

University of Delaware. Its catalog for 1953-54 contains the following data on its origin under church auspices:

The University of Delaware had its inception in a little institution of colonial days founded in 1743 near New London, Pennsylvania, by a

Presbyterian clergyman, the Reverend Francis Alison. The academy was made the official educational institution of the Synod of Philadelphia on May 25, 1744. When the Reverend Alexander McDowell succeeded Dr. Alison as principal in 1752, he removed the school to his manse located in the northwestern corner of Cecil County, Maryland, near Lewisville, Pennsylvania. It was removed thence to Newark, Delaware by Mr. McDowell in 1765 and chartered by Thomas and Richard Penn on November 10, 1769. Instruction in the academy was interrupted by the Revolutionary War in the period between 1777 and 1780 and again by financial difficulties between 1796 and 1799. From this time until 1834 it continued as one of the outstanding academies of its day.

When the degree-granting institution known as Newark College was opened on May 8, 1834, under a charter granted by the General Assembly of Delaware on February 5, 1833, Newark Academy was merged with it as its preparatory department. The name of the institution was changed to Delaware College by an Act of the General Assembly on February 7, 1843. As a result of a succession of financial misfortunes, the collegiate department of the institution was closed from 1859 to 1870, although the academic department continued to function throughout these years. Instruction in the collegiate department of the institution was resumed on September 14, 1870, and work below the collegiate grade was discontinued.

The College had meanwhile been designated by an Act of the General Assembly of March 14, 1867, as beneficiary under the Act of Congress, approved on July 2, 1862, and known as the Morrill Act, which apportioned to each of the several states large areas of public lands to form the bases of endowments for colleges which must include in their curricula courses in agriculture, the mechanic arts, and military tactics. The College remained under combined private and State ownership and until March 19, 1913, when by an Act of the General Assembly it came into the sole possession of the State.

The Women's College, a college for women affiliated with Delaware College, was established by an Act of the Delaware Legislature on March 13, 1913, and was opened to students on September 15, 1914. On March 28, 1921, by an Act of the Legislature Delaware College and the Women's College were united under the name of the University of Delaware. Separate classes were still held for men and women, however.

On September 16, 1944, the Board of Trustees adopted a new administrative structure for the University, according to which the two existing Colleges were completely merged into the University organization.

In the *University News* (Delaware), there is an article entitled "Ten Little Irish Lads," written by Thomas C. Pears, Jr.* This is an excerpt from his lectures given in 1942 at the Princeton Theological Seminary on the A. P. Stone Foundation. The "ten lads" comprised the first class of Presbyterian Alison's Academy, opened in 1743. They were George Read, James Smith, and Thomas McKean, signers of the Declaration of Independence; Hugh Williamson, member of the Constitutional Convention; Charles Thomson, Secretary of the Continental Congress; John Cochran, Director-General of Hospitals during the Revolution; John Ewing, mathematician, member of the commission which surveyed the Mason-Dixon Line and the first provost of the University of Pennsylvania; James Latta, Moderator of the General Assembly of the Presbyterian Church; Paul Jackson, who succeeded Alison as master of the Latin School in the Academy of Philadelphia; Mathew Wilson, Delaware pastor and physician.

Principal Alison was known as one of the greatest classical scholars of the time in America. Among other prominent alumni of the Academy forerunner of the University of Delaware are: David Ramsey, historian of the Revolution; George Duffield, chaplain of Congress; James McHenry, a Maryland delegate to Congress in 1783-86, member of the Constitutional Convention and Secretary of War under President Washington in 1796.

KANSAS

Washburn University of Topeka. A summary of the evolution of this institution from a college founded by the church to one controlled and operated by the municipality is to be found as the first item under the heading "General Information" in its current catalog:

Washburn College was founded by the General Association of Congregational Ministers and Churches of Kansas. Like other colleges of its type, loyal to Puritan traditions and ideals, it was independent in its govern-

* Vol. VIII, June 1943.

ment. Its charter declared that its purpose was "the diffusion of knowledge and the advancement of virtue and religion . . ."

Plans for founding such an institution as Washburn College were laid as early as 1857. In the spring of that year at a meeting of the Congregational Association a committee was appointed to "obtain information in regard to the location of a college under the patronage of this body and if they deem it expedient to secure a location."

There was spirited rivalry among the young and ambitious cities of Kansas for the possession of the proposed college; and it was not until May, 1860, that Topeka was finally chosen. During the period of the Civil War little could be done toward development of the project, although it was not forgotten. On February 6, 1865, a charter was secured under the name of Lincoln College, and a Board of Trustees was elected. In November, 1868, in recognition of a gift of twenty-five thousand dollars from Ichabod Washburn of Worcester, Massachusetts, the name was changed to Washburn College.

The first building was erected on the corner of Tenth and Jackson streets in the city of Topeka, and the first classes were formed in January, 1866. The first building on the present site, erected in the years 1872-73 was opened for school purposes in the fall of 1874.

The work at first was largely secondary, there being no high schools in Kansas. The college department soon developed and in 1918 all preparatory work was discontinued. In 1903 a School of Law was organized and the work in music was expanded into a School of Fine Arts, later termed the School of Music. In 1903, also, a merger was formed with the Kansas Medical College whereby it became the Medical School of Washburn College. The school was discontinued July 1, 1913.

In the autumn of 1940 the Board of Trustees of Washburn College announced its willingness to make available to a municipal university, if such an institution were approved by the voters of Topeka, the assets of the college. On April 1, 1941, by vote of four to one the citizens of Topeka indicated their approval of the establishment of a municipal university. Official transfer of the property to Washburn Municipal University was made by court order dated June 13, 1941. The net income from the endowment funds of the college is transferred to the University each year. The University, on its part, agrees to maintain a liberal arts college with the spirit and traditions of Washburn College. On January 2, 1952, the Board of Regents voted officially to change the name of the institution to Washburn University of Topeka.

The charter contains this challenging *raison d'être*: "an institution of learning of a high literary and religious character, to be named Lincoln College, which shall commemorate the triumph of liberty over slavery in our nation and serve as a memorial of those fallen in defense of their country."

Other articles of incorporation indicated that there should be no color distinctions and that deserving young men should be fitted "for the gospel ministry, thereby helping to supply the pressing demand for laborers in the States and Territories west of the Mississippi River."

Before Washburn lost its Congregational connections it had seven presidents over a period of seventy-two years from 1869 to 1941, one serving for over twenty-four years and another for sixteen years.

Just previous to the dying gasp of Washburn as a Congregational college, its president, Philip C. King, made a desperate effort to rally financial support from the alumni, churches, and townspeople. As a climax to the endeavor, he had the college sponsor a dinner program which included some oratory, imported and local. The author, having a reputation of considerable experience in the administration of church colleges, was the one imported. The reason for the failure to produce sufficient funds through such an intensive campaign can be shared by the other two dinner speakers: Alfred M. Landon, former Governor of Kansas, and the late Reverend Doctor Charles M. Sheldon, author of the former best-seller, *In His Steps*.

The Municipal University of Wichita. The "history," to be found in the early part of the current catalog of the university, begins with these two sentences: "The University of Wichita was created by a referendum vote of the people of Wichita on April 24, 1926. In June of the same year the Board of Trustees of Fairmount College, founded in 1895 under the auspices of the Congregational Church, formally deeded the property of the college to the University." Considerable aid for the establishment of Fairmount College had been given by the Boston Education Society.

Here is another evidence of the enthusiasm of church groups outrunning their business acumen. If a careful study had been made it would seem that cooperation between the church bodies concerned could have maintained through church support one of the two fine colleges established in the Kansas towns of Topeka and Wichita. However, local municipal pride doubtless weighed heavily in the transformation of the church schools to tax-supported institutions in the capital and the metropolis of the Sunflower State.

KENTUCKY

University of Kentucky. Although the Presbyterians had cooperated graciously with the Congregationalists in organizing a great number of colleges throughout the West and Far West, the Kentucky brand showed considerable reluctance to act similarly in their aspirations for improved higher education in that state. In 1783 the Virginia legislature chartered Transylvania Seminary to be established with assets of 8000 acres of escheated lands donated by the legislature in 1780 for a "publick school or seminary of learning" in the District of Kentucky. The "Seminary" was opened on February 1, 1785, near Danville in the "dog trot" home of a Presbyterian clergyman, the Reverend David Rice. The sole teacher was another Presbyterian minister, the Reverend James Mitchell. Enticed by an offer that would improve the financial condition of the institution, the trustees moved the "seminary" to Lexington in 1788.

When James Moore, a Presbyterian clergyman, was defeated in re-election as head of Transylvania Seminary in 1794, the majority of the board of trustees elected as president the Reverend Harry Toulmin, a Unitarian minister. The Presbyterian members of the Board resigned forthwith since they considered Toulmin "an apostate Baptist preacher," a deist if not an infidel. In short order they set up a school of their own, known as "Kentucky Academy."

In 1796 Toulmin resigned because of insurmountable problems of an economic nature. The Transylvania trustees re-elected as president the Reverend James Moore who had become an Episcopal minister in the meantime. Shortly thereafter the Presbyterian dissidents again became interested in the older school that they had founded. By an act of the General Assembly of Kentucky, under date of December 22, 1798, Transylvania Seminary and Kentucky Academy were merged under the name of Transylvania University. Rector James Moore continued as president, although the Presbyterians were largely in the majority on the board of trustees, of which the Governor of Kentucky continued as a member. Moore was professor of logic, moral philosophy, metaphysics, and belles-lettres, while two other clergymen taught the other subjects of ancient languages and mathematics, the chief components of the curriculum current throughout the country. The title of *university* was justified by the establishment of a department of medicine and a department of law and politics.

Lack of funds, factional quarrels, the War of 1812, soon caused the discontinuance of the two professional departments and later the disruption of the university. Since income from the lands donated by the parent state of Virginia was slight indeed, the trustees had great difficulty in balancing budgets and finding competent persons to act as presidents. After opposing for two years the nomination of the Reverend Doctor Horace Holley of Boston, the Presbyterian members of the board of trustees resigned when Holley was elected president in October 1817. Shortly thereafter, this group of trustees took the lead in organizing a college of their own, Centre College, chartered and opened in 1819.

These Presbyterian trustees of Transylvania had no doubts about the capacity and talents of Dr. Holley, nor did they consider his "moral conduct" and "Christian deportment" reproachable, but they feared "he had adopted some sentiments formerly entertained by the celebrated orator (Joseph) Priestly, which did not exactly quadrate with Calvanistic orthodoxy."

With grants from the state, donations and bequests, and the small tuition fees charged at the time, Transylvania University flourished for a few years, attaining to such a reputation that by 1820 Thomas Jefferson wrote a friend that, if the Virginia legislature did not "heartily push" forward his plans for a state university, "we must send our children for education to Kentucky or Cambridge."

After Holley resigned in 1827, primarily because the governor had openly criticized him for extravagance, there came a succession of acting presidents and two more Episcopal clergymen as presidents. In desperation due to financial straits, the trustees turned over without legislative sanction the college department of the university to the Kentucky Conference of the Methodist Episcopal Church. In the fall of 1842, Transylvania opened with the Reverend H. B. Bascom as acting president: he had been a professor in Augusta College, a college chartered by the Methodists, December 7, 1822. The historic schism of Methodism in 1844 prevented its General Conference from carrying through the proposal to adopt Transylvania as one of its approved colleges. However, the newly formed Methodist Episcopal Church South did take the institution under its aegis until 1850.

Transylvania then drifted along until 1855 when the state legislature appropriated $12,000 per annum toward the support of its normal school division. This action brought an increase of attendance, with the future looking rosy under the new head, the Reverend Lewis W. Green, formerly president of Hampden-Sydney College, a Presbyterian college in Virginia. When he resigned in 1857 to become president of Centre College, there arose noisy opposition to state aid which brought about legislative repeal of state support.

Georgetown College was chartered by the Kentucky Baptists in 1829. Seven years later three of its faculty members resigned in anticipation of impending dismissal because they had been branded as heretics for accepting the teachings of Alexander Campbell, the founder of the church known as the Disciples of Christ. These three obtained in 1837 without even a board of trustees, a charter from the state to establish Bacon College. Without endowment and suitable buildings the college could not survive in Georgetown, so an offer from Harrodsburg was avidly accepted, which resulted in the removal of Bacon College there in 1839. With the usual desperate struggles of such enterprises, the college floundered along until interest could be aroused among the wealthier members of the rapidly growing new Christian church, resultant in the chartering of Bacon College as Kentucky University on January 15, 1858.

As was the case of all other Southern church colleges, the War Between the States had a severe crippling effect on Kentucky University. However, it was claimed that Kentucky University suffered no loss in endowment nor were its classes interrupted by the war, although the enrollment dropped from 194 to 62 in four years. The college buildings were burned in 1864 after being used for some months as a hospital by the Confederates. The classes were then carried on temporarily in the Harrodsburg Christian Church until a merger with Transylvania was consummated in 1865, with transfer of all operations to the latter's campus in Lexington. By legislative act, under date of Ferbuary 28, 1865, all the assets of Transylvania, as well as its debts, were transferred to Kentucky University.

About that same time the Agricultural and Mechanical College of Kentucky was chartered as a department of Kentucky University, but with a separate Board of Visitors to be appointed by the governor. It is of historic interest that this new college had as part of its campus "Ashland," the former home of Henry Clay which became the residence of John B. Bowman, the Regent of Kentucky University. He had been elected from the Board of Curators to serve as head of the university.

In 1878 Regent Bowman was ousted from the presidency under a revival of sectarian opposition. The Agricultural and Mechanical College was then completely separated from Kentucky University. Not until 1908, thirty years later, was the Agricultural and Mechanical College re-organized as the State University of Kentucky. At that time Kentucky University agreed to change its name to Transylvania University, taking the name of Transylvania College in 1915. Only in 1916 came the official change of name from State University of Kentucky to University of Kentucky.

This record of revolutionary changes cannot obscure the fact that the Presbyterians took the lead in founding the forerunners of the state university now located on a beautiful and well-equipped campus in Lexington, Kentucky. Among the fine results of their efforts is the evolution of the oldest college under the aegis of the Disciples of Christ, the present Transylvania College, which is still chartered under the name of Transylvania University.

There is insufficient space to comment on the list of distinguished alumni that received their education in the congeries of colleges that eventuated in the University of Kentucky. In the chapel of Transylvania the author noticed hanging on the wall the portrait of one of the best known former students, Jefferson Davis, elected President of the Confederate States of America in February 1862 in the capitol at Montgomery, Alabama.

MARYLAND

Morgan State College in Baltimore came under the ownership and control of the state of Maryland in 1939. Shortly after the author had become executive director of the Association of American

Colleges he was asked, in a meeting in the office of Federal Judge Morris Soper, Chairman of the Morgan College Board, his candid opinion as to whether the Methodists should attempt to struggle further to maintain the first-class Negro college, or turn it over to the state which had received a command and funds from the legislature to establish a first-class college for Negroes in Maryland. Of course, the response to the query was in the affirmative.

November 27, 1867, marks the date of the chartering of Centenary Biblical Institute of the Methodist Church of Baltimore. In the Act of Incorporation, thirteen persons were "designated by the Bishops of the Methodist Episcopal Church in the United States of America as trustees to become organized into a body politic and corporate for the education of such pious young men, especially colored, for the ministry of the Methodist Episcopal Church as shall have been judged by a Quarterly Conference to be divinely called thereto."

The first chairman of the Board of Trustees was Bishop Levi Scott, a Negro. He was successful in getting the cooperation of various church groups in support of the institution. The early leaders were anxious to improve the education, academic standing, and religious training of the recently emancipated slaves.

The second chairman of the board of trustees was the Reverend Littleton F. Morgan, of the Baltimore Methodist Conference, who was responsible for raising the Institute to college level. In recognition of his gifts and services the name was changed to Morgan College in 1890.

In addition to the financial contributions of Dr. Morgan, land and other contributions were made to the college by Dr. and Mrs. John F. Goucher. He was the first president of the Womans College of Baltimore, chartered in 1885, also established by the Maryland Methodists. In appreciation for the land and substantial funds given by the Gouchers, this latter college received in 1910 the name of Goucher College. Later it severed all church connections.

While Dr. Goucher served as the third chairman of the Morgan board of trustees he was responsible for moving Morgan College to its present site in a fine section of Baltimore and for securing in 1902 the services of a well-known Methodist clergyman, Dr. John O.

Spencer, who served as president of Morgan College for thirty-five years.

The school was located originally in the heart of downtown Baltimore in the normal school room of the Association for the Moral and Educational Improvement of the Colored People. In a short while these quarters became too small and the college was moved to West Baltimore where it remained until removal in 1918 to its present site, a campus of 85 acres.

Upon retirement of President Spencer in 1937, a well-educated and distinguished Negro, Dwight O. W. Holmes was elected president. During his administration, the State of Maryland took over the institution in 1939 as indicated above. Notable expansion in facilities and other improvements through state aid have come to pass under the present president, Martin D. Jenkins, who succeeded Dr. Holmes in 1948.

Among the outstanding graduates of Morgan College while it was under Methodist control are: Benjamin O. Bird, first principal and founder of Princess Anne Academy, branch preparatory school of Morgan College, now Maryland State College; William F. Crockett, lawyer and outstanding judge in Honolulu, H. I.; Matthew W. Clair, elected Bishop of the Methodist Episcopal Church in 1920; Joseph H. Lockerman, principal of Baltimore Normal School, now Coppin State Teachers College; William A. Warfield, physician, chief surgeon and medical administrator of Freedmen's Hospital, Washington, D. C.; Sampson W. Brooks, elected Bishop in A.M.E. Church, 1920; W.A.C. Hughes, elected Bishop of the Methodist Church (Central Jurisdiction), 1940; Theophilius R. Parker, missionary in Liberia, Africa, and later president of Alabama A. & M. College, Normal, Alabama; Thomas H. Kiah, president of Maryland State College, Princess Anne, Maryland; Edgar A. Love, elected Bishop of the Methodist Church (Central Jurisdiction) 1952; Harold L. Trigg, president of St. Augustine's College, Raleigh, North Carolina; Leonidas S. James, president of State Normal School, now Maryland State Teachers College, Bowie, Maryland; Houston R. Jackson, Assistant Superintendent of Public Schools, Baltimore, Maryland; Elmer W. Henderson, Assistant Superintendent of Public Schools, Baltimore, Maryland, and hundreds of successful graduates in the professions, many of whom have earned the highest academic degrees.

MISSISSIPPI

Jackson College for Negro Teachers. This name was given on March 20, 1944, by legal enactment of the Mississippi legislature, to what had been briefly called Mississippi Negro Training School. The same legislature had passed a law under date of May 6, 1940, by which the state had accepted all the assets, including buildings and campus, of Jackson College which had been founded by the American Baptist Home Missionary Society sixty-seven years before.

This society, which was organized in 1832, had established the Natchez Seminary on October 23, 1877. The Seminary was intended primarily for the education of Negro preachers and teachers for whom educational facilities were woefully lacking at that time in Mississippi. Recalling that most of the students, who were ex-slaves, were unqualified for a college education, the Society simply required that students desiring admission to the Seminary should be capable of self-government and able to read the Bible. With the admission of twenty students it began a new era in Negro education in Mississippi and nearby Southern states.

The American Baptist Home Missionary Society sent Dr. Charles Ayer as the first president of this educational venture. Dr. Ayer was born at Clinton, New York, in 1823 of a family of culture and some wealth. He was a graduate of Hamilton College and of Newton Theological Seminary. He served Natchez Seminary as president for seventeen years, moving it from Natchez to Jackson in 1883, with the change of name to Jackson College.

In the beginning President Ayer had two other members on his faculty, his wife and Inman Page. The latter was selected because of the fine impression he made on President Ayer when giving the graduation address at Brown University a few years earlier. In spite of an outbreak of yellow fever which delayed the opening of the second year of the college, the enrollment did increase threefold by the end of the school year in 1878.

Upon the removal of the institution to Jackson, it held classes in the Mount Helm Baptist Church in what was then the outskirts of the city of Jackson. The encroachment of white residents and the chartering of Millsaps College in 1890 on an adjacent piece of land caused the trustees of Jackson College to accept the offer of Major Millsaps to purchase the Jackson College campus for $40,000. It is now a part of the grounds of Millsaps College.

When President Ayer resigned in May 1894, he was succeeded by the Reverend Luther G. Barrett, a New Englander and also a graduate of Newton Theological Seminary. He had received his bachelor's degree from Harvard University.

Although Jackson College had been removed to a section that was primarily Negro, the enrollment dropped for a short while but within four years had increased from 107 students to 442. Some students came from nearby Alabama and Louisiana, but none was above grammar school in preparation. By 1905 the grammar school became the practice school of the college; the majority of the students were at that time preparing to become teachers.

After seventeen years of service, President Barrett retired in 1911 to accept a position as a Baptist pastor in the state of Massachusetts. He was succeeded by Zachary Taylor Hubert, the first Negro president of the college. President Hubert was a native of White Plains, Georgia, and an A.B. graduate of Morehouse College, Atlanta, in the class of 1901. He did graduate work at Boston University and the Massachusetts Agricultural College, taught Science and Agriculture at the Florida Agricultural and Mechanical College in Tallahassee, and served as Superintendent of Buildings and Grounds at Spelman College in Atlanta.

In spite of the mores of the community, harmonious relations existed between the white and Negro members of the Jackson College faculty. Feeling that a large number of Negro teachers were available, President Hubert decided on an all-Negro faculty. He also persuaded the Missionary Society to permit the expansion of the curriculum to college rank by 1921. The college awarded its first Bachelor of Arts degree in 1924 to Mrs. Annie May Brown McGhee. In addition to expanding the curriculum for the benefit of others than those planning to become teachers or clergymen, the college became full-fledged by the establishment of a football team.

In September 1927, Dr. Hubert resigned to become president of

Langston University, the Negro land-grant college of Oklahoma. He was succeeded by B. Baldwin Dansby, who at that time was doing graduate work at the University of Chicago on a $1500 grant by the General Education Board of the Rockefeller Foundation. Like many new college presidents he found serious financial problems which became greatly aggravated during his first year because of the failure of the cotton crop. President Dansby had received his Bachelor of Arts degree from Morehouse College in 1906, where he had been class orator on graduation day. He taught mathematics and languages at the Florida Normal College in St. Augustine, an institution that had its start as Jacksonville Baptist Academy. In October 1911, he had accepted the appointment by the Home Missionary Society as Professor and Dean of Mathematics at Jackson College.

As the financial condition became progressively more difficult, a number of schemes were developed which would not only help the college but the constituents: (a) "Get Acquainted with the College" brought increased interest throughout the state of Mississippi as well as a cash contribution of $1700 from the Negro constituents during the year 1927; (b) a Ministers' Institute and a Summer School for Teachers were organized, the latter receiving approval of the Mississippi State Department of Education for training teachers in elementary and high school subjects. Help was also obtained from the Rosenwald Foundation for the construction of a library. Climaxing the financial problems came a notice from the American Baptist Home Missionary Society that it was no longer able to continue support of the college.

On April 5, 1933, the local trustee board under the chairmanship of W. F. Bond, State Superintendent of Education of Mississippi, held a meeting to decide whether to close the school as suggested by the American Baptist Home Missionary Society or rally the community to its support. The local board, composed of distinguished citizens, white and Negro, which included President J. W. Provine of Mississippi College, the white Baptist college at Clinton, and several leading white business men of Jackson, obtained the support of the local chamber of commerce and the Jackson newspapers. The local group then instituted a plan to have the State of

Mississippi take over the college. This proposal was finally approved by the Mississippi legislature in April 1940. The American Baptist Home Missionary Society readily agreed to transfer all their holdings and interests in Jackson College to the state of Mississippi.

Upon President Dansby's resignation in 1940, the board elected Jacob L. Reddix, who continues as president. He is a native of Mississippi, was educated in a normal school in Alabama, and obtained his college work at the Illinois Institute of Technology, with graduate work at the University of Chicago. At the beginning of his administration, the Rosenwald Foundation made a grant of $30,000 a year and the state of Mississippi gave an annual subsidy of $10,000. The Rosenwald Fund added $45,000 for building repairs while a similar grant of $5000 was made by the Mississippi State Building Commission. Thus the college has a new lease on life as a full-fledged state college. The records indicate that the gifts of the American Baptist Home Missionary Society over a period of fifty-five years totalled nearly $580,000, with more than half of this amount going to teachers' salaries. In addition to the Rosenwald Grants, Jackson College received donations of $196,000 from the General Education Board of New York.

A far greater contribution made by this college while under church auspices is the group of distinguished alumni and former students. Of the two members in the first graduating class of 1883, Pazavia O'Connel, with a Doctor of Philosophy degree from the University of Pennsylvania, became a well-known faculty member at Morgan College in Baltimore, and Mrs. Lillie Granderson Diggs became an accomplished music teacher, dying in 1937 at the home of her son, Senator Charles Diggs of Detroit, Michigan. Other distinguished graduates include former President J. M. Gandy of the Virginia State College at Petersburg, President Lynch of Central Mississippi College at Kosciusko, and Harry H. Jones, M.D., who is both a minister and a physician and is still rendering conspicuous service as a missionary in Liberia.

NEBRASKA

Bellevue College. This college was incorporated October 16, 1880, by the Presbyterian Synod of Nebraska. It opened three years later in Bellevue, located a few miles south of Omaha. Its charter was revised in 1891 so as to change its name to the University of Omaha though it maintained the Bellevue location. This title was justified by its affiliation with the Omaha Law School, the Omaha Medical College, and the Omaha Dental College.

Since the trustees did not yield to the pressure to move the collegiate department to Omaha, it changed its name again in 1908 to Bellevue College. However, some of the Presbyterian leaders did organize themselves into a board of trustees of the University of Omaha under the presidency of Professor Daniel Jenkins of the Omaha Theological Seminary. Failure to receive sufficient financial support elsewhere resulted in the success of a movement to make the university a municipal institution which was finally legally authorized in 1930. When this legislation was passed, the assets accumulated by the Presbyterian group totalled some $200,000, which were turned over to the new Municipal University of Omaha. Among the distinguished alumni of the old Bellevue College are Rear Admiral Stanton Salisbury, former Chief of Chaplains of the United States Navy, Judge Arthur C. Thomsen, and Professor Harrison A. Trexler, formerly head of the Department of History at Southern Methodist University. When Bellevue College ceased operations as an independent institution, its records were transferred to Hastings College, the nearest Presbyterian college in the state, and the graduates of the former Bellevue College were officially voted to be considered alumni of Hastings College in 1934.

New Jersey

Rutgers University, The State University of New Jersey, received its first charter as Queen's College in 1766 in the name of King George III from Governor William Franklin of the Colony of New Jersey, the Tory and disowned son of the great American patriot, Benjamin Franklin. Chapter I outlines in some detail how the fortunes of Queen's College ebbed and flowed under the control and intermittent interest of the Dutch Reformed Church. It got under way in 1771 shortly after receiving a second charter from the same Governor Franklin to replace the earlier one that had disappeared. After being closed for two intermittent periods, the college was re-opened in 1825 under the name of Rutgers College. In 1864 its Science School became the New Jersey Agricultural and Mechanical College and the college was designated the State University of New Jersey in 1917.

NORTH CAROLINA

North Carolina College at Durham opened its doors on July 10, 1910, having received a charter the previous year. In the beginning it was known as the National Religious Training School and Chautauqua. Its purpose was the development in its students of fine character and the giving of "sound academic training requisite for real service to the nation." From the beginning there was a lack of money but a "wealth of enthusiasm and high endeavor." The project was kept afloat principally by student fees and some donations collected by the president and founder, the late Dr. James E. Shepard. For a while the late Mrs. Russell Sage of New York made generous donations to the school.

In 1923 funds were appropriated by the General Assembly of North Carolina for the purchase and maintenance of the school as the Durham State Normal College. In 1925 the college was changed by the North Carolina legislature into the North Carolina College for Negroes, with a curriculum offering liberal arts with emphasis on teacher preparation. With gifts from the Duke family and other citizens of Durham, the college has rapidly grown so that in 1937 it received accreditment as a class A institution. In 1947 the name was changed again by the state legislature to North Carolina College at Durham.

OHIO

The University of Akron had its origin as Buchtel College, which was founded in 1870. It was chartered the same year by the legislature of Ohio. The college was founded by the Ohio Universalist Convention.

The Universalist Church has been responsible for the establishment of a number of other fine liberal arts colleges, all of which seem to have become independent institutions or have been combined with other colleges. In this group should be included *Tufts*

College, Medford, Massachusetts; *St. Lawrence University,* Canton, New York; and *Lombard College,* Galesburg, Illinois. In 1930 the latter became an integral part of Knox College in the same city.

Buchtel College was named for John Richards Buchtel, an industrious farmer and ardent Universalist churchman of the community. He gave $31,000 to start the project and considerably more later, after he had become a successful farm machinery salesman and president of the company that manufactured the Buckeye mowers and reapers. He was one of the incorporators of the college and chairman of its board of trustees until his death, May 23, 1892.

The Universalist Church put some $200,000 into the Buchtel College enterprise. Because of its location in a rapidly growing city, because the institution thus became a community college with fewer and fewer Universalists in attendance and because the latter group were unable to continue to meet the expenses necessary for this type of college, the trustees donated the plant and assets to the city of Akron in 1913. Doubtless these trustees were greatly influenced in their decision by the success of the University of Cincinnati, a municipally controlled institution in a neighboring city. The liberal arts division is still called Buchtel College of Liberal Arts, University of Akron.

Among the many distinguished graduates before the college was turned over to the city of Akron can be listed two college presidents, Parke R. Kolbe, who died while president of Drexel Institute of Technology, Philadelphia, and H. E. Simmons, former president of the University of Akron; two presidents of the Firestone Tire and Rubber Company, John W. Thomas of the class of 1904 and Lee R. Jackson of the class of 1913; Mary E. Gladwin, chief nurse of the United States Army in 1898; Theron S. Jackson, a world-famous surgeon; Frank Pixley, editor and dramatist, author of *The Prince of Pilsen.*

Central State College. This college is an offshoot of Wilberforce University. Unlike other state colleges mentioned in this chapter, it is not exactly a direct descendant of a church college. However, it does owe its origin to the leaders of the African Methodist Episcopal Church who took over the support and control of Wilberforce from the Methodist Episcopal Church in 1863.

At the September 28, 1853, session of the Cincinnati Conference of the Methodist Episcopal Church, a committee was appointed to inquire into what could be done for the many colored people in that section of Ohio. The result of this action was the opening of Wilberforce University at Tawawa Springs, Greene County, Ohio, in October 1856. Understandingly, the group discarded the proposed name of Ohio African University for Wilberforce in recognition of the famous William Wilberforce who was largely responsible for the emancipation of the Negroes in England.

Since the recently freed Negroes were not ready for college instruction, the school was originally quite elementary in its character and functioned briefly under a principal. In 1858, deeming it was possible to offer advanced courses, the trustees called the Reverend Richard S. Rust of the New Hampshire Methodist Conference to be the university's first president. He later became so successful in advancing the interests of Negro education that Rust College, now an accredited college in Mississippi, was named in his honor. However, local adverse economic and political conditions were too strenuous for him to overcome so that he and the supporting Cincinnati Conference of the Methodist Episcopal Church felt obliged to close the college in the summer of 1862. Under the valiant leadership of Bishop Daniel S. Payne, a son of freedmen of Charleston, South Carolina, the African Methodist Episcopal Church took over all the assets (and some debts) of the school by a payment of $10,000. While continuing as bishop, the heroic Daniel A. Payne served as president of Wilberforce from 1863 to 1876.

Among the early trustees was Salmon P. Chase, then governor of Ohio and later Secretary of Treasury under President Lincoln who appointed him in 1864 the Chief Justice of the United States Supreme Court. Chase contributed over $10,000 toward the upbuilding of Wilberforce.

Under the leadership of the third president, S. T. Mitchell, an alumnus of the class of 1873, serving from 1884 to 1900, the Ohio legislature passed a law in 1887 appropriating $5000 a year for the support of the combined Normal and Industrial Department of Wilberforce University. There was from the beginning an autonomous board for this division, comprising at first three of the

166 THE CHURCH AND THE FOUR-YEAR COLLEGE

regular board of trustees plus three others appointed by the governor.

By later amendments to the law, the governor appointed six trustees and the trustees named three, including the president of the university. It can be readily appreciated that this arrangement would engender friction which increased over the years. It culminated in 1947 in the establishment of a completely independent institution, Central State College. The latter, with generous state support, located on property contiguous to the original Wilberforce campus, is showing fine growth which overshadows the physical equipment of the parent institution. Charles H. Wesley, a distinguished scholar, educator, and former high official in the African Methodist Episcopal Church was president of Wilberforce from 1942 to 1947. In 1947 he became the first president of Central State College when it severed all connections with Wilberforce.

OREGON

Oregon College of Education. Organized at Monmouth in 1856 as Monmouth University, it became Christian College in 1865 when it merged with Bethel College. The charter for the college under its new name was obtained in 1866 under the sponsorship of an agency of the Disciples of Christ. There is no available record of the amount of money involved in its establishment: the building erected for college purposes was a rather modest one.

After a precarious existence the institution was turned over to the state in 1882, when it received the name Oregon State Normal School. However, the state did not assume full control until 1892. In 1911 the name was changed to Oregon Normal School and in 1937 it received its present title.

PENNSYLVANIA

Mansfield State Teachers College was chartered in 1854 as the Mansfield Classical Seminary under the auspices of the East Genesee Conference of the Methodist Episcopal Church. The board of trustees, April 17, 1856, elected as principal and preceptress the Reverend J. E. and Mrs. H. L. Jaques at a combined salary of $900 per annum. On January 7, 1857, the seminary was finally opened with

105 students. This number had increased to 150 at the opening of the second term, April 16, 1857. Six days thereafter the college buildings burned to the ground. Although there was some insurance, the ensuing 1857 panic finished one insurance company and caused the other to refuse to pay.

In spite of continued financial difficulties the institution re-opened November 23, 1859, but continued to have great financial embarrassment, with the continuous threat of being sold out by the sheriff. Quite readily and unanimously the trustees voted on July 2, 1862, to apply to the state of Pennsylvania for the transformation of the institution into a state normal school. The examiners appointed by the governor met at Mansfield on December 11, 1862, and after a study of the situation reported in favor of the transfer proposal. On December 12, 1862, the Mansfield Classical Seminary became officially the State Normal School of the Fifth District. In 1927 the name was changed to Mansfield State Teachers College.

VIRGINIA

College of William and Mary. The days during which William and Mary flourished under the domination and with the support of the Church have been briefly chronicled in Chapter I. After many years of precarious and intermittent existence due to the lack of sufficient financial support, dating from the incipience of the American Revolution, the college was completely taken over by the state of Virginia in 1906. It was closed from 1861 to 1865 when all of the faculty and 90 per cent of the students had entered the Confederate service at the beginning of the War Between the States. The buildings were twice destroyed by fire, in 1859 through the carelessness of a servant and in 1862 by the willful wantonness of drunken Union soldiers. For the latter loss, partial reimbursement was made by the United States Congress in 1893.

Although prominent Episcopalians and other friends made substantial gifts toward the rebuilding and general support of the college, it could not overcome its financial difficulties and was obliged to close again in 1881. Its trustees were able to re-open the college in 1888 on a grant of $10,000 per annum by the Virginia legislature, made with the understanding the college would maintain a "normal" course for those planning to teach in Virginia. At this re-opening the trustees chose as president, Lyon Gardiner Tyler, son of John Tyler, the tenth President of the United States who himself was a graduate of William and Mary in 1807. Lyon Tyler became president emeritus in 1919, after thirty-one years in office.

WEST VIRGINIA

Marshall College. This college began operations in 1837 as Marshall Academy in a log structure, in what is now downtown Huntington, which had housed a school previously known as Mount Hebron. It received the official name of Marshall Academy by an act of the General Assembly of Virginia, dated March 13, 1838.

The leading spirit in the founding of Marshall Academy was John O. Laidley, an eminent lawyer, who was prosecuting attorney for Cabell County from 1817-60. He was a close friend of the famous Chief Justice, John Marshall, who died in 1835; this friendship accounts for the name of the academy. An additional acre and a quarter of land was purchased with the understanding that the building erected thereon should be ever after used for school purposes. In a new four-room structure one room was set aside as a chapel, which was used as a church on the Sabbath by the Presbyterians, who contributed somewhat generously with that understanding. Previously the Presbyterians had been worshipping in a church across the Ohio river in the state of Ohio. The first Presbyterian minister, the Reverend E. C. Thom, supplemented his salary by teaching in the academy. After Parson Thom had accepted a parish at Paris, Kentucky, he was succeeded by the Reverend Josiah Poage, a graduate of Princeton, who served part time also as principal of the Academy from 1843-49. Through his church connections Poage attracted a number of students from eastern Kentucky as well as from other areas in the western part of Virginia.

In 1850 the West Virginia Conference of the Methodist Episcopal Church, South, took over the support and control of the School. However, they made it clear that the institution would maintain a nonsectarian atmosphere, as a Presbyterian would continue to be principal of the academy. With the approach of the War Between the States the Academy was beset with such financial difficulties that the Methodists allowed the college to be sold at auction to a Mrs. Salina C. Mason who moved her family into the main building, though maintaining a school throughout the period of the war.

During the period of Methodist ownership Marshall Academy changed its name to Marshall College through action of the Virginia Assembly, under the control of twenty-one trustees, eleven Methodist ministers, and ten Methodist laymen.

The new state of West Virginia had been carved out of Virginia in 1863. In 1866 the West Virginia Conference of the Methodist Church made a vain effort to raise sufficient funds to gain back ownership and control of the institution.

In 1867 the legislature of the new state passed an act which converted Marshall College into a State Normal School, with the understanding that the Cabell County Board of Supervisors would purchase the lands and buildings of the college and turn them over to the state. This they did by repurchase of the property from the aforementioned Mrs. Salina C. Mason. State authority was given to the granting of Bachelor's degrees in 1920, the teachers college conferred its first degree in June 1921. The College of Arts and Sciences awarded the first liberal arts degrees in 1925.

A memorandum is in order concerning the early presidents of Marshall College under state control. James E. Morrow was president 1872-73: during this year was born his distinguished son, Dwight Morrow, who became Ambassador to Mexico and United States Senator from New Jersey. During 1873-74 the president was James Beauchamp Clark, who was twenty-one years old and a recent graduate of Bethany College. He holds a position in American history as the well-known Champ Clark of Missouri, who was Speaker of the United States House of Representatives, 1911-15. It will be recalled that at the famous Democratic convention held in Baltimore in 1912, he almost defeated Woodrow Wilson for nomination as President of the United States by the Democratic party. During his presidency he sang regularly in the choir of the Southern Methodist Church.

John Marshall has the distinction of having had another college named in his honor, Marshall College. This college was established at Mercersburg, Pennsylvania, in 1836, by the German Reformed

Church. Falling into hard financial straits, its trustees accepted an invitation to join with Franklin College in Lancaster in the formation of Franklin and Marshall College in 1853.

THREE BORDER CASES

One competent authority in the field of higher education asserts that the *College of Charleston* and the *University of Tennessee* were established under church auspices, the first by the Episcopalians and the second by the Presbyterians.

A careful search of the records indicates clearly that both were undenominational when they were founded, and this fact is so indicated in the legal papers relating to their origin.

Blount College. Named for the first governor of Tennessee, Blount College was chartered by the territorial government on September 10, 1794. It was located in the central area of Knoxville. Its first and only president was the Reverend Samuel Carrick, a well-known Presbyterian clergyman of the area. When financial problems became insurmountable, the trustees turned the college over to the state of Tennessee in 1807. The name was then changed to East Tennessee College, which was again changed to East Tennessee University in 1840 and in 1879 to the University of Tennessee. The Reverend Mr. Carrick carried on as president of the college after it came under state control until his demise in 1809 at the age of forty-nine.

College of Charleston. This college was established by a group of distinguished citizens of Charleston, including the Reverend Robert Smith, Rector of St. Philip's Church. They obtained the official charter from the state of South Carolina in 1785. On July 3, 1785, Robert Smith opened in his home an academy which offered courses "in the English, Latin, Greek and French Languages— Writing, Arithmetic and Geography" which was "resorted to by parents of all ranks and conditions in life."

At a meeting of the board of trustees on February 6, 1786, Rector Smith was elected the first president of the board. On March 14, 1789, the record indicates "the Reverend R. Smith proposed to the trustees to lay the foundations of the college by giving up to it on the first day of January next the youth in his academy, amounting to sixty Scholars." It is worthy of note that while in other cases land and buildings were transferred from one set of owners to another, in this case the gift was simply sixty students.

The trustees accepted the offer of Robert Smith and forthwith elected him unanimously "principal" of the college which was officially opened in 1790. Rector Smith continued as principal until 1797 although he had been elected the first Episcopal Bishop of South Carolina in 1795.

Robert Smith had been educated in Cambridge University in England, was ordained an Anglican Priest in 1756, and became Rector of St. Philip's Church in "Charles Town" in 1759. He was a man of considerable means, joined with the colonists against the mother country during the Revolution, and served as a common soldier when the British tried to capture the city.

In the transfer of the academy to the college it was deemed advisable to add to the building equipment. Other trustees being indifferent, or financially unable to assist, Principal Smith bought the necessary materials and paid the bricklayers out of his own purse. For this he received a bond from the trustees but there is no record that this bond was ever redeemed. At his death the college still owed him $14,000, which debt was finally settled with his heirs in the sale of some land he had accumulated for the college.

In 1794 the College of Charleston had its first graduation exercises. The six members in the class submitted to a two-day examination on the "learned languages, arts and sciences" in which both trustees and faculty participated as examiners. One of the six members of the original class was the Reverend Nathaniel Bowen who was twice principal of the college for a total period of nine years and who was later Episcopal Bishop of South Carolina.

In the early faculty were four other clergymen: Dr. Simon Felix Gallagher, born in Dublin, Ireland, Rector of St. Mary's Catholic Church, who taught mathematics and natural philosophy; the Reverend Jean Paul Coste, Pastor of the Huguenot Church, who taught French; the Reverend Thomas Mills, rector of St. Andrews Episcopal Church, who taught Latin; the Reverend Thomas Frost, Assistant Rector of St. Philip's Episcopal Church.

Further evidence of the religious influence predominating in the early days of the College of Charleston is indicated by the regulation that the college day should start with a Latin prayer and should be closed with a prayer in English. When Bishop Smith resigned in 1797 because of pressure of episcopal duties, he was succeeded by a layman, Thomas Bee, Jr.

Finally financial difficulties became so harassing that the trustees turned over their independent institution to the city council of Charleston in 1837. Thus it became the first municipally controlled institution of higher learning in the United States. Recently it has become again an "independent" college, with no municipal support or control.

West Liberty State College. Located in West Liberty, West Virginia, West Liberty State College is another accredited college that had its origin as an independent school with church leadership distinctly in evidence. On March 30, 1837, the legislature of Virginia passed "An Act to incorporate the trustees of West Liberty Academy in the county of Ohio." This academy was opened with sixty-five students in 1838. The Reverend Doctor Nathan Shotwell and Mrs. Shotwell comprised the original faculty. He continued as principal of the West Liberty Academy until about 1854. Most of his successors in the school's leadership were Presbyterian clergymen until 1870, when the new state of West Virginia bought the property and renamed the school West Liberty State Normal School. By legislative action in 1931 its name was changed to West Liberty State Teachers College, having received shortly before the authority to confer baccalaureate degrees. In the spring of 1943 it was legally empowered to change its name to West Liberty State College.

OTHER TRANSFORMATIONS

There are three instances of colleges whose transformation followed an opposite direction from those described previously in this chapter. Centenary College of Louisiana evolved from a state college into one controlled by the Methodist Church. Mississippi College, the Baptist College of Mississippi, was originally operated under the auspices of the state. The present independent Tulane University began as the University of Louisiana, with state support and control.

Centenary College of Louisana received its charter from the Louisana legislature in February 1825. It was founded at Jackson with state funds, having been called originally "College of Louisiana." The Jackson area was too sparsely settled at the time to make the project successful. After a struggle of twenty years, during which only twenty-four students obtained the baccalaureate degree, the state turned over in 1845 the campus and buildings to the Mississippi Conference of the Southern Methodist Church. This group brought over from Mississippi the assets and records of a college they had established in 1839, the centennial of the arrival of leaders of the Wesleyan movement in the United States. This explains the change of name. The college has continued under Methodist control and support, being closed, like most Southern colleges, from 1861 to 1866. By the fall of 1861 most of the students had enlisted in the Confederate Army, with nearly every member of the Senior Class paying the supreme sacrifice.

Mississippi College in Clinton was first chartered by the Mississippi legislature in 1826 as Hampstead Academy. It became known as Mississippi Academy in 1827 and in 1830 the name was changed to Mississippi College. This did not mean, as many friends of the institution ardently hoped, that the state was taking over the college entirely. According to the records, all the assistance that the state gave was the donation over a period of five years of rents from the leased portions of thirty-six sections of lands granted to Mississippi by the United States Congress in 1819 "for the aid of an institution of learning." In addition the state made a loan of $5000 for construction of buildings.

With contraction in annual donations and failure of further state aid, the trustees were impelled to seek more substantial support. By a majority vote of one the Mississippi Conference of the Methodist Church meeting in its 1841 session declined to accept the Mississippi College property, "with all its improvements and apparatus" plus $20,000 in cash. They voted instead to locate their college at Brandon Springs, which institution was later transferred to Louisiana to become what is now the strong accredited Centenary College of Shreveport. The trustees then turned over the college in 1842 to the Clinton Presbytery of the Presbyterian Church, U. S.

After a brief period of prosperity the college again became so involved financially that the Presbyterians turned it back to its original sponsors.

In 1850 the college with all its equipment was transferred to the Mississippi Baptist Convention. From that date it has had a steady and noteworthy growth, continuing under Baptist control.

Tulane University started as a Medical College in 1834. All the founders were physicians, affiliated with the Louisana State Charity Hospital. They gave their first lectures in a nondenominational church in downtown New Orleans.

Encouraged by the success attained by the medical college, local civic leaders agitated for a state university and were successful in having their plan incorporated in the state constitution, adopted in 1845. On February 16, 1847, the legislature passed an act incorporating the University of Louisana which then included not only the Medical College of Louisana but also law and preparatory departments. The collegiate department was not opened until 1851.

Although Paul Tulane, a prosperous merchant who had migrated to New Orleans from New Jersey, had started his benefactions, the university soon was in grave financial distress. The climax was reached in 1861 when all four departments, one after another, were closed until the fall of 1865. In 1882 Paul Tulane set up the Tulane Educational Fund with a gift of over a million dollars "for the advancement of learning and letters the arts and sciences therein." In 1884, by an act of the legislature, the properties of the University of Louisiana were turned over by the state to the administrators of the Tulane Fund. The institution thus reorganized is officially known as The Tulane University of Louisiana.

Indiana University. No organized church group had any official connection with the establishment in 1820 of the State Seminary of Indiana, which changed its name to Indiana College in 1828 and expanded into Indiana University in 1838. Rivalry between church groups caused considerable instability at the college in its early days. Some church enthusiasts were so uncharitable that they called their state college a Godless institution with the result that it was almost closed on one occasion. On another occasion the Methodists became greatly perturbed because all three faculty members happened to be Presbyterians. Doubtless this unsuccessful contest resulted in the founding in 1837 of Indiana Asbury College, now DePauw University. When the Methodists finally got one of their clergymen elected president of Indiana College, his opponents opined his main assets were that he was a Democrat and a Methodist. David Starr Jordan, professor of biology and president of Indiana University before leaving to become the first president of Leland Stanford University, quipped that there were "three kinds of Presbyterians in Bloomington: Reformed Presbyterians, United Presbyterians, and Presbyterians that are neither united nor reformed."

CHAPTER XII

Church Boards of Education

THE church boards of education working primarily through their executive secretaries and other officers have been of utmost value in establishing and strengthening the church-related colleges of the United States. Some of these boards have been in operation for more than half a century. In the early nineteenth century they invited to their annual meetings the presidents of their respective affiliated colleges.

In 1914 the Council of Church Board Secretaries voted to organize the Association of American Colleges. This organization was begun at a meeting in Chicago with the election of Robert L. Kelly as president. Dr. Kelly had been for some years president of Earlham College, the well-known Quaker institution in Indiana.

A little over a year later President Kelly gave up the Earlham presidency to become full-time executive officer of the Association of American Colleges and Executive Secretary of the Council of Church Boards of Education. At first the latter group financed the combined office. Within a few years other liberal arts colleges were accepted to membership in the Association of American Colleges; later the collegiate departments of state and independent universities also joined.

The expanding work of the Association soon demanded the full time of Dr. Kelly, thus resulting in his relinquishing the duties of Executive Secretary of the Council of the Church Boards of Education. In this office he was succeeded in 1934 by Dr. Gould Wickey,

Executive Secretary of The Board of Education of The United Lutheran Church in America.

The church-related colleges as a federated group have had an interesting evolution over the past forty years. When the Council of Church Boards of Education organized the Association of American Colleges in 1915, the latter's membership included only 204 Protestant colleges. Eventually other Protestant colleges joined and the membership was gradually opened to independent, Roman Catholic, and Jewish colleges. Later the college departments of the independent and state universities were invited to membership, so that at present there are over seven hundred members of the Association of American Colleges. Naturally the four-year colleges, whatever their connection or affiliations, have much in common, with practically the same problems of administration, curriculum, finances, etc.

At the concluding session of the Association of American Colleges on January 16, 1930, when the author was president for the year, a motion made by President A. N. Ward of Western Maryland College resulted in the organization on that evening of the Liberal Arts College Movement. This group had as its chief ideal a desire to cooperate in a nation-wide campaign for funds for the small independent church-related college. The steering committee of the group was entertained at the White House by President Herbert Hoover, who lent encouragement to this proposal which shortly was found to be impractical. Insurmountable were the problems of combined campaigns and a just division of prospective receipts.

The Liberal Arts College Movement published an inspirational magazine under the editorship of B. Warren Brown. The movement languished during the depths of the Depression with the result that at the Annual Meeting of the Association of American Colleges in St. Louis on January 15, 1934, the group voted, after conference with officials of the Association and of the National Council of Church Boards of Education, to become "The National Conference of Church-Related Colleges." This conference continued from February 1934 to January 1944, under the direction of a commission of fifteen members, composed of church board secretaries and presidents of Catholic and Protestant colleges. During this period Gould

Wickey, Secretary of the United Lutheran Board of Education, served as the Commission's secretary and executive officer.

The conference maintained a quarterly magazine known as *College and Church*. It held its annual meeting the day before the annual meeting of the Association of American Colleges. In complete harmony the two associations held a joint meeting on the evening prior to the first business session of the annual meeting of the Association of American Colleges. The program of this joint session consisted mainly of two addresses from outstanding Catholic and Protestant clergymen, a policy still in vogue at the first session of the annual meetings of the Association of American Colleges.

In due time it seemed to the leaders of both groups that an amalgamation was in order. Thus on January 14, 1944, the National Conference of Church-Related Colleges became a semi-autonomous commission of the Association of American Colleges with the name of the Commission on Christian Higher Education. For three years this Commission maintained a full-time paid secretary in the person of the Reverend Robert N. DuBose, who had been for some years Chaplain of Duke University. He has returned to his native state of South Carolina to re-enter the Methodist ministry.

The following is a list of chairmen of the conference during the period of its separate existence:

1934–1935—President Harry M. Gage, Coe College
    1936—President E. E. Rall, North Central College
    1937—President E. V. Stanford, Villanova College
    1938—President Ralph W. Lloyd, Maryville College (Tennessee)
    1939—President Rees E. Tulloss, Wittenberg College
    1940—Chancellor David Shaw Duncan, the University of Denver
    1941—Professor William F. Cunningham, Notre Dame University
    1942—President Irving Maurer, Beloit College
    1943—President Charles E. Diehl, Southwestern at Memphis.

The National Council of Churches of Christ in the United States of America has established a huge division of Christian Education with a subdivision known as the Commission on Christian Higher Education, which carries on in an expanded form the activities and influence of the original independent Council of Church Board Secretaries organized some fifty years ago.

The National Council of Churches came into being in November 1950, at a large gathering of church leaders in Cleveland, Ohio. The Council is a merger of twelve organizations, among the better known ones of which were the Federal Council of Churches and the International Council of Religious Education. One of the principal contributions of the latter has been the compilation of the Uniform Lessons used annually by most of the Protestant Sunday Schools. The author was a consultant at the merger made in Cleveland, having been for many years a director of the International Council of Religious Education and chairman of the host committee when the Council held its quadrennial session in Birmingham, Alabama, in the spring of 1926.

The first chairman of the National Council's Commission on Christian Higher Education is John O. Gross, who was formerly president of two Methodist colleges, Union in Kentucky and later Simpson in Iowa.

The first secretary of this Commission is Raymond F. McLain, former president of two colleges affiliated with the Church of the Disciples, Eureka in Illinois and later Transylvania in Kentucky. He was elected president of the American University at Cairo, Egypt, early in 1955.

Here follow the names and addresses, as of July 1, 1954, of the executive officers of the Church Boards of Education affiliated with the Commission on Christian Higher Education of the National Council of Churches of Christ in the United States of America:

CHURCH BOARDS OF HIGHER EDUCATION

African Methodist Episcopal
Church
S. L. Greene, Jr.
414 Eighth Avenue, S.
Nashville, Tennessee

African Methodist Episcopal Zion
Church
James W. Eichelberger
128 East 58th Street
Chicago 37, Illinois

American Baptist Convention
Ronald V. Wells
152 Madison Avenue
New York 16, New York

American Evangelical Lutheran
Church
Ernest D. Nielsen
Grand View College
Des Moines 16, Iowa

CHURCH BOARDS OF HIGHER EDUCATION (*Continued*)

Augustana Evangelical Lutheran
   Church
Karl Mattson
Augustana Seminary
Rock Island, Illinois

Central Methodist Episcopal
   Church
B. J. Smith
4043 S. Drexel Avenue
Chicago 15, Illinois

Church of The Brethren
C. Ernest Davis
22 South State Street
Elgin, Illinois

Church of God
Adam W. Miller
1303 East Fifth Street
Anderson, Indiana

Church of the Nazarene
S. T. Ludwig
2923 Troost Avenue
Kansas City 41, Missouri

Churches of God in North America
Roy Schreiner
13th and Walnut Streets
Harrisburg, Pennsylvania

Congregational Christian Churches
Bryant Drake
19 South LaSalle Street
Chicago 3, Illinois

Disciples of Christ
Harlie L. Smith
222 S. Downey Avenue
Indianapolis 7, Indiana

Evangelical Lutheran Church
J.C.K. Preus
421 S. Fourth Street
Minneapolis 15, Minnesota

Evangelical and Reformed Church
Franklin I. Sheeder
1505 Race Street
Philadelphia 2, Pennsylvania

Evangelical United Brethren
   Church
Reuben H. Mueller
1900 Knott Building
Dayton 2, Ohio

Five Years Meeting of Friends
Clyde A. Milner
Guilford College
Guilford College, North Carolina

Mennonite Church
Williard K. Claassen
722 Main Street
Newton, Kansas

Methodist Church
John O. Gross
1001 Nineteenth Avenue S.
Nashville 2, Tennessee

Moravian Church in America
B. K. Horne
Linden Hall School for Girls
Lititz, Pennsylvania

National Baptist Convention
   of America
Henry A. Boyd
523 Second Avenue N.
Nashville 3, Tennessee

CHURCH BOARDS OF HIGHER EDUCATION (*Continued*)

National Baptist Convention,
U.S.A.
Benjamin E. Mays
Morehouse College
Atlanta, Georgia

Presbyterian Church, U.S.
Hunter B. Blakely
8 North Sixth Street
Richmond 9, Virginia

Presbyterian Church, U.S.A.
E. Fay Campbell
808 Witherspoon Building
Philadelphia 7, Pennsylvania

Protestant Episcopal Church
Roger Blanchard
281 Fourth Avenue
New York 10, New York

Reformed Church in America
Bernard J. Mulder
156 Fifth Avenue
New York 10, New York

United Lutheran Church in
America
Gould Wickey
2633 16th Street N.W.
Washington, D. C.

United Presbyterian Church of
North America
Lee Edwin Walker
209 Ninth Street
Pittsburgh 22, Pennsylvania

Other churches that have Boards of Higher Education not affiliated
with the NATIONAL COUNCIL:

American Lutheran Church
William L. Young
57 East Main Street
Columbus, Ohio

Brethren in Christ Church
Ervin W. Thomas
Nappanee, Indiana

Church of Latter Day Saints
Ernest L. Wilkinson
Provo, Utah

Cumberland Presbyterian Church
Ernest Gross
Dyersburg, Tennessee

Free Methodist Church
Charles V. Fairbairn
McPherson, Kansas

Lutheran Missouri Synod Church
Walter F. Wolbrecht
210 N. Broadway
St. Louis 2, Missouri

Seventh Day Adventist Church
E. C. Cossentine
6840 Eastern Avenue N.W.
Takoma Park
Washington 12, D. C.

Seventh Day Baptist Church
Neel D. Mills
P.O. Box 742
Alfred, New York

Southern Baptist Church
R. Orin Cornett
127 Ninth Ave. North
Nashville 5, Tennessee

United Danish Evangelical
Lutheran Church in America
Alvin M. Petersen
1200 N. 37th Street
Lincoln, Nebraska

Wesleyan Methodist Church of
America
Roy S. Nicholson
330 East Onondaga Street
Syracuse 2, New York

The National Catholic Educational Association includes in its membership the universities, colleges, parochial elementary and secondary schools, a large organization that rivals in attendance at annual meetings the record of the National Education Association. There is a well-staffed division of the Association known as the College and University Department. The Director of this department is the Right Reverend Monsignor Frederick G. Hochwalt, whose office is at 1785 Massachusetts Avenue, N.W., Washington, D. C.

This College and University Department operates through regional divisions which in turn have annual meetings. The department issues an informative and inspirational journal. Its executive committee holds regular meetings in connection with the annual meeting of the Association of American Colleges.

In the latest report issued by the College and University Department, data compiled for 1952-53, is to be found not only the list of approved member colleges which has been given in Chapter IX, but also statistics on courses offered particularly in the field of religion. Every Catholic college requires its students to take at least one course in religion. Throughout the years this group has been protagonistic for the liberal arts and sciences.

The serious concern of the various church groups in their education programs is evidenced by the fact that the Board of Higher Education of the Church of the Latter Day Saints is composed of their twelve apostles. Up to the Quadrennium beginning in 1952, all the thirty-seven Bishops of the Methodist Church served with other clergymen and a large number of distinguished laymen on their board of education.

The state and independent colleges and universities are not unmindful of their responsibilities in the area of religion. Many of them have regular courses in religion. All of them welcome church foundations for their students. There is a strong organization for

Jewish students known as the Hillel Foundation; the Catholics maintain Newman Clubs; the Methodists, Wesley Foundations; many of the other churches maintain "Student Associations." There are also flourishing College Young Men and Young Women's Christian Associations.

The combined efforts of the religious forces in the church-related colleges as well as in the independent and state-supported institutions are constantly needed to keep our nation on the path to the goal of the early settlers and founding fathers.

CHAPTER XIII

The Church College Tomorrow

A summation of the impact of the colleges established by the church is in order before observations are made concerning their future. Throughout the previous chapters is to be found ample evidence of their contribution to the leadership given in all realms—state, church, the professions, industry, home life, and social improvements. The church colleges have maintained a high level of culture and have played a leading role in elevating the standards of living in the United States so as to create not only admiration and imitation but also envy and caviling in other countries.

It is to be noted that these results arrive naturally when the ideals of many church colleges are made crystal clear in the mottoes placed on their seals by their founders. Pro christo et republica is the motto of one well-known college whose myriad alumni have attained distinction as clergymen, and in all types of other professions and in industry. These alumni have held high office in national, state, and county government. Many colleges can boast of similar mottoes with similar contributions of leadership in all realms of human endeavor. The idea is well summarized in the refrain of a nationally known college glee club whose last number of a program usually concludes with the phrase: For God, for Country, and for Yale.

The church-related colleges blazed the trail in organizing and developing strong professional schools. Some still maintain outstanding schools of Law, Medicine, Engineering, Journalism, Fine Arts, as well as Theology which is their obvious responsibility. They have set the pace over the years in elevating standards for teacher education. They still educate a great share of teachers employed in all levels of instruction. The leadership of the church colleges in the realm of standards is outlined briefly in Chapter I in the section referring to the organization of the Regional Accrediting Associations.

With the tremendous increase of persons of college age and interests expected during the next decade the church colleges must and will continue to play a leading role. Later in this chapter it will be shown how they can meet this challenge. Obviously much extra expense will be entailed, but these colleges have met and solved emergencies before and can and will do so again. With much better support from the church and their alumni, and with increasing aid from industry, they will continue to educate many of the leaders of our great country and of the world.

The churches of the United States have over the years been highly successful in educating leaders in foreign lands through the well-known colleges they have established there. Notable are the American universities in Beirut and Cairo, Robert College and its co-ordinate Woman's College in Istanbul, Yenching and some fifteen other universities and colleges in China, Isabella Thoburn College in India, and many other schools and colleges in Syria, Iraq, Iran, and other sections of the Near and Middle East, in Africa, and throughout Central and South America. Now that the China colleges have disappeared behind the Bamboo Curtain their United Boards have boldly proceeded to organize high grade colleges in Formosa, Hong Kong, and Singapore. Most promising is the future of the new Japanese International Christian University at Tokyo.

Higher Education for American Democracy is the title of a book, highly thought-provoking, issued in 1947 as the Report of a Commission on Higher Education appointed by President Harry S. Truman. In the section on "Financing Higher Education" occurs this disturbing observation:

Although the financial program for the future of higher education outlined in this chapter contemplates a balanced budget for the privately controlled institutions, this Commission is fully aware of the serious financial problems facing many of these institutions. The Commission is also aware of the fact that its proposals for a great expansion of higher education in publicly controlled institutions may make it extremely difficult for many private institutions to survive. A system of tuition-free education up through the fourteenth year and relatively low fees above the fourteenth year and in graduate and professional schools of publicly controlled institutions will undoubtedly force many of the weaker private schools out of existence and profoundly affect the whole pattern of private institutional support. Furthermore, the strengthening of publicly supported institutions, as recommended by this Commission, may have the effect of further increasing the gradual upward trend in the flow of private benefactions to state institutions.*

The Commission's Report, among many recommendations for federal aid to higher education, advises strongly against such assistance to privately controlled colleges. Here is its philosophy on this point:

Sound public policy demands, furthermore, that State and local public educational bodies be able to exercise at all times the right to review and control educational policies in any institution or agency for which public monies are appropriated and expended. Public responsibility for support of education implies public responsibility for the policies which are supported. It follows, therefore, that the acceptance of public funds by any institution, public or private, should carry with it the acceptance of the right of the people as a whole to exercise review and control of the educational policies and procedures of that institution. Such acceptance by privately controlled institutions would, in the opinion of this Commission, tend to destroy the competitive advantages and free inquiry which they have established and which are so important in providing certain safeguards to freedom. It would be contrary to the best interests of these institutions as well as to those of society in general.**

These observations, supported by substantiating statistics, are a challenge to all friends of the four-year college. The demise of the independent college would be the death-knell of free enterprise.

The strength of a nation depends upon the strength of its citizens. The strength of its citizens depends upon the amount, quality, and type of their education.

* Pages 46-47.
** Page 58.

As indicated in Chapter II, all but one of the nine surviving colonial colleges were founded under the direct influence of the church. There is strong evidence that that one college, now called the University of Pennsylvania, received considerable impetus in its origin from that eloquent Methodist revivalist, George Whitefield. The record shows that of the first 120 colleges founded in our country, about 100 were established under church auspices. It should be a matter of real regret that so many of these colleges have slipped from their moorings and have severed all church connections.

In the *Education Directory* issued by the United States Office of Education in 1954, there are listed 751 accredited four-year liberal arts colleges in the United States. Of this number 189 are state supported. These include the college departments of the state universities, land-grant colleges, and municipal colleges and universities. Thus there are 562 other colleges, including those which are component parts of universities which are independent of control and support by a state or municipality. Of these 292 are affiliated with some Protestant church group, 149 are founded, controlled, and supported by the Roman Catholic Church, 2 by Jewish groups, with the remaining 119 independent of church and state control.

In spite of the fact that the independent institutions, which include the church-related colleges, outnumber the state-supported institutions by a ratio of nearly three to one, until recently the enrollments in each of the two types of colleges stood about the same. During 1954-55 there were about one million and a half students in state-supported colleges and universities and slightly more than another million in those operated independently of the state, with a total enrollment of over 2,500,000. This is an increase of nearly 2,000,000 since 1920, or 1000 per cent advance in thirty-five years. There is good evidence that college attendance will go beyond 4,000,000 within the next decade.

The phenomenal growth of college enrollment in the past fifty years is indicated by the statistics in the table below which were furnished by the United States Office of Education. No other nation in the world can begin to adduce a comparable record.

TOTAL ENROLLMENT IN HIGHER EDUCATION 1900-50

1900.........238,210	1930.........1,082,443
1910.........339,578	1940.........1,499,109
1920.........531,339	1950.........2,439,910

The two types of institutions of higher education have budgets of about the same size. Because of lack of campus space and buildings in addition to a desire in many cases to remain small, the independent colleges have deliberately set a limit to their enrollments. Many are obliged to do so because of limitations of dormitory space, others out of preference.

This dual system of higher education which has prevailed in our country has been the chief bulwark of our Republic since its establishment. In no other section of the world, save in some parts of the British Commonwealth of Nations, does such a system of higher education exist. For example, in France the few universities operated by the Roman Catholic Church are not permitted to confer degrees. Their graduates must pass examinations at a state university in order to receive their degrees. Even those ancient bulwarks of freedom, Oxford and Cambridge Universities, are now coming under the control of the government through receipt of annual sizable grants for operating expenses.

The two types of higher institutions in our country are needed to complement and supplement each other. There is little jealousy or friction between the administrators of the two types. From time to time distinguished state university presidents publish pronouncements pleading for the strengthening of the independent colleges and universities. Similar sentiments are shared and expressed by leading educators of the independent group.

Milton Eisenhower, the well-known president of Pennsylvania State University, stated in his presidential address to the Annual Meeting of the Land-Grant College Association, held in Washington in November 1953:

It is the private institutions that set traditions, the standards of academic freedom in America. And because the private institutions do set and maintain these standards, we of the public institutions also enjoy the benefit of such freedom. If private institutions were ever to disappear, the politicians would take over the universities, and there would then be neither educational freedom nor any other kind.

Similar opinions, even stronger in content, are voiced in the following two paragraphs taken from the early part of a Charter Day Address delivered at the University of California at Los Angeles on March 25, 1955, by President Gordon Gray of the University of North Carolina. In commenting on the tremendous pressure that will face state universities by the evident early increase in enrollment of college students, President Gray made these observations:

This necessarily raises questions, as I have indicated, about the maintenance of what I call the dual system of higher education. As a purely selfish matter, I think it is apparent that we in public institutions would hope that independent institutions can absorb at least a good part of the additional load; but I am concerned about the private institution on other grounds. It seems to be vital that we must preserve in a viable way this system. It would be an offensive exercise in the expression of fundamentals to point out the differences and similarities between the two types of institutions; nor need I go out of my way to defend the private institution. I should like to remind you, however, that, as we seek to meet our old functions in higher education and as we accept new ones, the private institutions have certain advantages, which the tax supported institution cannot emulate, but which must survive as guides and challenges to us. . . .

You will pardon me for a statement of conviction which may have very little practical import in the light of facts as we face them. However, even as President of the oldest state university in America, I would have to say that, if I were presented with a choice between a system of private higher education and a system of public higher education, I would select the former. Fortunately, no such alternative is presented. Indeed, my concern is that we do all we can to avoid having the other choice thrust upon us by circumstances. You should not suppose from this that I agree with those who assert that, because the principles of taxation affect the private institutions only indirectly, they should have exclusive access to gifts and grants. Indeed, I believe that state universities should continue to share in private philanthropy, both on practical and moral grounds.

The reverse of the shield is not so encouraging. Not far from Chicago not long ago the president of one of our greatest state universities was given peremptory permission to resign *instanter*.

Vivid in the memory of the author remain some jarring experiences with governors of two Southern states when he was secretary-treasurer of the Southern Association of Colleges and Secondary Schools. Thanks to the leadership of this group, standards were maintained in the state colleges and the governors failed of re-election.

The rapid trend of events in recent years forces one to conclude that a materialistic outlook of life is predominating in the colleges over one that would keep the spirit preeminent. Responsibility for this trend can fairly be laid at the doors of both types of higher institutions. It behooves those in the church-related colleges to think more seriously of the ideals of their founding fathers.

The best education for democracy and freedom will, on the college level, depend mostly on three factors—faculty, curriculum, and financial support. Campus equipment, library and laboratory facilities are taken for granted.

Whether the student leaves his *alma mater* with ideals predominantly materialistic rather than spiritual will depend to a great extent upon the faculty. The faculty will be largely responsible if the alumnus goes forth educated to think and act with honesty, with precision, with justice, with charity. The ideal teacher will be unselfish, patient, full of understanding, desirous to encourage both the laggard and the ambitious. For his arduous duties he will be inspired to have the best possible preparation for his highly rewarding task. He will ever continue to study and keep himself fully prepared.

A curriculum that overstresses offerings in any particular area is lopsided and augurs ill for a prospective leader or an educated follower in a free democracy. In this Atomic Age there seem to be threatening tendencies of an undue stress on studies in the natural sciences on one hand and an overweening interest in the social studies on the other hand. In the United States, courses in the humanities, religion (frankly called "theology" in the Catholic colleges), and the fine arts have too often and too long taken a back seat for the social and natural sciences, particularly since the dawn of the twentieth century.

The tide has been turned somewhat in the past decade. Notable influences in this direction have been the results of the studies of the Commission on Liberal Education of the Association of American Colleges (published in its *Bulletin* for May 1943), in the well-publicized Harvard Report, and in many other less advertised reports of studies in this area, issued by faculties of other distinguished colleges and universities.

Great emphasis on courses in the scientific and technological areas comes from industry in its restless search for engineers of many types. Further pressure comes from lures in the form of multitudinous scholarship and fellowship grants for students majoring in the sciences. Even our federal government has voted liberal largesse in the establishment of the National Science Foundation, ostensibly for the development of scientific personnel for the national defense.

Many fear a tendency to "creeping socialism" among leaders in the teaching of the social sciences. These feel that if our country is to remain free and democratic free enterprise must be allowed to thrive. Government checks and controls on local and national levels will be necessary: government ownership will mean political despotism.

Encouraging are strong pronouncements in recent years by leaders in the great professions of medicine, law, and ministry that they prefer candidates who have had a well-rounded undergraduate course rather than one slanted for their particular type of professional school.

The following extract from a letter written by John Paul Jones, our first Admiral, to the Naval Committee of the Continental Congress, September 14, 1775, is still valuable and timely:

It is by no means enough that an officer of the Navy should be a capable mariner. He must be that, of course, but also a great deal more. He should be as well a gentleman of liberal education, refined manners, punctilious courtesy, and the nicest sense of personal honour.

He should not only be able to express himself clearly and with force in his own language, both with tongue and pen, but he should also be versed in French and Spanish.

This early and appropriate advice lends support to an ideal long held by the author that the United States Military, Naval, and Air

Force Academies should be postgraduate rather than undergraduate institutions. At present these fine schools duplicate to a large extent what is being done in the better colleges of liberal arts and sciences. The "Academy" graduates now go to the better-known universities for advanced work that will be helpful, nay necessary, for their success as officers. By this proposed plan the federal government could contract its astronomical appropriations for the military and all the people could expect to obtain more readily a better-educated leadership in times of emergency.

To obtain and maintain a competent faculty of sufficient size to administer a worth-while curriculum adequate financial resources are needed. The usual sources of income include endowment interest, student fees, grants from church groups or state and municipal treasuries, and most recently in practically all colleges and universities annual gifts from alumni and other friends.

In face of rising costs and shrinking endowment income, the colleges are learning to balance their budgets through these annual gifts from alumni and friends. Thrilling is the spectacle of such universities as Yale, Princeton, Notre Dame, and Dartmouth receiving a million dollars or more in their annual appeals to the alumni.

Within the past quarter of a century church leaders have responded much more sympathetically to appeals for support of their church-related colleges. Too long had they exhibited an attitude of inertia or indifference to the fate of their foundlings. No wonder that so many of the colleges established by "blood, sweat and tears" of consecrated church men of yesteryear slipped off into the group of independent institutions.

Notable indeed has been the growth in annual contributions to the annual budgets of their affiliated colleges on the part of the Southern Baptists, Lutherans, and Methodists. Increase of financial support is particularly noteworthy among the Southern Baptists, who are concentrating their efforts on single institutions in individual states. As an illustration of increased support I can cite a well-known Methodist college that now receives about $90,000 annually from the church whereas twenty years ago it was glad to get $3500 a year, with plenty of free advice and some unjust criticism thrown in for good measure.

There is additional information to the effect that a number of colleges affiliated with the various Lutheran bodies receive annual contributions that average one dollar per communing member. A well-known Presbyterian college in the South received in the current year nearly one dollar per member from each of its four supporting synods, a tidy total that would more than balance its annual budget for operating expenses.

Many family Foundations have been established within the past 50 years with the chief purpose of aiding higher education. The largest of these include the Carnegie Corporation, the Rockefeller and the Ford Foundations. The first two have from time to time made conspicuous grants toward increasing college endowments. During 1955 and 1956 the Ford Foundation proposes to distribute $50,000,000 to colleges on a matching basis for additional endowment funds for the express purpose of raising faculty salaries.

Under the leadership of the Commission on Colleges and Industry of the Association of American Colleges, there has developed in recent years annual contributions of increasing dimensions by corporations. Heretofore corporations have been increasingly liberal in making grants to higher education for specific projects, generally of a research nature, from which they will receive some benefit in return. With legal approval in most states, corporations are starting to make annual donations for the general operative expenses of the colleges. A healthful sign for both the corporation and the college is the mushroom growth over the past three years of state college foundations working in full cooperation in search for corporate gifts.

These college foundations have been organized by some thirty states. They operate efficiently through college presidents going in pairs to visit corporation executives, so far with increasingly encouraging results.

The Standard Oil Company of Ohio has been cooperating notably with the college foundation in that state. The Standard Oil of Indiana made a grant of $150,000 during the current year to be divided among the accredited colleges in the eleven states in which the corporation does business. The Union Carbide and Carbon Corporation has established a plan whereby in selected colleges $600 scholarships will be awarded to competent and worthy students with the same amount for each student donated to the college. The Ford Motor Company has had for some years a similar plan which was limited in operation to children of its employees. During 1954 the United States Steel Corporation distributed $700,000 among approved colleges in the area of its operations. Another significant program has been initiated in 1954 by the Standard Oil Company of New Jersey, with their distribution of $450,000 to 138 selected accredited colleges and universities widely scattered throughout the country for use in the current operating expenses of their liberal arts divisions.

Another announcement made late in 1954 is the plan of the General Electric Company, effective in 1955, to match contributions up to $1,000 per annum made to colleges by their alumni who are in the employ of the company. Of the 23,000 college graduates on the rolls of General Electric many will surely be spurred to aid their alma maters, particularly with the encouragement given by the federal government in the remission of taxes on the first 30 per cent of their income if given to such a type of institution. If one tenth of their college graduates should be inspired to accept the General Electric challenge, the colleges would thus receive four times as much as they would from the other corporations just mentioned. The contributors must have been with the company a year and must make an outright gift, not a pledge, to the accredited college from which they had earned their baccalaureate degrees. It is devoutly hoped by the colleges that such a plan will become contagious.

The Westinghouse Educational Foundation announced on March 10, 1955 a $5,000,000 financial aid program to colleges and universities. Their expanded plan of aid to higher education will provide: (1) outright gifts of $1,700,000 to selected schools for buildings and equipment, (2) $650,000 toward annual operating expenses of selected institutions not receiving state support for such expenses, (3) the balance for use in scholarship and fellowship grants and for support of professorships.

Early in 1955 the General Motors Corporation announced a program of aid to higher education which will total $2,000,000 per annum. Scholarships will range from $800 to $2000 a year; they will be distributed among 306 colleges and universities, including state-controlled as well as independent institutions. Other corporations that have recently joined the movement to come to the aid of under-graduate liberal education include Armstrong Cork Company, Columbia Broadcasting System, General Foods Corporation, Walter Kidde and Company, and Merrill Lynch, Pierce, Fenner and Beane.

The following excerpts from a letter sent a small church-related college under date of November 4, 1954, is doubly significant in that it shows (1) a growing realization on the part of individual leaders of the value of this type of college and (2) a potent stimulus to the college authorities to expect other and continuing strong support for their enterprises:

Under the impetus of the wide publicity given the subject in the recent past, my company has become very interested in Corporate Aid to Education. We have always been appreciative of the contribution made to the religious, economic, social, and political life of our country by the graduates of the privately endowed and church-related liberal arts institutions. We have only recently become cognizant of the need of such institutions for financial assistance if their fine educational contributions were to be continued.

In my company there is a strong feeling that an industrial organization owes a debt to the economic system under which it can operate and thrive. This debt can in part be paid by the corporation by advocating good corporate citizenship. Such good citizenship would dictate financial assistance to education; particularly to education as represented by the privately endowed liberal arts colleges which are doing such a fine job of training future leaders of this country.

With the above premise in mind, we have conducted a survey to determine the colleges in our area worthy of our help. I am pleased that the institution which you head ranked high on our list. Therefore, I am enclosing [our] check in the amount of $3,000 as an unrestricted gift to your institution with the best wishes of the officers and directors of this company.

Most encouraging in this area is the establishment in New York, on November 1, 1953, of the Council for Financial Aid to Education, Inc., with the avowed purpose of promoting mutual understanding between American business corporations, labor organizations, foundations and citizens groups, and the nation's colleges and universities, toward encouraging more general private support of higher education. The trustees of the Council comprise outstanding leaders in industry and successful college and university presidents.

Acceptance of federal funds by independent colleges will mean the beginning of the end of free enterprise. Of course, this observation does not apply to government grants on a *quid pro quo* basis: a college could receive from the government as well as from a corporation or an individual a grant for research or for some other special project. In this connection it is interesting to note that the federal government in the past year made a larger total of grants for research to independent universities, while the corporations gave a larger total of funds for research to state universities.

In the past few years a great hue and cry has been raised about the overlooking of the better high school graduate who should be going to college. It would seem that this matter has been somewhat overstressed. The admissions officers of the accredited colleges can and should become more strict in keeping out the less competent students. The more capable with any ambition at all can find ways and means of enrolling in college far more readily than in any previous era.

Many philanthropic persons have established scholarship foundations. There are a large number of funds set up especially to loan money to college students. At the present time some of these whose funds total up in the millions are not having sufficient requests to use up the monies available at the moment. The ambitious boy or girl of today who desires a college education should be reminded of the old adage: "Where there is a will, there is a way."

Excellent ideals for the church-related college of tomorrow may be found in the following suggestions of D. Elton Trueblood, professor of philosophy and religion at Earlham College, Richmond, Indiana. He was led to make these observations after long experience as student and teacher in such large and small institutions as William Penn and Guilford Colleges and Stanford, Harvard, and Johns Hopkins Universities. He has also served as adviser on religious activities for the United States Information Agency.

A Ten-Point Platform for a College

1. *Adult Education.* Not juvenile at any point. Resist the tendency to have too many games and too many activities of any kind. Colleges now

compete with themselves in overactivity so that the drive for maturity is frustrated.

2. *A National Institution.* The college should serve the entire nation and not be sectional in any way, either in point of view or in selection of students.

3. *A Standard of Excellence.* The college must resist the tendency toward mediocrity at every point. If the college is not good it is not worth supporting.

4. *Emphasize Great Teaching.* Find great teachers and set them free to teach. Put more emphasis on teaching than on methods of organization; minimize committee work and thus set the teachers free to teach.

5. *Produce a Responsible Society.* Avoid both empty freedom and regimentation. Eliminate small rules such as the smoking rule and put the whole emphasis on becoming responsible persons.

6. *Develop a Passionate Devotion to the Ideal.* The college must reject the position of cold detachment. The religious conviction, without which there is no firm ideological basis, must become a matter of unapologetic witness.

7. *Coordinate Education Between Men and Women.* The education of men and women must be equal but not identical. There should be special courses for men and special courses for women with abundant opportunity for both to be in close contact with persons who can serve as models for their future careers.

8. *Emphasize the Residential Aspect.* There must not be any complete day students. The tuition should cover the cost of daily lunch as well as the use of study rooms in the dormitories. Once a week there should be a really dignified dinner for the entire community with musical and other programs and with the elimination of any competition for time.

9. *Graduation by Achievement.* Because the credit system is so open to abuse we must not allow anyone to graduate by the mere accumulation of credits. Genuine evidence of competence in both breadth and depth must be assured.

10. *Vocational Liberalism.* The conflict between vocational education and liberal education is both unreal and unnecessary. The college must seek the motivation which the idea of vocation provides and the breadth incurred in the promotion of the liberal arts and sciences.

All types of colleges have the obligation to encourage their alumni to be more concerned about their duties as citizens. If educated people would exercise their sovereign rights of suffrage, the demagogues and blatant leaders of selfish minorities would promptly be put in the background. The colleges must emphasize the importance of participation by every alumnus in local, state, and national affairs. He more than others could and should vote intelligently. When occasion arises he should not hesitate to run for office. Further, he should be intelligent in world affairs; the hegemony of our nation in international politics literally requires that he consider himself a world citizen.

To sum up, the main mission of a church-related college would be to turn out men and women who would live the more abundant, the more cheerful and richer life; to educate those who will become leaders, imbued with the spirit of the Golden Rule, in all professions and human activities, in a word those who would put "service above self"; to inspire all who pass through its portals to become active citizens in local, state, national, and international politics.

The church-related college should and will continue to be a veritable pharos "amid the encircling gloom" resultant from the threats of atom and hydrogen bombs.

BIBLIOGRAPHY

[Many data have been compiled from college catalogs]

ADAMS, HERBERT B., *Thomas Jefferson and the University of Virginia*, Washington, 1888.

ALEXANDER, ARCHIBALD, *Biographical Sketches of the Founder and Principal Alumni of Log College*, Philadelphia, 1851.

BEACH, ARTHUR G., *A Pioneer College, The Story of Marietta*, Chicago, 1935.

BELDEN, ALBERT D., *George Whitefield, The Awakener*, London, 1930.

BLACKMAR, FRANK W., *Higher Education in Kansas*, Washington, 1900.

BROWN, HALLIE Q., *Pen Pictures of Pioneers of Wilberforce*, Xenia, Ohio, 1937.

BULLOCK, HENRY MORTON, *A History of Emory University 1836-1936*, Nashville, Tennessee, 1936.

BUSH, GEORGE GARY, *Harvard, the First American University*, Boston, 1886.

———, *History of Education in New Hampshire*, Washington, 1898.

———, *History of Education in Vermont*, Washington, 1900.

CABANISS, JAMES ALLEN, *A History of the University of Mississippi*, University of Mississippi Press, 1949.

CASSIDY, F. P., *Catholic College Foundations and Developments in the United States, 1677-1850*, Washington, D. C., 1924.

CHAFFIN, NORA CAMPBELL, *Trinity College, 1839-1892, The Beginnings of Duke University*, Durham, North Carolina, 1950.

CHEYNEY, EDWARD P., *History of the University of Pennsylvania 1740-1940*, Philadelphia, 1940.

CHRISTENBERRY, DANIEL P., *A Semi-Centennial History of the Southern University*, Birmingham, Alabama, 1908.

CLARK, ELMER T., *The Small Sects in America*, rev. ed., Nashville, Tennessee, 1937.

CLARK, W. G., *History of Education in Alabama*, Washington, 1889.

COOPER, W. RAYMOND, *Southwestern at Memphis, 1848-1948,* Richmond, Virginia, 1949.

COULTER, E. MERTON, *College Life in the Old South,* Athens, Georgia, 1951.

DANSBY, R. BALDWIN, *A Brief History of Jackson College,* Jackson, Mississippi, 1953.

DEMAREST, WILLIAM H. S., *A History of Rutgers College, 1766-1924,* New Brunswick, 1924.

DEXTER, FRANKLIN B., *Founding of Yale College,* New Haven, 1916.

EARNEST, ERNEST, *Academic Procession—An Informal History of the American College, 1636 to 1953,* Indianapolis-New York, 1953.

EASTERBY, J. H., *A History of the College of Charleston,* Charleston, South Carolina, 1935.

ELLISON, RHODA COLEMAN, *History of Huntingdon College 1854-1954,* University, Alabama, 1954.

ERBACHER, SEBASTIAN A., *Catholic Higher Education for Men in the United States, 1850-66,* Washington, 1931.

ERSKINE, JOHN, *My Life as a Teacher,* Philadelphia, 1948.

FAY, EDWIN W., *The History of Education in Louisiana,* Washington, 1898.

FERRIER, WILLIAM WARREN, *Origin and Development of the University of California,* Berkeley, California, 1930.

————, *Henry Durant, First President, University of California;* the New Englander who came to California with college on the brain, Berkeley, California, 1942.

FISHER, SYDNEY G., *Church Colleges,* Philadelphia, 1895.

FITZPATRICK, EDWARD A., *The Autobiography of a College (Mount Mary College),* Milwaukee, 1939.

————, *LaSalle, Patron of all Teachers,* Milwaukee, 1951.

FLETCHER, ROBERT S., *A History of Oberlin College From Its Foundation Through the Civil War,* Oberlin, 1943.

FRANKLIN, FABIAN, *The Life of Daniel Coit Gilman,* New York, 1910.

FREEMAN, DOUGLAS S., *Robert E. Lee, A Biography,* 4 volumes, New York, 1934-36.

FRENCH, JOHN CALVIN, *A History of the University Founded by Johns Hopkins,* Baltimore, Maryland, 1946.

GARBER, PAUL N., *The Romance of American Methodism,* Greensboro, North Carolina, 1931.

GILBERT, DOROTHY LLOYD, *Guilford, A Quaker College,* Guilford, North Carolina, 1937.

GILMAN, DANIEL COIT, *The Launching of a University and Other Papers* (Johns Hopkins University), New York, 1906.

GODBOLD, ALBEA, *The Church College of the Old South*, Durham, 1944.

GOODSELL, CHARLES TRUE AND DUNBAR, WILLIS FREDERICK, *Centennial History of Kalamazoo College*, Kalamazoo, Michigan, 1933.

GOVAN, GILBERT E. AND LIVINGOOD, JAMES W., *The University of Chattanooga, Sixty Years*, Chattanooga, Tennessee, 1947.

GROSS, JOHN OWEN, *Cokesbury College*, Nashville, Tennessee.

HALL, THOMAS CUMING, *The Religious Background of American Culture*, Boston, 1930.

HALL, WILLIAM W., Jr., *The Small College Talks Back* (College of Idaho) New York, 1951.

HASKINS, CHARLES H. AND HULL, WILLIAM, *A History of Higher Education in Pennsylvania*, Washington, 1902.

HAUGHT, THOMAS W., *West Virginia Wesleyan College, First Fifty Years, 1890-1940*, Buckhannon, 1940.

HIGGINS, RUTH L. AND STURGEON, MARY S., *Beaver College: The First Hundred Years*, Jenkintown, Pennsylvania, 1954.

Higher Education for American Democracy: The Report of the President's Commission on Higher Education, New York, 1947.

HOLMES, D. O. W., *The Evolution of the Negro College*, New York, 1934.

HOPE, ARTHUR J., *Notre Dame, One Hundred Years*, Notre Dame, Indiana, 1943.

HOPKINS, JAMES F., *The University of Kentucky*, Lexington, 1951.

JAMES, HENRY, *Charles W. Eliot*, Cambridge, 1930.

JONES, WILLIAM CAREY, *Illustrated History of the University of California*, San Francisco, 1895.

KETLER, WEIR C., *An Adventure in Education, 75 Years of Grove City College (1876-1951)*, Grove City, Pennsylvania, 1953.

KLEIN, H. M. J., *Cedar Crest College 1867-1947*, Allentown, Pennsylvania, 1948.

———, *History of Franklin and Marshall College 1787-1948*, Lancaster, Pennsylvania, 1952.

KNIGHT AND COMMONS, *History of Higher Education in Ohio*, Washington, 1891.

KNIPP, ANNA HEUBECK AND THOMAS, THADDEUS P., *The History of Goucher College*, Baltimore, Maryland, 1938.

KROEZE, BAREND H., *A Prairie Saga (Jamestown College)*, Saint Paul, Minnesota, 1952.

LAMKIN, CHARLES FACKLER, *A Great Small College, Westminster College, Fulton, Missouri*, St. Louis, 1946.

LEWIS, A. F., *History of Higher Education in Kentucky*, Washington, 1899.

LINGLE, WALTER L., *Memories of Davidson College*, Richmond, Virginia, 1947.

MAXSON, C. H., *The Great Awakening in the Middle Colonies*, Chicago, Illinois, 1920.

MAYES, EDWARD, *History of Education in Mississippi*, Washington, 1899.

McGINNIS, FREDERICK A., *A History and an Interpretation of Wilberforce University*, Wilberforce, Ohio, 1941.

McTYEIRE, HOLLAND N., *A History of Methodism*, Nashville, 1884.

MERIWETHER, COLYER, *History of Higher Education in South Carolina*, Washington, 1888.

MERRIAM, LUCIUS S., *Higher Education in Tennessee*, Washington, 1893.

MIMS, EDWIN, *Chancellor Kirkland of Vanderbilt*, Nashville, Tennessee, 1940.

MODE, PETER G., *The Frontier Spirit in American Christianity*, New York, 1923.

MONROE, PAUL (ed.), *A Cyclopedia of Education*, New York, 1910-1913.

MONROSS, WILLIAM W., *A History of the American Episcopal Church*, Milwaukee, 1935.

MOORE, N. F., *An Historical Sketch of Columbia College*, New York, 1846.

MORISON, SAMUEL ELIOT, *Three Centuries of Harvard 1636-1936*, Cambridge, Massachusetts, 1936.

————, *The Founding of Harvard College*, Cambridge, Massachusetts, 1935.

MURRAY, DAVID, *History of Education in New Jersey*, Washington, 1899.

NELSON, NARKA, *The Western College for Women 1853-1953*, Oxford, Ohio, 1954.

NOBLE, STUART G., *A History of American Education* (Revised Edition) New York, 1954.

OTTERSBERG, GERHARD, *Wartburg College, 1852-1952*, Waverly, Iowa, 1952.

PERRY, BLISS, *And Gladly Teach*, New York, 1935.

PERRY, WILBUR DOW, *A History of Birmingham-Southern College 1856-1931*, Birmingham, Alabama, 1931.

PETERS, GEORGE L., *Dreams Come True—The Story of Culver-Stockton College*, Canton, Missouri, 1941.

PHELPS, WILLIAM LYON, *Autobiography*, New York, 1939.

PIERSON, GEORGE WILSON, *Yale College—An Educational History, 1871-1921*, New Haven, 1952.

POSEY, WALTER B., *La Grange, Alabama's Earliest College*, Birmingham, Alabama, 1933.

POWELL, LYMAN P., *History of Education in Delaware*, Washington, 1893.

RAMMELKAMP, CHARLES HENRY, *Illinois College, A Centennial History 1829-1929*, Yale University Press, 1928.

REEVES, F. W. AND RUSSELL, J. D., *College Organization and Administration, A Report of a Survey of Disciples Colleges*, Indianapolis, Indiana, 1929.

RUSH, BENJAMIN, *A Letter Describing the Consecration of the German College at Lancaster*, Lancaster, Pennsylvania, 1945.

SCHMIDT, GEORGE P., *The Old Time College President*, New York, 1930.

SHARPLESS, ISAAC, *The American College*, New York, 1915.

SHAW, CORNELIA REBEKAH, *Davidson College*, New York, 1921.

SHINN, JOSIAH H., *History of Education in Arkansas*, Washington, 1900.

SLATER, JOHN ROTHWELL, *Rhees of Rochester*, New York, 1946.

SMITH, ERNEST ASHTON, *Allegheny—A Century of Education, 1815-1915*, Meadville, Pennsylvania, 1915.

SMYTHE, GEORGE FRANKLIN, *Kenyon College, Its First Century*, New Haven, 1924.

SNYDER, HENRY NELSON, *An Educational Odyssey*, Nashville, 1947.

STEINER, BERNARD C., *History of Education in Connecticut*, Washington, 1893.

———, *History of Education in Maryland*, Washington, 1894.

SWEET, WILLIAM WARREN, *Religion on the American Frontier* (Presbyterians, Methodists, Baptists, 1783-1840), New York, 1936.

———, *The Rise of Methodism in the West*, New York, 1920.

———, *The Story of Religions in America*, New York, 1920.

———, *Methodism in American History*, Revised and Enlarged Edition, Nashville, 1953.

TAYLOR, JAMES B., *Memoir of Reverend Luther Rice*, Nashville, Tennessee, 1841.

TEWKSBURY, D. G., *The Founding of American Colleges and Universities Before the Civil War, With Particular Reference to the Religious Influences Bearing Upon the College Movement*, New York, 1932.

THOSTENSEON, JOSEPHINE E., *One Hundred Years of Service 1853-1953: A History of Central*, Pella, Iowa, 1953.

THWING, CHARLES F., *The American College in American Life*, New York, 1897.

——, *The American College and University*, New York, 1935.

——, *A History of Higher Education in America*, New York, 1906.

TOLMAN, WILLIAM H., *History of Higher Education in Rhode Island*, Washington, 1894.

TREUDLEY, MARY BOSWORTH, *Prelude to the Future, The First Hundred Years of Hiram College*, New York, 1950.

VANDERBILT UNIVERSITY, *Proceedings of the Semi-Centennial 1875-1925*, Nashville, Tennessee, 1925.

WAGNER, CHARLES A., Harvard, *Four Centuries and Freedoms*, New York, 1950.

WALLACE, DAVID DUNCAN, *History of Wofford College 1854-1949*, Nashville, 1951.

WATSON, ELMO SCOTT, *The Illinois Wesleyan Story 1850-1950*, Bloomington, Illinois, 1950.

WATTERS, MARY, *The First Hundred Years of MacMurray College*, Springfield, Illinois, 1947.

WHELAN, JAMES F., *Catholic Colleges of the United States of America At the Middle of the Twentieth Century*, Loyola University, New Orleans, Louisiana, 1954.

WHITE, MARIAN CHURCHILL, *A History of Barnard College*, New York, 1954.

WICKERSHAM, JAMES PYLE, *A History of Education in Pennsylvania*, Lancaster, 1886.

William and Mary, The History of the College of (including the general catalogue), *from its foundation, 1693 to 1870*, Baltimore, 1870.

WILLS, ELBERT VAUGHAN, *The Growth of American Higher Education, Liberal, Professional and Technical*, Philadelphia, 1936.

WOOD, GEORGE BACON, *Early History of the University of Pennsylvania*, Philadelphia, 1896.

WOODBURN, JAMES A., *History of Indiana University*, Bloomington, 1940.

WOODY, WALTER THOMAS, *The History of Women's Education in the U. S.*, Lancaster, Pennsylvania, 1929.

WOOLERY, W. K., *Bethany Years*, Huntington, West Virginia, 1941.

YOUNG, M. NORVEL, *A History of Colleges Established and Controlled by Members of the Churches of Christ*, Kansas City, Missouri, 1949.

INDEX

Abilene Christian College, 128
Academy of the New Church, 131
Adams, John, 16
Adams, Samuel, 16
Add Ran College, 82
Adrian College, 88, 98
Adrian, Roberts, 55, 87
Agnes Scott College, 106, 107
Akron, University of, 163, 164
Alabama Agricultural and Mechanical College, 139
Alabama Polytechnic Institute, 139, 140
Alabama State Teachers College (Florence), 141
Alabama, University of, 93
Albertus Magnus College, 119
Albion College, 87
Albright College, 132
Alden, Timothy, 93
Alderson-Broaddus College, 67
Alfred University, 73, 98
Alison, Francis, 39, 148, 149
Allegheny College, 87, 93, 94, 95, 104, 105
Allen, Richard, 99
Allen University, 98
Alma College, 102
Alverno College, 122
American International College, 136
American University, 87, 96
Amherst College, 3, 6, 30, 51, 57, 76
Anderson College (Indiana), 130
Anderson, Martin Brewer, 69
Andrew, Samuel, 23, 25
Andrews, Elisha B., 50
Angell, James B., 51
Angell, James R., 24
Anna Maria College for Women, 123
Annhurst College, 119
Antioch College, 51, 139
Aquinas College, 119
Arkadelphia Methodist College, 144
Arkansas Baptist College, 71
Arkansas College, 106
Asbury College, 96
Asbury, Francis, 67, 90, 91, 99
Ashland College, 126, 127
Association of American Colleges, ix, x, 5, 176, 177, 178, 182, 191, 193
Association of American Universities, 5

Association of Land-Grant Colleges and Universities, 5, 188
Association of Urban Universities, 5
Assumption College, 117
Athens College, 87, 143
Atlanta University, 76
Atlantic Christian College, 81
Atlantic Union College, 136
Atwater, Jeremiah, 30
Augsburg College and Theological Seminary, 85
Augusta College, 77, 92, 94, 154
Augustana College (Illinois), 85
Augustana College (South Dakota), 85
Aurora College, 126
Austin College, 106
Ayer, Charles, 158, 159

Backus, Azel, 30
Bacon College, 80, 154
Baker University, 87
Baldwin, Abraham, 27
Baldwin, E. W., 30
Baldwin-Wallace College, 87
Barat College of the Sacret Heart, 125
Barbour, Clarence A., 50
Bard College, 133
Barrett, Luther G., 159
Barry College, 119
Bartlett, Samuel Colcord, 65
Bascom, Henry B., 92, 153
Bates College, 67, 68
Baylor University, 71
Beard, Charles A., 63
Beaver College, 102
Bee, Thomas Jr., 172
Beecher, Lyman, 2, 30
Belcher, Jonathan, 33, 34
Belhaven College, 107
Bellarmine College (Kentucky), 119
Bellevue College, 161, 162
Belmont Abbey College, 117
Belmont College, 71, 112
Beloit College, 3, 31, 74, 75, 178
Benedict College, 67
Benedictine Heights College, 118
Bennett College, 87
Berea College, 77
Berkeley Bible Seminary, 82
Berkeley, George, 26, 43, 59, 60, 146

Berkeley, William, 19
Bessie Tift College, 71
Bethany College (Kansas), 85
Bethany College (West Virginia), 80, 81, 169
Bethany-Peniel College, 130
Bethel College (Kansas), 133
Bethel College (Minnesota), 67, 71
Bethel College (Oregon), 166
Bethel College (Tennessee), 110, 111
Bethune-Cookman College, 87
Billings Polytechnic Institute, 77
Bird, Benjamin O., 157
Birmingham-Southern College, 87, 95, 140
Bishop College, 68
Blackburn College, 102
Blair, James, 19, 20
Blair, Samuel, 32
Blakely, Hunter B., 181
Blanchard, Charles A., 101
Blanchard, Jonathan, 101
Blanchard, Roger, 181
Blount College, 170
Blue Mountain College, 71
Blue Ridge College, 127
Bluffton College, 133
Bond, W. F., 160
Boston College, 120
Boston University, 87, 159
Bowdoin College, 76
Bowen, Nathaniel, 171
Bowman, John B., 155
Boyd, Henry A., 190
Boyle, Robert, 21
Brandeis University, 133
Braxton, Carter, 22
Briar Cliff College, 123
Bridgewater College, 127
Brigham Young University, 129
Brooks, Sampson W., 157
Brown, B. Warren, 177
Brown, Francis, 61, 65
Brown, John, 80
Brown, Moses, 48
Brown, Nicholas, 48
Brown University, 35, 45, 48, 49, 50, 51, 158
Brown, W. W., 144
Bryn Mawr College, 133
Bryson College, 113
Buchanan, James, 95, 132
Buchtel College, 163, 164
Buchtel, John Richards, 164
Bucknell University, 68
Buena Vista College, 102
Burr, Aaron, 35
Burr, Reverend Aaron, 26, 27, 32, 33, 34
Butler College, 71
Butler, Nicholas Murray, 45
Butler, Ovid, 82
Butler University, 81
Byrd, William M., 142

Caldwell College for Women, 119
Calhoun, John C., 31

California, College of, 1, 60, 105, 145, 146
California School of Christianity, 82
California, University of, 1, 51, 60, 74, 104, 145, 146, 189
Calvert, George, 115
Calvin College, 135
Campbell, Alexander, 77, 79, 80, 81, 128, 154
Campbell, E. Fay, 181
Campbell, Thomas, 79
Cambridge University, 10, 11, 16, 44, 137, 171, 188
Campbell, William Henry, 57
Canisius College, 120
Capital University, 84
Cardinal Stritch College, 124
Carleton College, 68, 75
Carnegie Corporation, 193
Carrick, Samuel, 170
Carroll, Charles, 115
Carroll College (Montana), 119
Carroll College (Wisconsin), 102
Carroll, John, 17, 115
Carson-Newman College, 71
Carthage College, 83, 84
Cascade College, 136
Caswell, Alexis, 50
Catawba College, 131
Catholic University of America, 120
Cedar Crest College, 131
Centenary College, 31, 87, 172, 173
Central Christian College, 129
Central College (Iowa), 69, 135
Central College (Missouri), 87
Central Mississippi College, 161
Central State College, 164, 166
Centre College, 102, 106, 107, 153, 154
Chapman College, 81, 82
Charity School, 37, 38, 39
Charleston, College of, 170, 171, 172
Chase, Philander, 134
Chase, Salmon P., 165
Chattanooga, University of, 89
Chauncy, Charles, 12
Chestnut Hill College, 123
Cheyney, Edward P., 37, 40
Chicago, University of, 68, 71, 78, 160, 161
Choate, Rufus, 62, 64
Christian University, 82
Churchill, Winston, ix
Cincinnati, University of, 164
Claassen, Williard K., 180
Claflin College, 87
Clair, Matthew W., 157
Clap, Thomas, 27, 28, 29
Clark College, 87
Clark, James Beauchamp, 169
Clarke College, 122
Clay, Cassius M., 77
Clay, Henry, 56, 92, 155
Clemens, Jeremiah, 142
Cochran, John, 149
Coe College, 102, 178
Coke, Thomas, 90

Coker College, 73
Cokesbury College, 90
Colby College, 68
Coleman, Benjamin, 15
Colgate University, 49, 68, 69
College Misericordia, 123
Colorado College, 76
Colorado School of Mines, 146, 147
Columbia College (South Carolina), 88
Columbia University, 40, 42, 45, 55, 56, 134
Columbian College, 50, 66, 67, 69, 72
Compton, Henry, 20, 21
Conant, James B., 18
Concordia College (Minnesota), 85
Concordia Teachers College (Illinois), 85
Concordia Teachers College (Nebraska), 85
Condict, Daniel, 55
Condict, Ira, 55
Contra Costa Academy, 145
Conwell, Russell H., 69
Cooke, Thomas, 28
Cooper, Myles, 44
Cornell College, 88
Cornell University, 50
Cornett, R. Orin, 181
Corpus Christi, University of, 72
Cossentine, E. S., 181
Cossitt, F. R., 111, 112
Coste, Jean Paul, 171
Cotton, John, 11
Cotton, Simeon, 30
Council for Financial Aid to Education, 195
Creighton University, 121
Crockett, William F., 157
Culver-Stockton College, 81, 82
Cumberland College, 110, 111, 112
Cumberland University, 111, 112
Cunningham, William F., 178
Cushing, Jonathan P., 108
Cutler, Timothy, 25

Daggett, Naphtali, 27, 28, 29
Dakota Wesleyan University, 88
Daleville College, 127
Dana College, 86
Dana, Daniel, 65
Dansby, B. Baldwin, 160, 161
Dartmouth College, 6, 26, 27, 30, 48, 58, 59, 60, 61, 63, 65, 76, 108, 134, 192
Dartmouth College Case, 61
Dartmouth, Earl of, 59
David Lipscomb College, 128
Davidson College, 107, 109
Davies, Samuel, 33, 35, 107
Davis and Elkins College, 102, 106, 107
Davis, C. Ernest, 180
Davis, Henry, 30
Davis, Jefferson, 8, 155
Day, Jeremiah, 30, 31
Dayton, University of, 125
Defiance College, 75
Delaware College, 148
Delaware, University of, 39, 104, 105, 147, 149

Demarest, William H. S., 58
Denison University, 50, 68
Denver, University of, 89, 178
De Paul University, 118
De Pauw University, 88, 175
Detroit, University of, 121
Dew, Thomas R., 20
DeWitt, Simeon, 54
Dickinson College, 57, 88, 93, 95, 96, 104, 105
Dickinson, John, 95
Dickinson, Jonathan, 32, 33
Diehl, Charles E., 178
Diggs, Charles, 161
Diggs, Lillie Granderson, 161
Dillard University, 75, 77, 88
Doane College, 75
Dodds, Harold Willis, 37
Dominican College, 119
Dominican College of San Rafael, 119
Douglass, David B., 30
Dowdell, James F., 141
Drake, Bryant, 180
Drake University, 81
Drew University, 88
Drexel Institute of Technology, 164
Drury College, 75
DuBose, Robert N., 178
Dubuque, University of, 102
Duchesne College, 125
Dudley, Joseph, 13
Duffield, George, 149
Due West Female College, 113
Duke University, 88, 93, 98, 178
Dunbarton College of Holy Cross, 119
Duncan, David Shaw, 178
Dunster, Henry, 11, 12
Duquesne University, 120
Durant, Henry, 145, 146
Dwight, Sereno E., 30
Dwight, Timothy, 27, 29, 30, 31
D'Youville College, 120

Earlham College, 132, 176, 196
East Alabama Male College, 139, 140, 144
East Texas Baptist College, 71
Eastern Baptist College, 68
Eastern Mennonite College, 133
Eastern Nazarene College, 130
Eaton, Nathaniel, 11
Edgewood College of the Sacred Heart, 120
Edinburgh, University of, 34
Edwards, Jonathan, 25, 27, 30, 34, 60, 108
Edwards, Morgan, 46
Eichelberger, James W., 179
Eisenhower, Dwight D., 45, 127
Eisenhower, Milton, 188
Elchanan, Isaac, 133
Eliot, Charles W., 7, 18
Elizabethtown College, 127
Ellis, Matt L., 144
Elmhurst College, 131, 132
Elmira College, 105
Elon College, 75, 77

Emmanuel College, 123
Emmanuel Missionary College, 136
Emory and Henry College, 88, 96
Emory, John, 96
Emory University, 31, 88, 93, 96, 98
Emporia, College of, 102
Erskine College, 113
Etz Chaim Yeshiva, 133
Eureka College, 81, 179
Eureka Lutheran College, 85
Evansville College, 88
Ewing, John, 41, 149

Fairbairn, Charles V., 181
Fairfield University, 121
Fairmount College, 151
Faunce, William Herbert Perry, 50
Fee, John G., 77
Findlay College, 130
Finley, Samuel, 33, 35
Fisk University, 75
Fisk, Wilbur, 93
Fitch, Ebenezer, 30
Flora Macdonald College, 107
Florence Wesleyan University, 141, 143
Florida Christian College, 129
Florida Normal and Industrial Memorial College, 68, 160
Florida Southern College, 88
Fontbonne College, 124
Ford Foundation, 193
Ford Motor Company, 194
Fordham University, 121
Foster, Randolph S., 92
Fournier Institute of Technology, 118
Franeker, University of (Netherlands), 11
Franklin, Benjamin, 14, 37, 38, 39, 40, 41, 53, 132, 162
Franklin College of Indiana, 68
Franklin and Marshall College, 95, 131, 132, 170
Franklin, William, 52, 162
Frelinghuysen, Frederick, 53
Frelinghuysen, John, 53
Frelinghuysen, Theodore J., 32, 56, 57
French American College, 136
French Protestant College, 136
Friends University, 133
Frost, Thomas, 171
Furman, Richard, 72
Furman University, 71, 72

Gage, Harry M., 178
Gallagher, Simon Felix, 171
Galloway Woman's College, 144
Gambier, Lord, 134
Gandy, J. M., 161
Garfield, James A., 82
Garland, Landon C., 93
Gates, Merrill Edward, 57
Gates, Thomas S., 37
General Electric Company, 194
General Motors Corporation, 194
Geneva College, 113, 114

Geneva Hall, 113, 114
George Fox College, 133
George Peabody College for Teachers, 35, 112
George Pepperdine College, 128
George Washington University, 66, 67
George Williams College, 136
Georgetown College, 67, 71, 154
Georgetown University, 115, 121
Georgia, University of, 92, 107
Georgian Court College, 122
Gettysburg College, 83, 84
Gilman, Daniel Coit, 28, 145
Gladwin, Mary E., 164
Glenn, Wilbur Fisk, 141
Golden Gate College, 136
Gonzaga University, 121
Good Counsel College, 124
Goshen College, 133
Goucher College, 97
Goucher, Dr. and Mrs. John Franklin, 97, 156
Grand Canyon College, 71
Gray, Gordon, 189
Great Falls, College of, 122
Green, Ashbel, 36
Green, Eleanor, ix
Green, John Findley, ix
Green, Lewis W., 154
Greene, S. L. Jr., 179
Greensboro College, 88
Greenville College, 100
Griffin, Edward Dorr, 30
Grinnell College, 3, 74, 75
Griswold, A. Whitney, 24
Gross, Ernest, 181
Gross, John O., 179, 180
Grove City College, 102
Guilford College, 132, 196
Gustavus Adolphus College, 85

Hadley, Arthur T., 24
Hale, Nathan, 29
Hamilton, Alexander, 34, 44
Hamilton College, 30, 105, 158
Hamilton, John, 32
Hamline University, 88
Hampden-Sydney College, 30, 35, 36, 106, 107, 108, 154
Hampton Institute, 76
Hancock, John, 16
Hanover College, 6, 102
Hardenbergh, Henry Janeway, 54
Hardenbergh, Jacob Rutsen, 53, 54
Hardenbergh, William P., 54
Hardin-Simmons University, 71
Harding College, 128
Harrison, Benjamin, 22
Harrison, William Henry, 108
Harrocks, James, 20
Hartwick College, 83
Harvard, John, 11
Harvard University, 1, 6, 7, 10, 12, 13, 14, 16, 17, 18, 21, 23, 24, 26, 27, 29, 32, 33, 34, 45, 60, 64, 76, 107, 159, 196

Hasbrouck, Abraham B., 30, 56
Haskell, Daniel, 30
Hastings College, 102, 162
Haverford College, 133
Hay, John, 51
Heath, John, 23, 91
Heidelberg College, 131
Henderson-Brown College, 144, 145
Henderson, C. C., 144
Henderson, Elmer W., 157
Henderson State Teachers College, 144
Hendrix College, 88, 144
Henry, Patrick, 108
Hesperian College, 82
High Point College, 88, 98
Hillsboro College, 84
Hillsdale College, 68
Hiram College, 81, 82
Hobart College, 133
Hochwalt, Frederick G., 182
Holley, Horace, 30, 153
Hollins College, 73
Hollis, Thomas, 14, 15
Holmes, Dwight O. W., 157
Holmes, John, 61
Holy Cross, College of the, 120
Holy Family College, 120
Holy Names College, 124
Holy Names, College of the (California), 124
Holyoke, Edward, 15, 16
Hood College, 131
Hooker, Thomas, 11
Hoover, Herbert, 177
Hope College, 135
Hopkinson, Josiah, 61
Horne, B. K., 180
Houghton College, 100
Howard College, 71
Howard Payne College, 71
Hubert, Zachary Taylor, 159
Hudson, William, 142
Hughes, Charles Evans, 51
Hughes, W. A. C., 157
Hull, Cordell, 112
Humphrey, Heman, 30
Huntingdon College, 60, 88
Huntingdon, Countess of, 60
Huntington College, 136
Huron College, 102
Huston-Tillotson College, 75
Hutchins, Francis S., 78
Hutchins, Hobert M., 78
Hutchins, William J., 78

Idaho, College of, 103
Illinois College, 3, 6, 74, 75, 103
Illionis Institute of Technology, 161
Illinois State University, 84
Illinois, University of, 138
Illinois Wesleyan University, 88
Immaculata College, 124
Immaculate Heart College, 124
Incarnate Word College, 118

Indiana Central College, 132
Indiana University, 94, 138, 174, 175
International Council of Religious Education, 179
Iona College, 118
Iowa Wesleyan College, 88

Jackson College, 158, 159, 160, 161
Jackson, Houston R., 157
Jackson, Lee R., 164
Jackson, Paul, 149
Jackson, Theron S., 164
James, Leonidas S., 157
Jamestown College, 103
Jaques, J. E. and Mrs., 166
Jarvis Christian College, 81
Jay, James, 40, 43
Jay, John, 44
Jefferson, Thomas, 21, 22, 108, 137
Jenkins, Daniel, 162
Jenkins, Martin D., 157
Jennings, Samuel K., 91
John Carroll University, 121
Johns Hopkins University, 7, 28, 145, 196
Johnson, Samuel, 24, 42, 43, 44, 45
Johnson, William Samuel, 27, 45
Johnson C. Smith University, 103
Jones, Harry H., 161
Jones, John Paul, 191
Jordan, David Starr, 175
Jubilee College, 134
Judd, Bethel, 30
Judson, Adoniram, 51, 66
Judson College, 51, 71
Juniata College, 127

Kalamazoo College, 68
Kansas Wesleyan University, 88
Kellog, Martin, 145, 146
Kelly, Robert L., 176
Kent, Aratus, 31
Kent, Chancellor, 61
Kentucky, University of, 80, 104, 105, 152, 154, 155
Kentucky Wesleyan College, 88
Kenyon College, 30, 31, 133, 134
Kenyon, Lord, 134
Keuka College, 68
Kiah, Thomas H., 157
Kindrick, Nathaniel, 69
King Charles I, 115
King George II, 36, 42, 43
King George III, 40, 52, 53, 58, 60, 63, 162
King College, 107
King, Philip C., 151
King's College (New York), 40, 42, 45, 56, 134
King's College (Pennsylvania), 121
Kirk, Grayson, 45
Kirkland, John Thornton, 17, 18
Knox College, 6, 74, 75, 101, 105, 164
Knox, John, 35
Knoxville College, 109
Kolbe, Parke R., 164

Lafayette College, 103
Lafayette, Marquis de, 141
La Grange College (Alabama), 92, 141, 142, 143, 144
LaGrange College (Georgia), 88
Laidley, John O., 168
Lake Forest College, 103
Lambuth College, 88
Landon, Alfred M., 151
Lane College, 99
Langdon, Samuel, 16, 17
Langston University, 160
LaSalle College, 118
LaSalle, John Baptiste de, 117
La Sierra College, 136
Latta, James, 149
LaVerne College, 127
Lawrence College, 88
Lebanon Valley College, 132
Lee, Charles, 35
Lee, Henry, 35
Lee, Robert E., 109
Leland College, 68
LeMoyne College (New York), 121
LeMoyne College (Tennesee), 75
Lenoir Rhyne College, 83
Leverett, John, 13, 14
Lewis and Clark College, 103
Lewis College of Science and Technology, 118
Lewis, David P., 142
Leydt, Matthew, 54
Liberal Arts College Movement, 177
Limestone College, 73
Lincoln, Abraham, 51, 146, 165
Lincoln University (Illinois), 111
Lincoln University (Pennsylvania), 105
Lindenwood College, 103
Linfield College, 68
Lipscomb, David, 128
Livingston, John H., 55
Livingston, Peter Van Brugh, 32
Livingston, Philip, 28
Livingston, Robert R., 44
Livingston, William, 42, 44
Livingstone College, 99
Llewelyn, Thomas, 48
Lloyd, Ralph W., 178
Locke, Samuel, 16
Lockerman, Joseph H., 157
Loehe, Wilhelm, 85
Log College, 32, 34, 35
Lombard College, 164
Longfellow, Henry Wadsworth, 7, 17, 93
Longstreet, Augustus H., 31
Loras College, 119
Lord, Nathan, 65
Loretto Heights College, 122
Lothian, Marquis of, 60
Louisiana College, 71
Louisiana, University of, 172, 174
Love, Edgar A., 157
Low, Seth, 45
Lowell, A. Lawrence, 18

Lowell, James Russell, 7, 17
Loyola College, 121
Loyola, Ignatius, 116
Loyola University (Illinois), 121
Loyola University (Louisiana), 117, 121
Loyola University of Los Angeles, 121
Ludwig, S. T., 180
Luther College, 85
Luther, Martin, 83
Lycoming College, 88
Lynchburg College, 81

Macalester College, 103
Maclean, John, Jr., 36
MacMurray College, 88
Madison College, 92, 113
Madison, President James, 20, 35, 92, 108, 116
Madison, Right Reverend James, 20
Madonna College, 120
Malik, Charles H., ix
Mallet, E. J., 147
Manchester College, 127
Manhattan College, 118
Manhattanville College of the Sacred Heart, 125
Mann, Horace, 49, 51, 138, 139
Manning, James, 46, 47
Mansfield Classical Seminary, 166, 167
Mansfield State Teachers College, 166, 167
Marian College (Indiana), 119
Marian College (Wisconsin), 124
Marietta College, 6, 75
Marion College, 100
Marquette University, 121
Marsh, Freeman, 91
Marshall College, 132, 168, 169
Marshall, John, 22, 23, 62, 64, 132, 168, 169
Mary Allen College, 71
Mary Baldwin College, 107
Mary Hardin-Baylor College, 71
Mary Manse College, 125
Marygrove College, 124
Maryknoll Teachers College, 121
Marylhurst College, 124
Marymount College (Kansas), 123
Marymount College (Los Angeles), 122
Maryville College (Missouri), 125
Maryville College (Tennessee), 103, 178
Marywood College, 124
Mason, Mrs. Salina C., 169
Mather, Azariah, 24
Mather, Cotton, 13, 14, 25
Mather, Increase, 13
Mattson, Karl, 180
Maurer, Irving, 178
Maxcy, Jonathan, 48
Maxwell, William, 30
Mays, Benjamin E., 181
McClellan, George B., 146
McCosh, James, 36
McDowell, Alexander, 148
McGhee, Annie May Brown, 159

McHenry, James, 149
McKean, Thomas, 149
McKendree College, 88
McLain, Raymond F., 179
McLean, John J., 96
McMurry College, 88
McPherson College, 127
McTyeire, Holland N., 97, 100
Meiklejohn, Alexander, 51
Mercer University, 71
Mercy College, 123
Mercyhurst College, 123
Meredith College, 71
Merrimack College, 117
Messer, Asa, 48
Messiah College, 127
Methodist Woman's College of Alabama, 60
Michigan Union College, 98
Michigan, University of, 51, 138
Middle States Association of Colleges and Secondary Schools, 4
Middlebury College, 6, 30, 76, 93, 111
Midland College, 83
Miles College, 99
Millikan University, 103, 111
Milledoler, Philip, 55, 56
Miller, Adam W., 180
Mills, Neel D., 181
Mills, Thomas, 171
Millsaps College, 88, 158, 159
Milner, Clyde A., 180
Milton College, 73
Milwaukee-Downer College, 74, 76
Minnesota, University of, 138
Mission House College and Theological Seminary, 131
Mississippi College, 30, 71, 160, 172, 173, 174
Mississippi Industrial College, 99
Mississippi, University of, 31
Missouri Valley College, 103, 111
Mitchell, James, 152
Mitchell, S. T., 165
Monmouth College, 109
Monmouth University, 166
Monroe, James, 22
Montana, College of, 77
Montana Wesleyan College, 77
Montreat College, 107
Moore, Benjamin M., 45
Moore, James, 152, 153
Moor's Indian Charity School, 59
Moravian College, 133
Moravian College for Women, 133
Morehouse College, 68, 159, 160
Morgan, Littleton F., 156
Morgan State College, 155, 156, 157, 161
Morningside College, 88
Morrill Act, 8, 49, 57, 138, 146
Morrill, Justin Smith, 138
Morris College, 71
Morris Brown College, 98
Morris, Gouverneur, 44
Morrow, Dwight, 169

Morrow, James E., 169
Morse, Samuel F. B., 31
Mount Angel Women's College, 118
Mount Holyoke College, 76
Mount Mary College, 122
Mount Mercy College, 122
Mount Morris College, 127
Mount St. Agnes College, 123
Mount St. Joseph-on-the-Ohio, College of, 122
Mount St. Mary College, 122
Mount St. Mary's College (California), 124
Mount St. Mary's College (Maryland), 119
Mount St. Scholastica College, 118
Mount St. Vincent College, 122
Mount St. Vincent, College of (New York), 122
Mount Union College, 88
Mueller, Reuben H., 180
Muhlenberg College, 83
Mulder, Bernard J., 181
Mundelein College, 122
Municipal University of Wichita, 151
Muskingum College, 109, 110

Nashville, University of, 35, 112
Nassau Hall, 34, 36
Natchez Seminary, 158
National Association of Accrediting, 5
National Association of State Universities, 5
National Catholic Educational Association, 182
National Conference of Church Related Colleges, 177, 178
National Council of Churches of Christ in the U. S. A., 178, 179
National Science Foundation, 191
Nazareth College (Kentucky), 122
Nazareth College (Michigan), 123
Nazareth College (New York), 123
Nebraska, University of, 50
Nebraska Wesleyan University, 88
Nelson, Thomas, 22
New England Association of Colleges and Secondary Schools, 4
New Jersey, State University of, 58
New Orleans University, 77
New Rochelle, College of, 125
New York, State University of, 73
New York University, 57, 96, 105
Newberry College, 83
Newberry, Farrar, 144
Newton College of the Sacred Heart, 125
Newton, Sir Isaac, 24
Niagara University, 118
Nicholson, Roy S., 182
Nicholson, William R., 142
Nielsen, Ernest D., 179
Nisbet, Charles, 95
North Carolina College at Durham, 163
North Carolina, University of, 35, 137, 189
North Central Association of Colleges and Secondary Schools, 4

North Central College, 132, 178
Northland College, 75
Northwest Association of Secondary and Higher Schools, 4
Northwest Christian College, 81
Northwest Nazarene College, 130
Northwestern Christian University, 81
Northwestern College, 86
Northwestern University, 88
Notre Dame College, 123
Notre Dame, College of (California), 123
Notre Dame College of Staten Island, 124
Notre Dame of Maryland, College of, 122
Notre Dame, University of, 121, 178, 192
Nott, Cyrus, 94
Nott, Eliphalet, 106
Nottingham Academy, 35

Oakland City College, 71
Oakwood College, 136
Oberlin College, 76, 78
Occidental College, 103
Occom, Samson, 59, 60
O'Connel, Pazavia, 161
Oglethorpe College, 109
Ohio Northern University, 88
Ohio State University, 138
Ohio Wesleyan University, 88
O'Kelly, James, 77
Oklahoma Baptist University, 71
Oklahoma Christian University, 82
Oklahoma City University, 88
Olin, Stephen, 92, 93, 142
Olivet College, 75
Olivet Nazarene College, 130, 131
Omaha,, University of, 162
O'Neal, Edward A., 142
Oregon College of Education, 166
Ottawa University, 68
Otterbein College, 132
Ouachita Baptist College, 72
Our Lady of Cincinnati College, 123
Our Lady of the Elms, College of, 123
Our Lady of the Lake College, 122
Our Lady of Mercy, College of, 122
Our Lady of Victory College, 124
Oxford University, 10, 16, 38, 53, 79, 137, 188
Ozarks, College of the, 103, 110

Pacific Bible College, 130
Pacific, College of the, 88
Pacific Lutheran College, 85
Pacific Union College, 136
Pacific University, 3, 74, 75
Page, Inman, 158
Paine College, 99, 143
Paine, Robert, 100, 142, 143
Park College, 103
Parker, Theophilius R., 157
Parsons College, 103
Pasadena College, 130
Patton, Francis Landey, 37
Paul Quinn College, 98

Payne, Daniel S., 165
Peabody, George, 49
Peale, Charles Willson, 36
Pears, Thomas C., Jr., 149
Pearson, Abraham, 23
Pearson, Eliphalet, 17
Pemberton, Ebenezer, 32
Pendleton, William Kimbrough, 81
Penn, Richard, 37, 148
Penn, Thomas, 37, 40, 148
Pennsylvania College, 84
Pennsylvania College for Women, 105, 106
Pennsylvania State University, 188
Pennsylvania, University of, 37, 38, 39, 40, 41, 60, 134, 161, 187
Peters, Absalom, 1
Peters, Richard, 39, 41
Petersen, Alvin K., 182
Phi Beta Kappa, 23
Philander Smith College, 89
Philadelphia Academy, 37, 39
Philadelphia, College of, 43, 47, 96, 134
Phillips University, 81, 82
Pierce Christian College, 82
Pierce, George E., 31
Pierson, John, 32
Pipkin, Charles W., 144
Pitt, William, 40
Pittsburgh, University of, 106
Pixley, Frank, 164
Poage, Josiah, 168
Polk, Leonidas, 8
Pomona College, 76
Porter, Noah, 31
Portier, Michael, 116
Portland Bible Institute, 136
Portland, University of, 121
Pound, Roscoe, x
Presbyterian College, 107
Preston, John, 11
Preus, J. C. K., 180
Princeton University, 3, 26, 27, 32, 33, 34, 36, 37, 46, 47, 55, 56, 64, 104, 105, 106, 108, 109, 192
Principia, The, 128
Providence College, 121
Provine, J. W., 160
Puget Sound, College of, 88
Pusey, Nathan M., 18

Queen Charlotte, 53
Queen of the Holy Rosary College, 120
Queen's College (New Jersey), 51, 52, 53, 54, 55, 56, 57, 105, 162
Queen's College (North Carolina), 107
Quincy College, 120
Quincy, Josiah, 18

Rall, E. E., 178
Ramsey, David, 149
Randall, George M., 146, 147
Randolph, Edmund, 22
Randolph-Macon College, 89, 92, 93, 96, 142
Randolph-Macon Woman's College, 89

Randolph, Peyton, 22
Read, George, 149
Reddix, Jacob L., 161
Redlands, University of, 68
Regis College (Colorado), 121
Regis College (Massachusetts), 123
Rhees, Rush, 69
Rhode Island, College of, 45, 46, 48, 50
Rhode Island College of Agriculture, 50
Rice, David, 152
Rice, Luther, 66, 67
Richmond, University of, 72
Ricker College, 68
Ricks College, 129
Rio Grande College, 69
Ripon College, 74, 76
Rivers, Richard H., 143
Rivier College, 124
Roanoke College, 84
Roberts, B. T., 100
Roberts Wesleyan College, 100
Robinson, E. G., 50
Rochester, University of, 68, 69
Rockefeller Foundation, 193
Rockefeller, John D., Jr., 51
Rockford College, 74, 75
Rockhurst College, 121
Rocky Mountain College, 75, 77, 103
Rogers, William, 47
Rollins College, 76
Romeyn, Dirck, 54, 105
Roosevelt University, 136
Rosary College, 120
Rosary Hill College, 123
Rosemont College, 125
Rush, Benjamin, 95
Russell, Samuel, 23
Rust College, 89, 165
Rust, Richard S., 165
Ruter College, 95
Ruter, Martin, 94, 95
Rutgers, Henry, 55
Rutgers University, 30, 51, 55, 57, 58, 135, 162, 163
Ryland, John, 47

Sacred Heart, College of the (Louisiana), 125
Sacred Heart, College of the (Puerto Rico), 125
Sacred Heart Dominican College, 120
Sage, Mrs. Russell, 163
St. Ambrose College, 119
St. Anselm's College, 117
St. Augustine's College, 133
St. Basil's College, 119
St. Benedict, College of, 118
St. Benedict of Nursia, 117
St. Benedict's College, 117
St. Bernadine of Siena College, 120
St. Bonaventure University, 120
St. Catherine, College of, 124
St. Edward's University, 118
St. Elizabeth, College of, 122

St. Francis College (Illinois), 119
St. Francis College (Indiana), 121
St. Francis College (New York), 120
St. Francis College (Pennsylvania), 125
St. Francis, College of (Wisconsin), 120
St. Francis Xavier College for Women, 123
St. John College, 119
St. John Fisher College, 117
St. John's College, 30
St. John's University (Minnesota), 117
St. John's University (New York), 118
St. Joseph's College (Connecticut), 123
St. Joseph's College (Indiana), 125
St. Joseph's College (Maryland), 116, 119
St. Joseph's College (Pennsylvania), 121
St. Joseph's College for Women, 123
St. Lawrence University, 164
St. Louis University, 121
St. Martin's College, 117
St. Mary College, 122
St. Mary, College of, 123
St. Mary of the Springs, College of, 119
St. Mary of the Wasatch, College of, 119
St. Mary of the Woods College, 123
St. Mary's College (Indiana), 119
St. Mary's College (Michigan), 119
St. Mary's College (Minnesota), 118
St. Mary's College of California, 118
St. Mary's Dominican College, 120
St. Mary's University of San Antonio, 125
St. Michael's College, 118, 125
St. Norbert College, 118
St. Olaf College, 85
St. Peter's College, 121
St. Procopius College, 117
St. Rose, College of, 124
St. Scholastica, College of, 118
St. Teresa, College of (Minnesota), 124
St. Teresa, College of (Missouri), 124
St. Thomas, College of, 119
St. Thomas, University of, 117
St. Vincent College, 117
Salem College (North Carolina), 133
Salem College (West Virgniia), 73
Salisbury, Stanton, 162
Salve Regina College, 123
Sam Huston College, 77
Samford, William F., 141
San Antonio Female College, 112
San Antonio, University of, 112
San Diego College for Women, 125
San Francisco College for Women, 125
San Francisco, University of, 121
Santa Clara, University of, 121
Scarritt College, 89
Schauffler College, 75
Schreiner, Roy, 180
Scott, Austin, 58
Scott, Levi, 156
Scranton, University of, 121
Scripps College, 76
Sears, Barnas, 49, 50
Seattle Pacific College, 100
Seattle University, 121

Seton Hall University, 119
Seton Hill College, 122
Sewell, Joseph, 14
Seymour, Charles, 24
Sforza, Count Carlo, ix
Shaw University, 68
Sheeder, Franklin I., 180
Shephard, James E., 163
Sheldon, Charles M., 151
Sherman, David A., 30
Shippen, William, 34
Shorter College, 72
Shotwell, Dr. and Mrs. Nathan, 172
Shurtleff College, 68
Siena College, 120
Siena Heights College, 120
Simmons, H. E., 164
Simpson College, 89, 179
Simpson, Matthew, 92, 94
Sims, Edward D., 142
Sioux Falls College, 68
Smith, Asa Dodge, 65
Smith, B. J., 180
Smith College, 76
Smith, Harlie L., 180
Smith, Hezekiah, 47
Smith, James, 149
Smith, Jeremiah, 54
Smith, John Blair, 106, 108
Smith, Robert, 34, 170, 171, 172
Smith, Samuel Stanhope, 36, 106, 108
Smith, Thomas M., 31
Smith, William, 32, 39, 40, 41, 43, 96
Smith, William Peartree, 32
Society of Jesus, 116
Society for the Promotion of Collegiate and
  Theological Education at the West, 2
Soper, Morris, Judge, 156
South, University of the, 4, 8, 134
South Carolina, University of, 31, 48
Southern Association of Colleges and Sec-
  ondary Schools, 4, 190
Southern California, University of, 89
Southern Methodist University, 89
Southern Missionary College, 136
Southern Union College, 77
Southern University, 140
Southwestern College, 89
Southwestern at Memphis, 107, 109, 178
Southwestern University (Texas), 89, 95
Spelman College, 68
Spencer, John O., 157
Spring Hill College, 116, 121
Springfield College, 136
Standard Oil Company (Indiana), 193
Standard Oil Company (New Jersey), 194
Standard Oil Company (Ohio), 193
Stanford, E. V., 178
Stanford University, 175, 196
Steele, Sir Richard, 24
Steelman, John R., 144
Sterling College, 109, 110
Stetson University, 72
Steubenville, College of, 125

Stiles, Ezra, 25, 29, 30
Stillman College, 107
Stone, Barton W., 128
Stonehill College, 121
Straight College, 77
Stuart, John Leighton, 108
Stuart, Moses, 49
Susquehanna University, 84
Swarthmore College, 133
Syracuse University, 89

Tabor College, 133
Talbott, Fanning, 128
Talladega College, 75
Taney, Roger Brooke, 95
Tarkio College, 109
Taylor, Colonel John, 53
Taylor University, 96, 97
Taylor, William, 97
Temple University, 68, 69
Tennent, Gilbert, 32, 33
Tennent, William, Jr., 32
Tennent, William, Sr., 32, 34
Tennessee, University of, 170
Tennessee Wesleyan College, 30, 89
Tewskbury, Donald G., 6
Texas Christian University, 81, 82
Texas College, 99
Texas Lutheran College, 84, 85
Texas Wesleyan College, 89
Thiel College, 84
Thom, E. C., 168
Thomas, Ervin W., 181
Thomas, John W., 164
Thomsen, Arthur C., 162
Thomson, Charles, 47, 149
Thorpe, George, 18, 19
Tichnor, George, 17
Tillotson College, 77
Tougaloo Southern Christian College, 76,
  81, 82
Toulmin, Harry, 152
Transylvania College, 30, 67, 81, 92, 152,
  153, 154, 155, 179
Treat, Richard, 33
Trent, W. J., 99
Trent, W. J., Jr., 99
Trevecca Nazarene College, 130
Trexler, Harrison A., 162
Trigg, Harold L., 157
Trinity College (Connecticut), 31, 134, 135
Trinity College (District of Columbia), 123
Trinity College (Vermont), 123
Trinity University (Texas), 103, 111, 112
Trueblood, D. Elton, 196
Truman, Harry S., ix, 185
Tucker, William Jewett, 65
Tufts College, 163, 164
Tulane, Paul, 174
Tulane University, 172, 174
Tulloss, Rees E., 178
Tulsa, University of, 103
Turner, Daniel, 26
Tusculum College, 103

Tyler, Bennett, 30, 65
Tyler, John, 20, 168
Tyler, Lyon Gardiner, 168
Tyler, William S., 3

Union Carbide and Carbon Corporation, 193
Union College (Kentucky), 89, 179
Union College (Nebraska), 136
Union College and University (New York), 35, 48, 53, 105, 106, 108, 135
Union University, 72
United States Steel Corporation, 194
Upland College, 127
Upsala College, 85
Ursinus College, 131
Ursuline College (Kentucky), 125
Ursuline College for Women (Ohio), 125

Valparaiso University, 85
Vance, Rupert B., 144
Vanderbilt, Cornelius, 97
Vanderbilt University, 4, 93, 97, 100
Varnum, James Mitchell, 47
Vermont, University of, 30, 51
Villa Madonna College, 119
Villa Maria College, 123
Villanova College, 117, 178
Virginia State College, 161
Virginia Union University, 68
Virginia, University of, 137, 138
Viterbo College, 118

Wabash College, 6, 30, 105
Wadsworth, Benjamin, 15
Wagner Lutheran College, 84
Wake Forest College, 72
Walker, Lee Edwin, 181
Walla Walla College, 136
Ward, A. N., 177
Ward-Belmont College, 112
Warfield, William A., 157
Wartburg College, 84, 85
Washburn University of Topeka, 76, 149, 150, 151
Washington, Bushrod, 23, 62
Washington College, 41, 96, 109
Washington, George, 20, 29, 36, 109, 149
Washington and Jefferson College, 35, 94, 105
Washington and Lee University, 109
Washington Missionary College, 136
Wayland College, 72
Wayland, Francis, 48, 49, 50, 51
Waynesburg College, 103, 111, 113
Webster College, 122
Webster, Daniel, 61, 62, 63, 64
Webster, Noah, 30
Wellesley College, 76
Wells, Ronald V., 179
Wentworth, John, 59
Wesley, Charles, 79
Wesley, Charles H., 166
Wesley College, 89

Wesley, John, 38, 60, 79, 89, 90, 91, 96
Wesleyan College, 89
Wesleyan University, 89, 93, 96, 97, 142, 143
West Lafayette College, 98
West Liberty State College, 172
West Virginia Wesleyan College, 89
Western College Association, 4
Western College for Women, 105
Western Maryland College, 89, 98, 177
Western Reserve Eclectic Institute, 82
Western Reserve University, 3, 6, 31, 74, 76
Westinghouse Educational Foundation, 194
Westmar College, 132
Westminster College (Missouri), ix, 103, 106, 107
Westminster College (Pennsylvania), 109, 110
Westminster College (Utah), 103
Westmoreland College, 112
Wheaton College, 101
Wheaton, Nathaniel, S., 31
Wheeler, Benjamin Ide, 51
Wheelock, Eleazar, 26, 27, 58, 59, 60, 61, 65
Wheelock, John, 61, 65
Whelan, James F., 117
Whitefield, George, 15, 16, 27, 28, 30, 32, 34, 38, 59, 60, 79, 187
Whitman College, 76
Whitney, Eli, 30
Whittier College, 132
Whitworth College, 103
Wickey, Gould, 176, 177, 178, 181
Wigglesworth, Edward, 14
Wilberforce University, 98, 164, 165, 166
Wiley College, 89
Wilkinson, Ernest L., 181
Willamette University, 89
Willard, Samuel, 13
William Carey College, 72
William Jewell College, 68, 72
William and Mary, College of, 18, 19, 20, 21, 22, 134, 167, 168
William Penn College, 132, 196
William Smith College, 134
Williams College, 30, 66, 76
Williams, Elisha, 25, 26, 27
Williams, Roger, 45
Williamson, Hugh, 149
Wilmington College, 132
Wilson College, 103
Wilson, Joseph R., 109
Wilson, Matthew, 149
Wilson, Woodrow, 37, 109, 169
Wirt, William, 61
Wisconsin, University of, 138
Witherspoon, John, 35, 36, 106, 108
Wittenberg College, 84, 178
Wofford College, 89
Wolbrecht, Walter F., 181
Woolsey, Theodore D., 31
Wooster, College of, 103
Workman, James W., 145

Wren, Christopher, 21
Wriston, Henry M., 50
Wythe, George, 22

Xavier University (Louisiana), 125
Xavier University (Ohio), 121

Yale Band, 3, 23
Yale, Elihu, 25

Yale University, 3, 6, 23, 25, 26, 27, 28, 29, 30, 31, 32, 33, 34, 43, 45, 48, 60, 64, 76, 145, 192
Yankton College, 76
Yeshiva University, 133
York College, 132
Young, William L., 181
Youngstown College, 136

11/30/56

FAC.